Proven
Strategies
for Improving
Learning
& Achievement

Duane Brown, Ph.D.

ISBN 1-56109-086-7

This publication was funded in part by the US Department of Education, Office of Educational Research and Improvement, Contract no. ED-99-CO-0014. Options expressed in this publication do not necessarily reflect the positions of the US Department of Education, OERI, or ERIC/CASS.

Table of Contents

Foreword .... *III*

Preface .... *V*

Chapter 1 .... *1*
Student Support Personnel, Academic Performance, and Strategic Interventions

Chapter 2 .... *11*
Improving the Achievement of Racial, Ethnic, and Cultural Minorities Through Advocacy, Consultation, and Collaboration

Chapter 3 .... *33*
Improving Academic Achievement
Cooperative Learning

Chapter 4 .... *45*
Developing a Positive School Climate:
Influencing Student Perceptions and
Heightening Teacher Awareness

Chapter 5 .... *67*
A Study Skills Program
A Study Skills Course for Middle and High Schools
A Study Skills Course for Elementary Schools

Chapter 6 .... *99*
Improving Test Scores
Eliminating Test Anxiety

Chapter 7 .... *127*
Time Management: An Essential Habit

Chapter 8 .... *149*
Behavioral Contracting and Encouragement

Chapter 9 .... *167*
Establishing an Environment That Encourages
Academic Success

Chapter 10 .... *185*
Using Peers and Adult Volunteers as Academic Tutors

Chapter 11 .... *219*
Achievement Motivation Groups

Chapter 12 .... *233*
Establishing Homework Support Programs

Chapter 13 .... *239*
Parenting for Academic Achievement:
Promoting Resiliency and Academic Skills

Chapter 14 .... *259*
Resisting Peer Pressure to Underachieve:
A Refusal Skills Group

Chapter 15 .... *273*
Helping High-Potential Underachievers Set
Career and Educational Goals Using the Internet

Chapter 16 .... *291*
Summing Up: Principles and Practices

Appendix I *297*
Useful Resources

Appendix II *303*
Handouts

Appendix III *305*
Overheads

Appendix IV *305*
Figures

Foreword

A useful way to identify what is important is to note what types of books are displayed at locations which will catch attention, e.g., special shelves in bookstores, checkout counters at supermarkets, direct mail advertising and ads in student newspapers. All of these sources utilize the judgement of experienced sales personnel as to what a particular population sub group, e.g., students, teachers, parents, would purchase if they knew it was available. If you can register a hit with even one subgroup, e.g., students, you are on target. If you are able to identify a topic that cuts across the needs and interests of several groups and has real substance, you have a winner! Such is this monograph on proven strategies for improving learning and achievement.

It is no exaggeration to say that we live in a *learning society* and willy-nilly, we are all, young or old, destined for a *lifetime of learning*. We start life with one learning challenge after another and if we are to make our final years rewarding, we need to cope with a continuous succession of new learnings. You would think that anything as basic to living in this age as learning *efficiently* and *effectively* would be the subject of numerous courses and countless publications. If everyone has to learn new things on a daily basis, whether formally in classes or as a part of coping with daily tasks, one would think that we would have identified the need and responded to it with quality materials. Right!

Part of that scenario is true. There is a never-ending supply of publications, usually with catchy titles, that promise the reader a quicker, easier and better way to studying and learning than they currently possess. Most of them are short lived. They will be purchased, but their use seldom produces the dramatic improvements in learning which are promised. That many of them do offer some helpful ideas and do lead to improved learning if consistently used is understandable. The large majority of persons employ study and learning techniques which are relatively unexamined. Even graduate students who have been in formal training for over twenty years will often display archaic and ineffective methods of studying and learning. For many persons, it doesn't take much to offer an improvement over what they are doing.

What many, if not most, of the proposed quick fixes for learning and study problems lack, however, is a substantive, *proven* basis for the approaches to learning they offer. For the most part, they are (like many of the new diets which appear like dandelions on a lawn in the spring) the pet ideas of an enthusiastic originator which may or probably won't work as well for others.

What distinguishes the work of Dr. Duane Brown, a distinguished researcher, scholar, and career development theorist, is his painstaking examination of the research literature to identify those techniques/strategies which have demonstrated their worth and utility in the research literature. He then used the research findings to produce a body of strategies for responding to a wide variety of learning tasks that clearly employ the "best" that research and experience have to offer for dealing with a particular learning challenge.

The net result is that a counselor, school psychologist, or teacher who wants to assist students and learners of all ages to learn effectively can base his or her assistance on the ideas in the book knowing that they are as "good as you can get."

Suffice to say, this is a book which counselors and school psychologists can use to both enhance their own approaches to learning as well as recommend to students for their use and referral. It can be used by all, knowing that it is authoritative, up-to-date, and written in a direct and easy-to-understand manner. We are proud to publish it. It is our expectation that it will be used by persons of widely differing ages and specialities with a high degree of reward and satisfaction. Just what we like our publications to do!

Garry R. Walz
Co-Director and Editor-in-Chief

Preface

The school reform movement has been gaining momentum for more than a decade. Among the results of this movement have been changes in educational practices for students and faculty. Students now face more rigorous curricula, end-of-grade tests to check on their academic progress, and stiffer graduation requirements in the form of more core courses and academic competency tests. In some instances, principals and teachers are faced with public ridicule – and worse – if their students do not meet the expectations of the public, state boards of education, and legislators. Entire school districts have been taken over by state boards of education because of their failure to raise academic performance. Principals have been placed on probation, and teachers have been threatened with loss of licensure to teach if their students do not perform better on tests. Not unexpectedly, teachers, principals, and local boards of education are pressing student support personnel to contribute to the overall task of improving student academic achievement.

School counselors, school psychologists, and school social workers can legitimately claim that they have always made contributions to the academic achievement of students. School counselors have taught study skills courses, led achievement groups, and helped students overcome the influence of debilitating emotional problems. School psychologists have promoted the academic achievement of mentally and physically challenged students in their assessment and consultation roles. Similarly, school social workers have contributed to the academic achievement of students by working with families and through direct interventions with students. However, according to many educators, these traditional efforts are clearly insufficient.

The purpose of this book is to give student support personnel tools that (1) will be recognized by educators as directly related to enhancing academic performance, (2) can be used with confidence that they will have the desired impact on achievement, and (3) are culturally sensitive. It is the

V

third criterion, cultural sensitivity, that is the most difficult to achieve because of the lack of empirical guidelines. Student support personnel who use any of these strategies are asked to use their own knowledge of the students with whom they work to embellish the work that is outlined in the chapters that follow.

Duane Brown, 1999

Acknowledgements

I want to thank Chevette Scott and Tony (T. J.) Hill for their assistance with this project. Their library work, proofreading, and suggestions for improving the manuscript were invaluable.

Duane Brown, 1999

Chapter One

Student Support Personnel, Academic Performance, and Strategic Interventions

School reform has been on the political and societal agenda of this country for 20 years. The idea that reform was needed comes partially out of, and continues to be fueled by, the concern that our students are not learning as much as students from western European and Pacific Rim countries. When students in these countries have been compared to students in the United States, U.S. students have never fared very well (e.g., Peak, 1997). A second, related impetus for the school reform movement resulted from a general concern by business and labor leaders that students graduating from our schools would be unable to perform the tasks required in the jobs of tomorrow (e.g., Daggett, 1997).

The school reform movement initially had little impact on the status quo and consequently on student performance. However, recent developments such as charter schools without many of the guidelines developed for public schools, local control options that allow educators to develop policies and utilize faculty and staff in nontraditional ways, end-of-grade testing programs that assess students' progress toward specific academic goals, the provision of incentives to schools that are successful in their efforts to promote achievement, and the takeover of low-performing schools by state school boards have had a variety of results. For example, some administrators are beginning to question the role of one group of student support personnel, school counselors, and wondering if they should not be replaced by additional teachers who could contribute directly to the achievement process. In one state (Virginia) the possibility has been raised that some or all elementary school counselors will be replaced by other educational personnel partially because of the misperception that counselors do not contribute to academic achievement.

The perception that school counselors do not make a contribution to educational achievement is incorrect, but some of their traditional effort can and probably should be expanded. School psychologists, who are legally linked to assessment for special education students, are viewed as necessary, but they may not be able to fill some desirable roles such as consultation, because of this linkage. In order to emerge from the narrow role of assessment, they must be able to demonstrate that they can make contributions to the academic achievement of all students. Social workers, like school psychologists, may be trapped in a range of narrow activities, such as dealing with attendance problems. However, social workers are in a position to promote academic achievement, particularly in their work with parents. They may also engage in collaborative efforts with other student support personnel, such as consultation with administrators and advocacy for students and their parents.

Examples of the efforts of student support personnel to improve achievement abound. Some counselors engage students in the development of study skills, educational and career goal setting that enhance motivation, social skills development that enable students to function more effectively in an educational setting, and SAT preparation course that improve students college entrance examination scores. Similarly, many school psychologists are engaged in ongoing consultation with classroom teachers to improve the learning environment in classrooms, and most school social workers are actively promoting academic achievement in their work with parents. In fact, all of the intervention strategies included in this book can be found being put into practice by school counselors, school psychologists, and school social workers. However, until now, no single reference is available that focuses on proven strategies to improve achievement. The more than 25 proven strategies that are presented in this book will allow student support personnel to enhance the achievement of their students if they choose to do so. Some of these strategies are easy to understand and implement while others are more difficult.

Service Delivery

Student support personnel have several options for delivering services to students including ad hoc, educational/developmental, and strategic interventions. In the ad hoc approach, services are provided to students, parents, and teachers on demand: no service delivery is preplanned. Student support personnel who use this approach often find themselves running from one crisis to another. The underlying philosophy of the educational approach, which is sometimes called developmental, is that all students need certain types of information and skills as they mature, and the student support program is structured to deliver the needed information and skills development activities. Although the educational/developmental approach must be included in all student support programs, it is not sufficient. Many children come to school with developmental deficits that cannot be addressed using educational approaches that are not geared to their specials needs. Moreover, some children who come to school without problems develop them because of the nature of the educational institutions and societal conditions that cannot be offset with educational approaches. The third service delivery strategy, strategic service delivery, involves designing and providing interventions based on the needs of students. These needs are identified through needs assessments that are administered to students, teachers, and parents. Although most student support personnel use all three approaches—ad hoc, educational/developmental, and strategic—when delivering services to students, the focus of this book is on providing services based on demonstrated needs, that is, the strategic approach.

Needs Assessment

Three sample needs assessment questionnaires that can be used as an initial step in identifying students who have problems that may lower their academic achievement are appended to this chapter. Other needs assessment inventories are presented throughout the book that can be used to conduct in-depth assessments of particular problems such as study skills. An initial needs assessment should be seen as a preliminary step in the delivery of strategic interventions to students. In-depth needs assessments can help focus interventions on the specific problems that students are experiencing.

In grades K through 3, the focus of needs assessment should be on parents and teachers. One of reason for this recommendation pertains to the reading level of students at this stage of their education. Many students in grades K through 3 will be unable to comprehend the language on most needs assessment devices. Moreover, caregivers, particularly teachers, often see the harbingers of serious academic problems soon after a child enters school and long before children and their parents are aware of the problem. Early detection and intervention can save students and their caregivers from anguish, and even failure. From grade 4 through 12, students should be included in the needs assessment process.

Designing Interventions

The best interventions are those that are matched to children's problems. Student support personnel have often assumed that interventions, such as those designed to improve self-esteem, will lead to enhanced school performance. The stance taken here is that self-esteem is the result of successful academic performance and interpersonal relationships as defined by the student. Moreover, high self-esteem may not lead to successful academic performance. Although people like Canfield (1986) have cited correlational data to support the idea that self-esteem is linked to academic achievement, this type of information does not infer that that there is a causal between self-esteem and achievement. For example, I helped an elementary school counselor administer, score, and interpret several hundred Piers-Harris Children's Self-Concept Scales (PCSCS). When we examined the data and compared the scores on the PCSCS to the achievement records of the children who took the inventory, it became clear that many of the students labeled as underachievers or low achievers by teachers had very good self-concepts. Somewhat surprisingly, many students that were labeled as aggressive and/or non-cooperative in the classroom, and as overall discipline problems, also had very positive views of themselves. As a result of this experience, I began to reconsider the relationship of self-esteem to school behavior.

Perhaps more importantly than the anecdotal information reported above, hundreds of studies have demonstrated that strategic interventions such as encouragement, behavioral contracts, and achievement motivation groups have been employed successfully when they have been applied appropriately. However, not all strategies work for all students. As Vasquez (1998) reported, there is a growing consensus that educational interventions must be tailored to fit the cultural values of the student. This issue will be taken up in detail in Chapter 3, and the concept of making interventions culturally sensitive will be stressed throughout this book.

The process of strategic making strategic interventions is simple and is depicted below.

Culturally Sensitive
Needs identified ------> Goals established ------> Interventions ------> Evaluation of Outcomes

---

This model is used throughout this book as the basis for presenting the interventions discussed.

A Word about Theory

Most student support personnel have been exposed to passionate discussions about the strengths and weaknesses of various theories. However, as practitioners, most student support personnel are less concerned about being purists from a theoretical point of view and more concerned with the pragmatic issue of what works. In this vein, the interventions outlined in this book have been taken from a variety of theoretical positions. Moreover, some of the best approaches to improving school achievement draw from several theoretical positions. For example, counselor or psychologist who is negotiating a behavioral contract (Behavioral) may use active listening (Humanistic) and provide encouragement (Adlerian) as a part of the process. In accord with the philosophy of most student support personnel, the perspective of this book is decidedly pragmatic.

About Strategies

Chapters 3 through 15 in this book will be devoted either to a single intervention or to a set of interventions that are designed to accomplish a specific purpose. Therefore, it is not necessary read each chapter in the book. Simply go to the chapter that is of interest and the process of delivering the intervention will be presented in its entirety. Moreover, the handouts needed to implement the strategy are provided at the end of each chapter (just as needs assessment devices are appended to this chapter). All handouts and other forms included can be copied without concern for copyright law. When classroom presentations are a part of the intervention and overheads are required, overhead masters are provided at the end of the chapter.

Summary

As a result of the education reform movement, some school administrators are questioning the roles of school counselors. Moreover, other student support personnel may be expected to step from their traditional roles as schools become increasingly concerned about the academic achievement level of students. However, the interventions used to improve academic performance must be geared to the specific problems being experienced by students, and they must be culturally sensitive as well.

References

Canfield, J. (1986). *Self-esteem in the classroom.* Culver City, CA: Self-Esteem Seminars.

Daggett, W. R. (1997). Getting schools ready for the technology of the future. *Model Schools News, 1,* 1-2.

Peak, L. (1997). *Pursuing excellence: A study of fourth grade mathematics and science achievement in an international context.* Washington, DC: National Center for Educational Statistics.

Vasquez, J. A. (1998). Distinctive traits of Hispanic students. *The Prevention Researcher, 5,* 1-4.

Needs Assessment Questionnaire
for High School Students
© 1998 Duane Brown

The faculty is trying to identify students who wish to improve their academic functioning because we are planning a number of individual and group activities to assist students to be successful in school. Please read the following items and check those that you believe you need to improve.

_____ 1. Completing homework
_____ 2. Class participation
_____ 3. Concentration in class
_____ 4. Test-taking skills
_____ 5. Preparing for the PSAT/SAT or ACT
_____ 6. Study skills
_____ 7. Educational goal setting
_____ 8. Getting along with teachers
_____ 9. Understanding my academic potential
_____ 10. Personal goal setting
_____ 11. Managing my time
_____ 12. Improving my academic skills such as reading and math
_____ 13. Setting career goals
_____ 14. Improving my public speaking
_____ 15. Decision-making skills
_____ 16. Personal problems that interfere with school work
_____ 17. Overload and stress
_____ 18. Staying in school/graduation
_____ 19. Resisting peer pressure not to do my best in school
_____ 20. Making money so I can stay in school
_____ 21. Anxiety about tests
_____ 22. Other (please list) _____

I would _____ would not _____ be interested in participating in activities that would improve the areas I have checked. If you would like to be contacted, sign your name below and indicate the best time for you to be contacted.

Name_____

Contact Me Time / Room Number _____

Assessing Academic Needs - Parent Survey

The counseling staff at XYZ School is developing a variety of strategies to help students enhance their achievement. The purpose of this survey is to give you an opportunity to identify any academic problems your student may be experiencing. Please identify your student and then check those areas that you believe could be improved.

Student's name _____

_____ 1. Being motivated to do homework
_____ 2. Study skills generally
_____ 3. Anxiety about tests
_____ 4. Preparing for tests (e.g., getting organized, spacing study time)
_____ 5. Preparing for the SAT/PSAT or ACT
_____ 6. Educational goal setting
_____ 7. Understanding his/her academic potential
_____ 8. Personal goal setting
_____ 9. Stress management /overload
_____ 10. Time management
_____ 11. Staying in school until graduation
_____ 12. Resisting peer pressure that leads to poor school performance
_____ 13. Career goal setting
_____ 14. Decision-making skills
_____ 15. Personal problems that interfere with academic performance
_____ 16. Improving specific academic skills such as math, writing, or reading
_____ 17. Dealing effectively with school officials such as teachers
_____ 18. Other (please list)

Check appropriate answer
Yes No
___ ___ 1. I would like the counseling staff to include my student in activities that improve his or her academic performance.
___ ___ 2. I would like to schedule a conference with my student's counselor.

If *Yes* to number 2, the best day and time to contact me is

_____

My telephone number is _____

Name _____

Handout 1-3

ASSESSING ACADEMIC NEEDS -
ELEMENTARY SCHOOL TEACHER SURVEY

The purpose of this survey is to identify students who are having various types of academic problems such as achieving below their potential, poor attending skills, poor study skills, and so forth. Once these students are identified, I plan to offer a variety of interventions that can help them overcome their academic deficits.

Teacher's Name _____

Grade Level _____

Academic Deficit	*Students Having This Problem*
1. Poor listening/ attending skills	1. _____
	2. _____
	3. _____
2. Often fails to get work in on time	1. _____
	2. _____
	3. _____
3. Capable but has low motivation.	1. _____
	2. _____
	3. _____
4. Poor study habits	1. _____
	2. _____
	3. _____
5. Is overly anxious about performance	1. _____
	2. _____
	3. _____
6. Poor test-taking skills	1. _____
	2. _____
	3. _____

7. Time-management deficits   1. _____

                                                 2. _____

                                                 3. _____

8. Specific academic deficits
    (e.g., math)   1. _____

                                                 2. _____

                                                 3. _____

9. Difficulty participating in class   1. _____

                                                 2. _____

                                                 3. _____

10. Other academic deficits (list)   1. _____

                                                 2. _____

                                                 3. _____

Many of the interventions I am planning, such as helping students develop study skills, can best be delivered to an entire class. Would you be interested in having your entire class exposed to a series of lessons on study skills? (Check one)   Yes _____ No _____

If you checked *Yes,* I will contact you in the near future to schedule an activity in your classroom.

Chapter Two

Improving the Achievement of Racial and Cultural Minorities Using Advocacy, Consultation and Collaboration

The problem of improving the achievement of cultural, ethnic, and racial minorities is one of the most pressing issues facing educators today. Wilson and Banks (1994) pointed out that this problem is particularly acute for African American males who are disproportionately labeled as underachievers and placed in special education classes. However, the problem goes far beyond this one group and includes African American females as well as males, American Indians (Thomason, 1995), Hispanics, (with the exception of Cubans) (Zapata, 1995), and some subgroups of Asian Americans (Yagi & Oh, 1995).

Understanding Cultural Values

Vasquez (1998) suggested a three-step process for improving the academic achievement of minority students based primarily on matching instructional techniques to the values of the students. Unfortunately, many educators are unaware of the differences that exist among the cultural values of European Americans, African Americans, Asian Americans, Hispanic Americans, and American Indians. Figure 2-1 depicts the traditional values of the major cultural groups in this country.

Values are beliefs that are experienced as standards that individuals use to judge themselves and others. Cultural values include clusters of beliefs held by cultural, ethnic, or racial groups that shape all aspects of their functioning, including their family structures, traditions, communication patterns, child rearing practices, and their perspective on the teaching/ learning process. Cultural values are also the basis for ethnocentrism, the belief that one's cultural group is superior to others. Taxonomies of cultural values, such as the one presented in Figure 2-1, are based on the pioneering research of Kluckhorn and Strodtbeck (1961). Typically these taxonomies include categories for values regarding human nature (human beings are good, bad, or neither), person-nature relationship (nature dominates people,

people dominate nature, living in harmony with nature is important). These values do not seem particularly important when viewed in relationship to achievement based on a review of the empirical and authoritative literature. Conversely, the values included in Figure 2-1 may influence cultural traits that interact with content, context, and teaching style to influence achievement outcomes. For example, time orientation, (future; past-future; present; circular, i.e., oriented to changes that recur in nature as opposed to time as measured by watches and calendars) may influence whether students see the relationship between what is learned in the classroom activity and the future events of their lives. Activity orientation (being, i.e., spontaneous self-expression is important; being-in-becoming, i.e., controlled self-expression is important; doing, i.e., action-oriented self-expression is important) may influence the response to critical problems that arise. Self-control values (it is either highly or moderately important to control one's thoughts and emotions) may influence certain aspects of classroom participation. However, it is unlikely that any of the values listed has more impact on classroom functioning than social relationship values (individualism, i.e., the individual is the most important social unit and collateral, i.e., it is important to put the group's concerns ahead of the

Figure 2-1

Value Orientations of Five Major U.S. Cultural Groups

Values

Cultural Groups	Self-Control	Time Orientation	Activity	Social Relationships	Achievement
European American	Moderately Important	Future	Doing	Individual	Competitive
Hispanics	Moderately Important	Present	Being	Collateral	Cooperative
American Indian	Very Important	Circular	Being/ Becoming	Collateral	Cooperative
African American	Moderately Important	Present	Doing	Collateral	Competitive
Asian American	Very Important	Past/ Present	Doing	Lineal	Cooperative

individual's concerns) and related values regarding cooperative versus competitive achievement. Most teachers expect independent behavior, and instruction is often organized to promote it. Moreover, the typical approach to achievement is competitive versus cooperative. Students who have been oriented to collateral relationships may not do as well in a competitive environment.

A cautionary note: Although the types of values included in the taxonomy presented in Figure 2-1 may be helpful in attempts to understand individuals, stereotyping individuals should be avoided. In the final analyses, each student should be considered as an individual who has a unique background. For example, some individuals who have the external characteristics of racial or ethnic minorities may have, because of the family structure and acculturation, adopted a traditional set of Eurocentric values. Handout 2-1, Your Cultural Values, can be used to gain a fuller understanding of your cultural values.

Strategies for Linking Values and Instructional Techniques

Numerous strategies for improving instruction are described in this book. The question that must be posed is, "How can new instructional strategies that will benefit minority students be infused into the instructional process?" Unfortunately, this is not an easy question to answer. School counselors, school psychologists, and school social workers must first familiarize themselves with potentially helpful strategies and become advocates for their usage. Advocacy is one of the many roles filled by school counselors, school psychologists and school social workers. Student support personnel should become advocates when students are not being well served by the school or its personnel. Advocacy is defined as "a process for protecting the rights and seeking assistance for those (students) who are unable to help themselves" (Kurpius & Lewis, 1988, p. 1). Because of language deficiencies, lack of information, value differences, and lack of experience with the educational bureaucracy, many minority students and their parents are unable to lobby for changes in their educational circumstances. Unfortunately, many of these circumstances, including certain instructional strategies, limit students' academic achievement. However, advocacy is not restricted to representing one student at a time. In some instances advocates will want to represent an entire group of students. One high school counselor sponsored several deserving African American students for membership in the National Honor Society of her school only to see them rejected. She decided to represent the entire group to the Society's sponsor, to the principal, and, if necessary, to the school board. The result was reconsideration of the manner in which students were admitted to the National Honor Society and the subsequent admission of several African American students. Advocates who are well armed with the facts can level the educational playing field that is tilted dramatically in favor of White, middle-class students in many instances.

School psychologists, school counselors, and school social workers must also engage in consultation and collaboration efforts with teachers as they strive to make instructional strategies more congruent with the cultural values of all students. Educational consultation occurs when a teacher works with a counselor, school psychologist, or school social worker for the purpose of assisting students improve their academic performance. The consultant (e.g., counselor, psychologist, or social worker) brings unique knowledge related to academic achievement to the process or the ability to tap resources that can yield solutions to students' problems to the consultee (teacher) to help the client (student) (Brown, Pryzwansky, & Schulte, 1998). Although the consultant may have information not known to teachers, the consultation process is equally dependent on the teacher's knowledge of the student and the teaching/learning process for success. The process of consultation includes five steps:

(1) development of an egalitarian relationship between the teacher and consultant,

(2) problem identification,

(3) goal setting,

(3) intervention selection,

(4) intervention implementation, and

(5) evaluation of outcomes.

With regard to the latter stage, evaluation of outcomes, two outcomes are expected to result from consultation. The first is that the client will receive better services from the teacher, and the second is that the teacher will be better able to cope with similar students in the future. Consultants play an active role in the consultation process, but the implementation of the intervention is left to the teacher.

Collaboration follows the same process as consultation — relationship development, problem identification, goal setting, intervention selection, intervention implementation, and evaluation—but the collaborator is involved in all of the steps including implementing the intervention and evaluating the outcomes (Dettmer, Dyck, & Thurston, 1996). The expected outcome of collaboration is that the student will be better served, but unlike consultation, there is no assumption that teachers will be better able to help similar students in the future.

There are no hard and fast rules regarding when to use consultation, collaboration, and advocacy. However, the following guidelines may be useful in determining which process to choose.

Use consultation when
- the intervention to be used is easy for teachers to understand and implement; and

- the consultant's presence in the classroom will not disrupt the teaching/learning process.

Do not use consultation when
- teachers are resistant;
- the same outcome can be achieved in simpler ways such as in-service training; and
- when the process adds work to the teacher's load.

Use collaboration when
- interventions are difficult to conceptualize and/or implement;
- the teacher lacks self-confidence; and
- when the solution to the problem literally requires more than one person to resolve. This might occur when there are several students in the same classroom who are underachieving.

Do not use collaboration when
- consultation can be used instead because of the time involved in implementing the intervention.

Use advocacy when
- the problem is embedded in institutional policies and practices that limit the educational opportunities for minorities and others, and they are unable to bring about change on their own.

Do not use advocacy when
- students or their parents can be empowered to represent their own interests successfully; and
- the conflict that inevitably flows from advocacy will permanently impair the functioning of the advocate.

Unique Knowledge and Consultation and Collaboration

Collaboration and consultation are both built on the premise that the consultant or collaborator brings specialized knowledge to the problem-solving process. Gladding and Pederson (1997) suggested that this "specialized knowledge" can be divided into three areas:
   (1) self-awareness of one's own skills and knowledge,
   (2) understanding of the perspective of the culturally different student, and
   (3) the ability to develop appropriate intervention strategies.

Dettmer, et al. (1996) indicated that, in the context of the classroom, the demonstration of specialized skills and knowledge that cover these three domains include
- understanding that not all students have Eurocentric values;
- avoiding offensive words and statements;
- working to increase information about, and sensitivity to, other cultural groups;

- counteracting prejudicial stereotypes when they occur;
- using books and materials that are free of stereotypes;
- including the contributions that members of minority groups have made in the curriculum;
- nurturing minority students in a manner that allows them to cope successfully with the dominant culture without giving up their own cultural identity;
- involving parents and others from various cultural backgrounds in the classroom;
- advocating for multiculturalism in all aspects of the school; and
- Establishing a classroom environment that promotes multicultural relationships, including pictures, displays, and posters.

Clearly what is missing from the Dettmer, et al. (1996) list is the skill and sensitivity needed to design culturally appropriate instructional strategies, section three in Gladding and Peterson's (1997) list of skills. Additionally, although it is implicit in the Dettmer, et al. list, it should be clear that consultants and collaborators will be unable to design culturally appropriate interventions unless they have knowledge about students from various minority groups. A brief quiz is presented in Figure 2-2 that can provide student support personnel with a quick look at their knowledge.

Figure 2-2

Assessing Your Knowledge

Complete this quiz by checking by True or False.

True   False

___   ___   1. I understand the cultural heritage of the minority students in my school including their values, customs, traditions, and religious views.

___   ___   2. I am aware of the stereotypes that people hold of the minority students in my school.

___   ___   3. I am aware of the behavioral differences (e.g., verbal expressiveness) between the minority students in my school and those of other students.

___   ___   4. I can explain the differences in the family structures of minority students and those typically found in our society.

___   ___   5. I am aware of the impact of historical discrimination on the views of some minority students.

___   ___   6. I am aware of the impact of current discriminatory patterns on the lives of minorities in my community and in this country.

_____ _____ 7. I am aware of the complex factors that may influence teacher/student interactions in the classroom, particularly as these relate to minority students.

_____ _____ 8. I am aware of the cultural limitations of the psychological assessment devices used in my school.

_____ _____ 9. I understand the limitations that impinge on English-as-a Second Language students in the learning process.

_____ _____ 10. I am aware of the differences that exist among the nonverbal patterns of communication of minorities and European Americans.

_____ _____ 11. I am aware of institutional policies and practices that limit the educational progress of minority students.

_____ _____ 13. I am aware of the cultural barriers that limit the ability of the families of minority students to intervene in the educational lives of children.

_____ _____ 14. I am aware of the prejudicial attitudes held by some members of the faculty that may limit their openness to changes that will enhance to achievement of minorities.

Next, complete the quiz that appears in Figure 2-3. This survey is designed to assess the skills and attitudes needed to make interventions with minority students.

Figure 2-3

**Skills And Attitudes Needed To Make
Interventions With Minority Students**

Complete this quiz by checking True or False.
True   False

_____ _____ 1. I recognize that some of my own stereotypes may interfere with my ability to work with minority students and constantly work to eliminate them.

_____ _____ 2. I have the skills needed to advocate for changes in institutional policies that may limit the educational progress of minorities.

_____ _____ 3. I have the skills needed to engage in successful cross-cultural consultation with the parents of minority students.

_____ _____ 4. I have the skills needed to consult/collaborate with teachers to assist them in their efforts to implement instructional strategies that will improve the achievement of minorities.

		5. I have the skills needed to carry on meaningful counseling and contract negotiation sessions with minority students.
—	—	
—	—	6. I can accurately interpret the assessment instruments used with minority students.
—	—	7. I have the skills needed to act as an advocate for minority students.

Linking Consultation, Collaboration and Advocacy to the Problems of Minority Students

As noted earlier, Vasquez (1998) outlined a process for developing instructional strategies for minority students, which he described generally as linking instructional interventions to cultural values. More specifically, the process outlined by Vasquez begins by identifying the "cultural traits" of students. Once the cultural traits of a particular student have been identified, three variables need to come into play: the content (subject matter) to be taught, the context (physical and psychological atmosphere of the classroom) in which materials are to be taught, and the mode or teaching style to be used in the presentation of the content. In Figures 2-4 to 2-7 an attempt will be made to identify some of the salient traits and other factors that grow out of the values and social context of cultural, ethnic, and racial minorities that may influence academic achievement. Later contextual variables that may influence the teaching/learning process of students from these groups are discussed and suggestions regarding the types of instructional strategies that may be most effective with each subgroup presented. In the final section of this chapter additional consideration will be given to how school counselors, school psychologists, and school social workers can use collaboration consultation, and advocate to get culturally sensitive instructional strategies adopted.

Figure 2-4

Cultural Factors That May Influence the Achievement of Hispanic American Students (Cuban, Puerto Rican, Mexican, Central and South American)

Factors That Promote Academic Achievement
- Strong family support
- Second or third generation in United States
- Higher socioeconomic status (SES)

Factors That Retard Achievement
- Non-conformance to classroom expectations

- English language deficiencies
- Late morning or afternoon preference (for learning)
- Culture shock if newly arrived (severe form includes elective mutism; withdrawal; alienation
- More sensitive to nonverbal; expression of feeling
- Preference for informal communication
- Preference for warm, personalized communication
- Relaxed attitude toward time
- Preferences for cooperative attainment of goals -discomfort with competition in the classroom
- Aversion to typical task-oriented styles of most teachers
- Less independence training (in traditional classroom
- Less positive toward education (Mexican Americans)
- Lower on need for achievement than Anglos
- Lower educational expectations/aspirations
- Preference for kinesthetic modality in learning (Mexican Americans) (in traditional classroom)
- Lower self-concept of ability
- Fatalistic (if poor)

Sources: Dunn, Griggs, & Price, 1993; Evans & Anderson, 1973; Ewing & Yong, 1992; Espinosa, 1998; Hernandez, 1973; Okagaki, Frensch, & Gordan, 1995; Ramirez, Taylor, & Petersen, 1971.

As can be seen in Figure 2-4, Hispanic American students may bring many deficiencies into the classroom rooted in the Eurocentric values of individualism, assertion, and competitiveness. Moreover, the instructional techniques in the typical classroom are typically formal in nature, and information is presented either orally or in written form. Hispanic American students who prefer informal communication and hands on learning experiences may find it more difficult to function academically than their Anglo counterparts. Because independence is not encouraged in some Hispanic families, students from those families may find it difficult to negotiate a classroom environment that expects a great deal of independent work. Further, because of their preferences for collateral social relationships, the peer group can become problematic if students in the group have low educational aspirations.

One instructional adaptation that may help Hispanic American students is cooperative learning (Slavin, 1990). This approach, which is described in detail in Chapter 3, emphasizes peer tutoring and group and individual performance appraisal. Many European Americans students and parents object to cooperative learning because of their concerns about individual performance and their competitive achievement values, but research suggests that the cooperative learning approach is superior to traditional instructional approaches in fostering learning. Importantly, when cooperative learning approaches utilize groups that include minority students, the racial climate in the classroom improves as judged by cross-cultural friendships and attitudes toward minorities (Slavin, 1990). An important aspect of cooperative learning is that it involves small group work in which peers are actively involved in assisting and encouraging each other. Cooperative learning strategies that are relatively easy to implement include

- partners: one individual in the partnership is asked to assist a less able student learn the material being taught.
- group projects in which all contribute: These are used by most teachers.
- jigsaw: All students are assigned groups for 6 to 8 weeks. For each task that is assigned to the group each student is given some of the material or information needed to complete the task.
- cross-grade tutoring: Students from higher grades are trained to tutor underachieving students.
- research projects: Students work cooperatively on projects and problems using library and or other resources (Schniedewind & Davidson, 1987).

The use of experiential learning techniques, such as simulations, may also be useful techniques for stimulating achievement. Students can learn about governmental process through the establishment of a simulated town in which all assume a role. A simulated business that borrows money at certain interest rates, prepares an annual budget, and computes profit and loss can provide a forum for teaching mathematical principles. Linking what is being learned to the "real world" (e.g., how math is used in day-to-day living) both now and in the future is another strategy that may be employed to stimulate interest among Hispanic American students. Independence training, or teaching students precisely what is expected in centers and other aspects of the instructional program, may also promote achievement. Hispanic American students should also be continuously encouraged to do better in school. Teachers who continuously express their faith in the ability of students to do the work and encourage them to try things that may be difficult may be more successful. In addition, many of the other group-based strategies suggested in other chapters in this book may also be helpful, but they require adaptation. For example, when contingency contracts are use with Hispanic American students, whenever possible they be group contracts (see Chapter 8).

Figure 2-5

**Cultural Factors That May Influence the Achievement
of African American Students**

Factors That Promote Achievement
- Peer support for achievement
- Optimism (if present)
- Altruism
- More expressiveness, particularly non-verbally (too much verbal expression can be a problem)
- Preference for visual modality in learning
- Perception of parent's achievement orientation critical
- Sense of control (if present)
- Involvement in school (if it occurs)

Factors That Retard Achievement
- High-risk neighborhood lowers achievement
- Value harmony (if peers are not achievers this is a problem)
- Imprecise expressions regarding facts (e.g., distances)
- Field dependent (need cues from the environment, prefer external structure, remember material in a social context, people oriented)
- Preference for social/affective learning situations
- Use of nonstandard English (in classrooms that emphasize standard English)

Sources: Ewing & Yong, 1992; Floyd, 1996; Ford, 1993. al., 1996; Johnson, 1992; Locke, 1995; Willis, 1989.

African Americans comprise the largest minority group in this country and have made great educational strides in the past 20 years. For example, the high school graduation rate of African American students is roughly equivalent to the graduation rate of European American students (Brown, 1998) in spite of the fact that they are more likely to be poor when compared to European Americans (Ponterotto & Casas, 1991). However, on average African American students achieve at a lower level than European Americans and Asian Americans, which places them at a disadvantage in college admissions, securing jobs, and other areas related to academic achievement.

As can be seen in Figure 2-5, African American students may bring a number of strengths to the classroom, but some of the factors listed are not present in all African American students. For example, not all African American students are optimistic and altruistic when they come to school. Moreover, their learning preferences for more informal and creative communication do not correspond to the formal and decidedly noncreative instructional styles of some teachers. For example, Hicks (1989) found that preschool children learned more when the content was presented in the form of "rap" music, and Locke (1995) recommended the use of music and dance to facilitate the communication of African American students.

Cooperative learning may also be an important way to improve the achievement of African American students. As noted in Figure 2-3, peer pressure can either facilitate or retard achievement. Unfortunately, some African American students see high levels of academic achievement as turning "White" and abandoning their African heritage. When this perception exists, it must be ameliorated or the chances of improving achievement for many African American students are greatly diminished. As emphasized in Chapter 8 and elsewhere, many of the strategies used by school counselors, school social workers, and school psychologists should be oriented to groups instead of individuals. This is particularly true when the target of the intervention is African American students.

In addition, the fact that many African American students speak nonstandard English, variously called Black English or Ebonics, has been widely discussed in the popular press. One side of the argument is that teaching using Ebonics is one way to facilitate the learning process and to move the African American students along the path of learning and the acquisition of standard English. Others disagree and take the stand that instruction should be done in standard English. At this point in time there is no resolution of this debate. However, lack of proficiency in writing and speaking standard English poses a barrier to African American students in the educational and vocational arenas; and African American students need to acquire high levels of proficiency in the use of standard English if they are to achieve at high levels regardless of the approach used to develop the skill.

Figure 2-6

**Cultural Factors That May Influence the Achievement
of Asian American Students (Chinese, Japanese, Korean,
Vietnamese; Cambodian, Laotian, Filipino)**

Factors That Promote Achievement
- Preference for visual modality in learning (in traditional classroom)
- Stronger work ethic, i.e., spending more time doing homework than other groups
- Peer support (so long as peers value achievement)
- Greater deference to parents
- Academic achievement brings honor to the family

Factors That Retard Achievement

22

- More reserved (if teacher is unaware of cultural values)
- Prefer cooperative learning (In competitive classroom environment)
- Cultural conflict with parents (as a result of adopting Eurocentric values)

Sources: Ewing & Yong, 1992; Peng & Wright, 1994; Yagi & Oh, 1995.

Asian American students have been characterized as the model minority because of their polite, reserved demeanor, their work ethic, and because they often do well in school. There are of course exceptions, particularly among the last group of immigrants who came to this country from Southeast Asia (Chuong, 1994). Although Asian American students have adapted well to the instructional strategies of the typical teacher, they are often more comfortable in cooperative learning situations. Additionally, Asian American students appear to be passive to many teachers (Chuong, 1994) and are stereotyped not only as being good in math and science but also as preferring classes and careers related to these areas (Sue & Sue, 1990). Additionally, many counselors, social workers, and psychologists who work with Asian American populations report conflicts between students who are adopting individualistic, democratic Eurocentric values and their parents who subscribe to collective values and who believe in hierarchical relationships (Brown, 1997). Because parental oversight appears to play a major role in the achievement of Asian American students, teachers and others need to nurture the student-parent relationship. This idea will be discussed in greater detail in Chapter 13.

Figure 2-7

**Cultural Factors That May Influence
the Achievement of American Indian Students
(Likely Variability Across 500 +Tribes)**

Factors That Promote Achievement
- Preference for observational or oral learning
- Strengths in visual memory

Factors That Retard Achievement
- Collective orientation and preference for cooperative learning (in traditional classroom)
- Quiet (teacher may not understand that this may mean respect)
- Inexpressive verbally or non-verbally
- Low educational self-esteem

- Lower educational aspirations
- Less parental support for education
- Less standard setting in the academic arena

Sources: Kleinfeld & Nelson, 1991; Peng & Wright, 1994; Thomason, 1995.

Although More (1990) indicated that there is considerable evidence that culture influences learning style, Kleinfeld and Nelson (1991) concluded there is no evidence to support the individualization of instruction for American Indian students based on learning style. Earlier, Gardner (1980) reviewed the literature regarding preferred learning mode and concluded that American Indian students prefer a visual mode of learning and have an affinity for subjects such as art, spelling, and penmanship. Although, Gardner's conclusions were based on logical extrapolations from learning style research, not empirical data, they make intuitive sense given the aural tradition of many American Indian tribes. Extrapolating even further from these sparse findings, it seems that the teaching/learning process for American Indians should be structured in a manner to accommodate all possible learning styles including the kinesthetic style apparently favored by some Hispanic American students. Other strategies that may enhance the achievement of American Indian students include cooperative learning experiences, peer tutoring, less formal analytical teaching, avoidance of stereotyping, and inclusion of classroom experiences that will enhance students' pride in their own culture. The starting points for the development of classroom activities is an extensive review of the history of the tribe, consultation with the elders of the tribe, and when possible, involvement of tribal representatives in the instructional process.

Linking Interventions to Minority Students

As noted earlier, collaboration and consultation involve a five-step process. The most critical of these steps is accurate identification of the problem and selection of an appropriate intervention. Although this not an easy task, some general recommendations can be made at this point that should probably be followed regardless of the nature of the problem.

Many of the students discussed in this chapter hold collective social values. For this reason, interventions should often include parents. This would be particularly true if the student holds a lineal-collective social value where parental authority is unquestioned. Specific recommendations for involving parents in the teaching/learning process are made in Chapter 13. Further, because of the collective value of many minority students, interventions should probably be aimed at peer groups instead of individuals. Many strategies for making these types of interventions are included in later chapters. However, in the classroom, cooperative learning should at least partially replace traditional instructional approaches to maximize the achievement of minority students. Peer tutoring programs may also be useful in the process of stimulating achievement (see Chapter 10).

Alienated students are unlikely to do well in school. The elimination of racism and sexism in the classroom is a good first step toward producing a friendlier learning environment for minority students. Developing culturally sensitive learning strategies is an excellent second step. For example, many elementary school counselors conduct self-esteem units that ask children to tell the class some of their strengths. This practice is likely to be embarrassing to students who hold collective values. Teachers who provide individual recognition may evoke the same response. Many students are placed in classroom situations in which they have to violate their own cultural values in order to fit into the classroom environment. Third, choosing material that is fair to all groups is a mandatory step toward producing a classroom environment that is conducive to learning for all students. Providing opportunities for the groups in the classroom to become familiar with each other's cultural heritage is a fourth step that should be taken.

Finally, although there are undoubtedly culturally specific learning styles and preferences, these are hard to identify. It therefore becomes important that Vasquez's (1998) strategy of careful observation of individuals be adopted as culturally sensitive learning strategies are developed. Specifically, Vasquez recommended that each student should be studied, specific problems be identified, and changes in instruction be made based on the observations. Once problems are identified they can be addressed, either through consultation or collaboration. If individual concerns are not addressed, or the broader issues of racism, inclusion, and cultural sensitivity are still problems, then advocacy becomes the intervention of choice.

Summary

The very difficult issue of underachievement among many minority groups is addressed in this chapter. Although consultation, collaboration, and advocacy have been discussed as techniques that can be used to facilitate the achievement of minorities, all of the strategies in this book may be useful if they are applied properly.

One of the major problems identified in this chapter is the mismatch between the instructional strategies employed in the typical classroom and the learning styles and values of minority students. This situation can be corrected to some degree by the inclusion of cooperative learning approaches, the use of peer tutoring, and the use of less formal communication styles. Cultural insensitivity, another major problem, also needs to be corrected in many instances to avoid the alienation of minority students.

References

Brown, D. (1997). Implications of cultural values for cross-cultural family consultation. *The Journal of Counseling and Development, 76,* 20-35.

Brown, D. (1998). *Leader's manual: hanging in or dropping out: What you should know before you leave school* (2nd Ed.). Lincolnwood, IL: VGM Books.

Brown, D., Pryzwansky, W. P., & Schulte, A. (1998). *Psychological consultation: Introduction to theory and practice* (4th ed.). Boston: Allyn & Bacon.

Chuong, C. H. (1994). *Vietnamese students: Changing patterns, changing need.* San Francisco: Many Cultures.

Dettmer, P.A., Dyck, N. T., & Thurston, L. (1996). *Consultation, collaboration and teamwork for students with special needs* (2nd ed.). Boston: Allyn & Bacon.

Dunn, R., Griggs, S. A., & Price, G. E. (1993). Learning styles of Mexican American and Anglo-American elementary school students. *Journal of Multicultural Counseling and Development, 21,* 237-247.

Espinosa, L. M. (1998). School involvement and Hispanic parents. *The Prevention Researcher, 5* (1), 5-6.

Evans, F. B., & Anderson, J. G. (1973). The psychological origins of achievement and achievement motivation. *Sociology of Education, 46,*396-416.

Ewing, N. J., & Yong, F. L. (1992). A comparative study of the learning style preferences among gifted African American, Mexican American, and American-born Chinese American middle-school students. *Roeper Review, 14,* 120-123.

Floyd, C. (1996). Achieving despite the odds. A study of resilience among a group of African American high school seniors. *Journal of Negro Education, 65,* 181-189.

Ford, D. Y. (1993). Black students' achievement orientation as a function of perceived family achievement orientation and demographic variables. *Journal of Negro Education, 62,* 47-66.

Gardner, R. C. (1980, November). *Learning styles. What every teacher should consider.* Paper presented at the Rocky Mountain Regional Conference of the International Reading Association, Boise, ID.

Gladding, S. T., & Pedersen, P. (1997). Multicultural counseling competencies: A self-examination. *ACES Spectrum, 58* (2), 4-5.

Gonzales, N. A., Cauce, A. M., Friedman, R. J., & Mason, C. A. (1996). Family, peer, and neighborhood influences on academic achievement among African American adolescents: One-year prospective effects. *Journal of Community Psychology, 24,* 365-387.

Hernandez, N. G. (1973). Variables affecting the achievement of middle school Mexican-American students. *Review of Educational Research, 43,* 1-39.

Hicks, P. T. (1997, August). *The relationship between an oral rhythmic style of communication (rap music) and learning in the urban preschool.* Paper presented at the Annual Meeting of the Association of Education in Journalism and Mass Communication. San Antonio, TX.

Johnson, S. T. (1992). Extra-school factors in achievement, attainment, and aspirations among junior and senior high-school-age African American youths. *Journal of Negro Education, 61,* 99-119.

Kleinfeld, J., & Nelson, P. (1991). Adapting instruction to Native Americans' learning styles: An iconoclastic view. *Journal of Cross-Cultural Psychology, 22,* 273-282.

Kluckhorn, F. R., & Strodtbeck, F. L. (1961). *Values in value orientations.* Evanston, IL: Row Paterson.

Kurpius, D. J., & Lewis, J. E. (1988). Introduction to consultation: An intervention for outreach and advocacy. In D. J. Kurpius & D. Brown (Eds.) *Handbook of consultation* (pp. 1-4). Alexandria, VA: Association of Counselor Education and Supervision.

Locke, D. C. (1995). Counseling intervention with African American youth. In C. C. Lee (Ed.) *Counseling for Diversity* (pp. 21-40) Boston: Longwood.

More, A. J. (1990, August). *Learning styles of Native Americans and Asians.* Paper presented at the Annual Meeting of the American Psychology Association, Boston, MA.

Morales, M., & Scheafor, J. (1986). *Social work: A profession of many faces.* Boston: Allyn & Bacon.

Okagaki, L., Frensch, P. A., & Gordan, E. W. (1995). Encouraging school achievement in Mexican-American children. *Hispanic Journal of Behavioral Science, 17,* 160-179.

Peng, S. S., & Wright, D. (1994). Explanation of academic achievement of Asian American students. *Journal of Educational Research, 87,* 346-352.

Ponterotto, J. G., & Casas, J. M. (1991). *Handbook of racial/ethnic minority counseling research.* Springfield, IL: Charles C Thomas.

Ramirez, M., Taylor, C., & Petersen, B. (1971). Mexican-American cultural membership and adjustment to school. *Developmental Psychology, 4,* 141-148.

Schniedewind, N., & Davidson, E. (1987). *Cooperative learning, cooperative lives.* Dubuque, IA: Wm. C. Brown.

Slavin, R. S. (1990). *Cooperative learning: Theory, research and practice.* Englewood Cliffs, NJ: Prentice Hall.

Sue, D. W., & Sue, D. (1990). *Counseling the culturally different* (2nd Ed.). New York: Wiley.

Thomason, T. C. (1995). Counseling Native American students. In C. C. Lee (Ed.), *Counseling for diversity* (109-126). Boston: Longwood

Vasquez, J. A. (1998). Distinctive traits of Hispanic students. *The Prevention Researcher, 5* (1), 1-4.

Willis, M. G. (1989). Learning styles of African American children: A review of the literature and interventions. *Journal of Black Psychology, 16,* 47-65.

Wilson, T. L. Y., & Banks, B. (1994). A perspective on the education of African American males. *Journal of Instructional Psychology, 21,* 97-100.

Yagi, D. T., & Oh, M. Y. (1995). Counseling Asian American students. In C. C. Lee (Ed.), *Counseling for diversity* (61-84). Boston: Longwood.

Zapata, J. T. (1995). Counseling Hispanic children and youth. In C. C. Lee (Ed.), *Counseling for diversity* (85-109). Boston: Longwood.

Your Cultural Values

by Duane Brown

Complete this survey of cultural values by circling the number that most clearly indicates the extent to which the statement pertains to you. Use the following rating scale:

    1. This statement does not describe my beliefs.

    2. This statement describes my beliefs to a small degree.

    3. This statement describes my beliefs to some degree.

    4. This statement describes my beliefs to a great degree.

    5. This statement describes my beliefs to a very great degree.

    6. This statement describes my beliefs with almost total accuracy.

A. Time Orientation

Rate the degree to which each statement describes your beliefs:

1. It is very important to plan for the future. 1 2 3 4 5 6

2. "Live for the moment." is one of mybeliefs. 1 2 3 4 5 6

3. I believe that the future is important.
but the past must not be forgotten.   1 2 3 4 5 6

4. I believe that nature's clock, as told by
things like the changing of the seasons,
is the best way to keep track of time. 1 2 3 4 5 6

5. The future is most important.   1 2 3 4 5 6

6. The present is most important.   1 2 3 4 5 6

7. The past and future are both important. 1 2 3 4 5 6

8. I prefer not to think about time in minutes,
hours, and days.   1 2 3 4 5 6

9. The important events are the ones that will
occur in the future.   1 2 3 4 5 6

10. The important events are the things that are
happening now. The future will take care
    of itself.   1 2 3 4 5 6

11. The events that have happened in the
past must be remembered as we move
into the future.   1 2 3 4 5 6

12. Time occurs in circles and many events
that have occurred in the past will repeat
themselves in some form.   1 2 3 4 5 6

B. Action Orientation

Rate the degree to which each statement describes your beliefs:

1. It is important to act when there is a problem
    to be solved.   1 2 3 4 5 6

2. Most problems do not need immediate
action.   1 2 3 4 5 6

3. Careful and controlled response is the best
way to take action when problems arise.   1 2 3 4 5 6

4. I feel better when I am doing something
about problems that arise.   1 2 3 4 5 6

5. Many problems will go away if you do nothing.
Sometimes I'm comfortable doing nothing.   1 2 3 4 5 6

6. I'm most comfortable when I respond to
problems after careful thought.   1 2 3 4 5 6

7. If I have someplace to go, I want to get
started.   1 2 3 4 5 6

8. If I have someplace to go, I don't worry
much about getting started.   1 2 3 4 5 6

9. Getting started on a trip is not very important.
When it is time to start I will know it.   1 2 3 4 5 6

C. Self-Control

Rate the degree to which each statement describes your beliefs:

1. Losing control of my emotions in public
would be embarrassing.   1 2 3 4 5 6

2. I'm not embarrassed when I lose control
of my emotions.   1 2 3 4 5 6

3. Keeping control of my thoughts and emotions
is very important.   1 2 3 4 5 6

4. It's okay to lose control of your emotions
sometimes.   1 2 3 4 5 6

5. It doesn't bother me when others get angry
or upset.   1 2 3 4 5 6

6. It makes me uncomfortable when others get
angry or upset.   1 2 3 4 5 6

D. Achievement Orientation

Rate the degree to which each statement describes your beliefs:

1. People need to compete with each other
to get ahead.   1 2 3 4 5 6

2. The best way to achieve is to work with
others.   1 2 3 4 5 6

3. It makes me feel good when my
accomplishments are recognized.   1 2 3 4 5 6

4. It makes me uncomfortable when others know
that I have performed better than they did.   1 2 3 4 5 6

5. Sometimes I tell others about my
accomplishments.   1 2 3 4 5 6

6. I rarely or never tell people about my
accomplishments.   1 2 3 4 5 6

E. Relationships
Rate the degree to which each statement describes your beliefs:

1. I believe that each individual should work to
   be independent.   1 2 3 4 5 6
2. It is important for people to work
   together cooperatively.   1 2 3 4 5 6
3. Although working harmoniously is
   important, some people's opinions are
   more important than others.   1 2 3 4 5 6
4. If you disagree it is important to state your
   opinion, even if it is different than the
   opinion of people in authority.   1 2 3 4 5 6
5. If you disagree with someone it is
   important to resolve the problem so that
   everyone agrees.   1 2 3 4 5 6
6. When disagreements arise it is not
   important to state your own opinion, and
   it is often necessary to go along with
   people in authority.   1 2 3 4 5 6
7. Personal decisions should be made by the
   individual.   1 2 3 4 5 6
8. Personal decisions should be made with
   other important people such as family
   members.   1 2 3 4 5 6
9. Sometimes when making personal
   decisions it is important to take the advice
   of others instead of making the decision
   yourself.   1 2 3 4 5 6

Scoring Your Cultural Values

Time Orientation

    1, 5, 9 = future orientation

    2, 6, 10 = present orientation

    3, 7, 11 = past/present orientation

    4, 8, 12 = circular

Action Orientation

    1, 4, 7 = doing

    2, 5, 8 = being

    3, 6, 9 = being-in-becoming

Maintaining Self-Control

    1, 3, 5 = very important

    2, 4, 6 = moderately important

Achievement Orientation

    1, 3, 5 = individual

    2, 4, 6 = cooperative

Relationships

    1, 4, 7 = individualism

    2, 5, 8 = collateral or collective

    3, 6, 9 = lineal

Return to the discussion of cultural values in this chapter for a fuller understanding of the values measured by Handout 2-1, Your Cultural Values.

Chapter Three

Improving Academic Achievement Through Cooperative Learning

The concept of cooperative learning was introduced in Chapter 2 as an approach that may be particularly helpful to many minority students because of the congruence of the concepts involved with collective values. Cooperative approaches to teaching and learning depart to some degree from competitive approaches to the teaching and learning that characterize most classrooms in this country (Johnson & Johnson, 1986). It is based on four simple but powerful ideas. First, students work together in teams to learn. Second, team members are responsible for their own learning *and* the learning of their teammates. Third, there is equal opportunity of success in the teams because they are structured in a manner that allows all members to contribute to the success of the team. Fourth, teams receive recognition for their collective efforts, but there is individual accountability, which means that although teams work together to learn, ultimately each student is judged on his or her merit (Johnson & Johnson, 1986; Slavin, 1990).

One of the expected outcomes of cooperative learning is increased achievement. Slavin (1990) reviewed 68 studies that met rigid methodological criteria and found that 72% of the studies favored cooperative learning while 12% favored traditional control groups consisting of students taught using traditional methods. There were no significant differences between control and experimental groups in the other studies (16%). Slavin also looked at other outcomes and found that cooperative learning improved friendships between handicapped and nonhandicapped, a conclusion identical to that of Johnson and Johnson (1986) after an earlier review. Moreover, Slavin (1990) concluded that the use of cooperative methodology in the classroom resulted in increased numbers of reciprocal friendships among students of different ethnic backgrounds.

Schniedewind & Davidson (1987, p. 9) also reviewed the outcomes of cooperative and competitive approaches to learning. They summarized their findings by contrasting the outcomes of cooperative learning versus competitive learning on the learner:

Competition outcomes - Learner believes	vs.	Cooperation outcomes - Learner believes
My goal is most important		Goals of others and my goal are both important
I work and live to benefit myself and others		I work and live to benefit myself and others
I consider my needs first		Both my needs and the needs of others are important
I have positive feelings when I win over others		I have positive feelings when everyone succeeds
I have positive feelings about myself when I win		I have positive feelings when all succeed together.
I am responsible and accountable only to myself		I am responsible and accountable to myself /others

Because of the potential of cooperative learning approaches to increase achievement for all students, two approaches–student learning teams and student learning teams with tournaments–that can be used in all types of classrooms will be presented in this chapter. (For additional information about the techniques presented here, as well as other specialized cooperative learning techniques, readers may contact John Hopkins Learning Team Project, 3305 North Charles Street, Baltimore, MD 21218.)

Note that many of the forms used in cooperative learning as outlined in this chapter are not included because they are copyrighted. The forms that are included were devised by the author unless otherwise indicated.

Student Learning Teams: Slavin (1990) reported that the approach to cooperative learning that has been around for the longest time is student learning teams. This approach involves eight steps:

1. Set up heterogeneous student teams: The makeup of teams should reflect the overall demographic composition of the classroom. Teams should be composed of four to five students from all achievement levels, both genders, and all ethnic groups. Groups should also include special education students who are being mainstreamed.

To establish teams made up of four students begin by ranking students in terms of their current achievement levels. If percentage grades are given, this is fairly easy. For example, students in a math class might be ranked 1 through 24 and assigned to teams based on the last three quiz grades in some phase of mathematics (see Figure 3-1). Note that if six teams are to be established, the order of assignment changes after the top six students are assigned. As is shown in Figures 3-1 and 3-2, the Devils were assigned the top student in round one. In the next round of assignments the Devils get the bottom student in the next tier of students. The Hoos, who were assigned to lowest ranking student in the first tier in round one get the top student in the second tier in round two. The Heels who were assigned the student with the second highest grade in round one get the student with the next to the lowest grade average in round two and the second highest student in the third tier in round three. The assignment process begins until all students are assigned to teams.

If teams are formed at the beginning of the school year, last year's averages or grades can be used to group students. (See Figure 3- 2). If possible, the weights assigned to grades should be based on the grading standard in the school. Also, if there are more than 24 students, some teams may be composed of 5 team members. Regardless of the number of team members assigned, the goal of the assignment process is to equalize the achievement level of the groups.

Figure 3-1

Preliminary Team Assignments Based on Test Averages

Student Names	Average	Student Rank	Student Assignments
Larry	94	1	Devils
Jamarcus	92	2	Heels
Jayne	90	3	Deacons
Felicia	89	4	Jackets
Lorenzo	88	5	Pack
J. R.	87	6	Hoos
Janet	86	7	Hoos
Latisha	85	8	Pack
Lawrence	84.5	9	Jackets
Bill	83	10	Deacons
Kim	82.5	11	Heels
Karen	82	12	Devils
Juan	81	13	Devils
Jake	80.5	14	Heels
Kristin	80	15	Deacons
Christina	79	16	Jackets
John	78	17	Pack
Johanna	76	18	Hoos
Caroline	74	19	Hoos
Campbell	72	20	Pack
Katherine	71	21	Jackets
Jed	70	22	Deacons
Jerry	66	23	Heels
Kittrel	62	24	Devils

Figure 3-2

Preliminary Team Assignments Based On Grades

Student Names	Grade/Weight	Student Ranks	Student Assignments
Larry	A / 93	1	Devils
Jamarcus	A- / 90	2	Heels
Jayne	B+ / 87	3	Deacons
Felicia	B+ / 87	4	Jackets
Lorenzo	B+ / 87	5	Pack
J. R.	B / 84	6	Hoos
Janet	B / 84	7	Hoos
Latisha	B - / 81	8	Pack
Lawrence	B- /81	9	Jackets
Bill	C+ / 78	10	Deacons
Kim	C+ / 78	11	Heels
Karen	C+ / 78	12	Devils
Juan	C / 75	13	Devils
Jake	C / 75	14	Heels
Kristin	C / 75	15	Deacons
Christina	C / 75	16	Jackets
John	C / 75	17	Pack
Johanna	C / 75	18	Hoos
Caroline	C- / 72	19	Hoos
Campbell	C- /72	20	Pack
Katherine	D / 69	21	Jackets
Jed	D / 69	22	Deacons
Jerry	D- / 66	23	Heels
Kittrel	F / 63	24	Devils
Carl *	F /63	25	

* Carl should be assigned to team with the highest average to make up a five-student team.

Once preliminary team assignments are completed, adjustments in team composition should be made based on gender, ethnicity (Slavin, 1990), and the nature of student handicaps (Johnson & Johnson, 1986). The resulting groups should be truly heterogeneous. This can be done by moving students from group to group based on their achievement scores.

2. *Teach material:* Once teams are established the instructional process begins. Typically, the teachers make presentations using traditional lecture-discussion methodology. However, regardless of the instruction strategy utilized, instruction must be focused on specific objectives if cooperative learning is to be successful.

3. *Prepare the team for cooperative learning:* Few students have been exposed to cooperative learning and thus even high school students must be prepared to learn using this approach. Younger students may need to be trained in active listening skills, asking questions, and other basic social skills. Basic tutoring skills should probably be taught to all students. All students need to know the goals of the cooperative learning group, the criteria for success for the group, and the nature of the individual accountability (grading) system. Johnson and Johnson (1986) pointed out that a common concern of nonhandicapped students is that their grades will be lowered as a result of having handicapped students in their groups. In many instances the individual accountability system included in cooperative learning will allay this fear, but some reassurance may be called for with some students

4. *Team study begins:* The team study component is the critical aspect of cooperation. Students are asked not only to master the material that has been taught, but to help others in the groups master the material as well. The rules of team study are as follows (Slavin, 1990):
- The group has completed its work when all team members have mastered the material.
- The key word is *mastered*. The work of the team is to make sure that each student will get a perfect score on the test.
- If questions arise, team members are to ask all other team members for help prior to asking the teacher.
- Move desks together and talk softly.
- Be positive and supportive, not critical or demeaning.

5. *Quiz the students:* After the teacher feels that a reasonable period of time has elapsed, a quiz should be administered to determine how much *each* student has learned. Students are not allowed to help each other on the quizzes. Some teachers will want to give practice quizzes prior to the test that is used to determine individual grades and team improvement scores.

6. *Process the learning experience:* Schniewind and Davidson (1987, p. 37) suggested that an important step in cooperative learning is to have students discuss their learning experiences, a step they called *processing*. Moreover, they suggested that processing be focused on both the content that was learned and the cooperative learning experience. Processing is done by asking questions such as the following:

About the cooperative learning experience
  • What were some of your feelings as you did the project?
  • Did anyone do something particularly positive? Negative?
  • How did the group work together to accomplish task?
  • What should the group do differently next time?
  • About the content
  • What were the most important ideas you learned?
  • What surprised you?
  • What more would you like to learn on this topic?

7. Recognize team performance: Determining the level of a team's performance can be done in a number of ways (cf. Johnson & Johnson, 1986). However, team quiz scores are used as the basis for determining what Slavin (1990, p. 63) calls *improvement points*. He suggested that improvement points be computed based on the following formula:

If the quiz score is
  • more than 10 points below the baseline average = 0 improvement points
  • 1 to 10 points below the baseline average = 10 improvement points
  • equal to 10 points above the baseline average = 20 improvement points
  • more than 10 points above the baseline average = 30 improvement points
  • perfect paper regardless of base score = 30 improvement points

After improvement points are computed, each team's total score is determined. In Figure 3-3 the improvement score for the Devils (from Figure 3-1) is shown.

Figure 3-3			
Individual and Team Improvement Scores for the Devils			
Student Score	**Class Average**	**Quiz**	**Improvement**
Larry	94	100	30
Karen	82	81	10
Juan	81	89	20
Kittrel	62	70	80
		Total Team Score =	80

Although it was mentioned in the introduction to this chapter, it is worth reiterating that in cooperative learning each team member has an opportunity to contribute to the success of the team. Kittrel, who has the lowest initial average, contributed as much or more to the team's score as did two other team members.

Once team improvement scores are computed, teams should be rewarded based on some predetermined criteria that should be determined logically. For example, it is not unreasonable to expect that every student in a group will maintain her or his level of performance. This would result in a team score of 80. Teams that meet this criterion could be recognized as All State (i.e., North Carolina)Teams. Teams that achieve scores of 90 could be recognized as All-American Teams, and teams that have team improvement scores of 100 or above could be recognized as All World Teams. This type of reward system allows all teams to gain recognition. In fact, it is conceivable that all teams in this system would achieve All World Team status. A team summary sheet such as the one shown in Figure 3-4 can be used to track team progress over a number of lessons.

Figure 3-4

Cooperative Learning Team Summary Sheet

Team Name _____

Team Members	1	2	3	4	5	6	7	8	9
_____	—	—	—	—	—	—	—	—	—
_____	—	—	—	—	—	—	—	—	—
_____	—	—	—	—	—	—	—	—	—
_____	—	—	—	—	—	—	—	—	—
_____	—	—	—	—	—	—	—	—	—
_____	—	—	—	—	—	—	—	—	—
Team Total Score	—	—	—	—	—	—	—	—	—
Team Average*	—	—	—	—	—	—	—	—	—
Team Award	—	—	—	—	—	—	—	—	—

* Team Average = team score ÷ number of team members

Note: From: *Cooperative Learning: Theory, Research and Practice* by R. E. Slavin, (p.156) 1990. Englewood Cliffs, NJ: Prentice Hall. Reprinted by permission of the publisher.

The mechanism for providing rewards should vary. Individual certificates, notes to parents, notices in school bulletins and school newspapers, and more tangible rewards if the school's budget permits have all been used for this purpose. Regardless of the approach used, team rewards are an essential component of cooperative learning. Certificates are particularly easy to produce on most word processing programs if a relatively sophisticated printer is available.

8. Ensure individual accountability: Because each student in the group takes quizzes on his or her own, individual accountability is preserved. Ultimately, the grade each student receives is the result of his or her own learning.

Recycling Student Learning Teams and Blending Approaches

Because students learn at different rates it is necessary to re-form student learning teams from time to time to correct achievement-level imbalances. In elementary school classes, students may belong to several student learning teams. Also, based on their achievement levels in math, reading, language arts, science, students may be assigned to four learning teams. Additionally, it is not necessary for teachers to use cooperative learning in all subjects. Students may be involved in cooperative learning in mathematics and traditional learning approaches in other subjects.

Student Learning Teams - Using Tournaments

The first four steps in setting up student learning teams with tournaments are the same as those outlined in the preceding section. Student learning teams are established, teachers provide instruction, learning teams are prepared for cooperation, and team study for mastery of the subject matter occurs. However, at step 5 in the cooperative learning process, tournaments are utilized instead of quizzes.

Tournaments are competitive events in which all representatives from each team compete with members of other teams who are at their same achievement level. In Figure 3-5 the six teams that were established in Figure 3-1 are shown. In tournaments each person is assigned to a table with two other students. In the case of the six teams described in Figure 3-5, the students in row 1 compete as would the students in row 2, row 3, and so forth. Slavin (1990) suggested that the numbers of the tables be scrambled so that the students could not automatically identify tables with students performing at various levels.

Figure 3-5

Teams from Figure 3-1

Devils		Heels		Deacons		Competitors	Scrambled #
Student	Average	Student	Average	Student	Average		
Larry	94	Jamarcus	92	Jayne	90	1	6
Karen	82	Kim	82.5	Bill	83	2	5
Juan	81	Jake	80.5	Kristin	80	3	4
Kittrel	62	Jerry	66	Jed	70	4	7
Jackets		**Pack**		**Hoos**			
Felicia	89	Lorenzo	88	J.R.	87	5	8
Lawrence	84.5	Latisha	85	Janet	86	6	1
Christina	79	John	78	Johanna	76	7	2
Katherine	72	Campbell	72	Caroline	74	8	3

Once students are seated at their tables, they should be given a deck of cards (these could be playing cards or simply a deck of cards constructed for the tournament). Each students should draw one card from the deck. The student who draws the highest card begins the tournament at that table, the one with the second highest cards goes second, and the student with the lowest card goes third. Students should also be given two sets of numbered cards, one with numbered questions that are to be answered during the tournament and one with correspondingly numbered answers. The number of question/answer cards given to each group should be divisible by three so that each student has an equal chance of going first when the tournament begins. Students should also receive numbered answer sheets on which to record the results of their answers to each question. At this point, the tournament begins and proceeds as follows:

5. Start the tournament: Simultaneously at each table, the student who drew the highest number selects a card from the deck and attempts to answer the question on it. Challenger one (the student who drew the second highest number) agrees or disagrees with the first student. If she or he disagrees with the answer that is given, he or she must provide an alternative answer. The student with the lowest number either agrees with or challenges either or both students who have preceded her/him. If she or he challenges both students, then an answer must be provided. After all students have responded, the answer to the question is drawn and read aloud. After each turn, students record the accuracy of their responses on their answer sheets (see Figure 3-6) with an X (correct) or an O (incorrect).

Table 3-6

Sample Student Tournament Scorecard

Science Tournament 1 - Climate

Team Name ————————————————————

Name ————————————————————————

Date ————————————————————————

Please place an X beside the number of each qustion you answered correctly and an O by each question that you answered incorrectly.

1.____	8.____	15.____
2.____	9.____	16.____
3.____	10.____	17.____
4.____	11.____	18.____
5.____	12.____	19.____
6.____	13.____	20.____
7.____	14.____	21.____

Record the number of X's on this sheet:_____

Tournament Points_____

6. *Compute tournament points for each individual:* Tournament points are computed as follows (Slavin, 1990, p. 72):

	No Ties	Tie for Top Score	Tie for Bottom Score	Three-way Tie
Low score at table	20	20	30	40
Middle score at table	40	50	30	40
High score at table	60	50	60	40

7. *Compute team points:* Computing the total number of team points involves adding the scores of the four-team members together. Slavin (1990) suggested that the awards be given on the basis of team averages, and, if this is the case, average scores should be computed. These computations can be handled by the teams if older students are involved. Calculation errors should result in disqualification.

Teachers may wish to provide teams with summary sheets and allow them to keep track of scores if several rounds are to be included in the tournament, which is typically the case (see Figure 3-7). This sheet should contain a space for the team name, a list of team members, a place for the individual, total and average scores for each round, and the nature of the award received, if any. Slavin (1990) suggested that team awards be given on the following basis: average score of 40 = good team; average score of 50 = great team, and average score of 60 = super team. However, teachers may wish to modify this system to reflect their goals for the class.

8. *Provide awards:* This process is very much like the one described earlier for Student Learning Teams. One difference is that awards can contain information about the number of rounds won. Also, awards may be cumulative, and thus tangible awards may replace certificates and announcements as teams pile up victories in rounds of continuing tournaments.

Recycling Teams

After one or two rounds, students should be reassigned to other groups based on their scores. Slavin (1990) suggests that the winners and losers from each table be reassigned. If there are ties, he suggests that a coin flip be used to decide who is to be reassigned. The basic principle involved in reassignment is that the students who are most successful are reassigned to tournament tables with stiffer competition and the least successful students are assigned to tables that are less competitive. The obvious problem with this is that the table with the highest achieving students will remain as the top table and the table with the lowest achievers is likely to remain the least competitive table. Figure 3-7 illustrates the principles involved in reassignment of students.

Figure 3-7
Reassigning Students

Table 1 (Highest achievers) Student who has lowest scores is reassigned to Table 2.

Table 2   Student who has highest scores is reassigned to Table 1;

                               Student who has the lowest scores is reassigned to Table 3;

Table 3 (Lowest achievers) Student who is highest achiever is reassigned to Table 2

Grading

The procedure outlined above is based largely on Slavin's approach to cooperative learning. Although, his approach does not provide a basis for grading students (individual accountability) because of the way questions and answers are presented in his tournament format, the quizzes, as they are outlined here, can be used as the basis for grading if the teacher chooses to do so. In the example provided, every student has an opportunity to provide answers to every question, although not in the traditional fashion. Teachers who use tournaments will probably use other individualized assessments as well.

Summary

Cooperative learning is introduced in Chapter Two as an approach that has great potential in the battle to increase the achievement level of minorities. However, the discussion of cooperative learning is placed in a separate chapter because its potential to increase achievement extends to all students. Just as important, cooperative learning has the potential to ameliorate the problems that develop in the traditional, competitive classroom. Increases in cross-cultural friendships and appreciation for handicapped students are two potential byproducts of cooperative learning.

References

Johnson, D. W., & Johnson, R. T. (1986). Mainstreaming and cooperative learning strategies. *Exceptional Children, 52,* 553-561.

Schniedewind, N., & Davidson, E. (1987). *Cooperative learning, cooperative lives.* Dubuque, IA: Wm. C. Brown.

Slavin, R. S. (1990). *Cooperative learning: Theory, research and practice.* Englewood Cliffs, NJ: Prentice Hall.

Chapter Four

Developing a Positive School Climate: Influencing Student Perceptions and Heightening Teacher Awareness

In Chapter 1 the importance of making strategic interventions, that is interventions that are tailored to the identified needs of students, was stressed. This chapter is about developing a school climate that can greatly reduce the need for strategic interventions by preventing problems from arising. Influencing the climate of the school is a major, but necessary, undertaking because negative school climates have been linked to factors such as dropping out of school (General Accounting Office, 1992) and lowered academic achievement (Nelson, Covin, & Smith, 1996). In order to make an impact on the climate of a school, a number of strategies are required, not all of which are focused on individual students. For example, system-wide policies regarding discipline and programs such as student assistance programs for smokers and alcohol users modeled after employee assistance programs in business and industry, influence the climate of each school. Given the political realities of most school districts that are governed by elected school boards and managed by an ever-changing administrative hierarchy, jousting with the system seems likely to be unproductive. However, most public schools have a great deal of latitude regarding the implementation of the school district's policies, and thus the emphasis in this chapter is on establishing a positive climate at the building, department, and classroom levels. These are the areas that most effect the day-to-day lives of students that are most amenable to influence by student support personnel.

What makes a positive school climate? Purkey and Schmidt (1996) emphasized that schools must be "inviting places." Schools are inviting–and have a positive climate–when

> (1) the people in the school are perceived as warm, caring, and concerned;
>
> (2) faculty, staff, and administrators see students as valuable and treat them with respect, even when they have misbehaved;
>
> (3) educational policies, including those affecting program admission, grading, promotion, and discipline, are designed

and administered so they foster personal and educational development;

(4) programs, including the curricula, are designed to be inclusive; and

(5) students are recognized for their accomplishments and encouraged to fulfill their potential.

Perhaps the inviting condition that is most often neglected is number 4, programs and the curricula are designed to be inclusive. Many schools celebrate Black History Month, honor Dr. Martin Luther King, Jr. on his birthday, note the arrival of the Chinese new year, make mention of the celebrations that coincide with Ramadan (the Muslim fast from sunup to sundown during the ninth month of the Muslim year to mark God's revelation of the Koran to the prophet Mohammed. It ends with a three-day feast, Eid al Fitra). They also make students aware of certain Jewish holidays such as Rosh Hashanah (the beginning of the Jewish New Year), Yom Kippur (The Day of Atonement), and Chanukah (marks the victor of the Maccabees over Syrians in 165 BC and the rededication of the temple in Jerusalem). However, with few exception public schools are more oriented to Christian traditions and holidays. More importantly, the curricula and the methods of teaching are based on assumptions drawn from values of western European culture, sometimes to the detriment of cultural, ethnic, and racial minorities.

This chapter focuses on the two aspects of a positive school climate listed above, ensuring that people are viewed as warm and caring and students are treated with respect and caring. The remainder of the factors that make up school climate, recognizing accomplishments and encouraging individuals to fulfill their potential, will be addressed extensively in later chapters (see Chapters 3, 7, and 8). The outcomes of these efforts should be that student perception of schooling is more positive

Orientation programs for continuing students are an important aspect of the effort to influence students' perceptions of the educational process, as are new student support groups and other types of support groups (MacGregor, Nelson, & Wesch, 1997). Training teachers to be more inviting, teaching them to communicate more effectively with students , and helping them develop positive disciplinary procedures are also important strategies that can influence students' attitudes toward school. Moreover, student support personnel are often involved in committees that either set building-level educational policy or make recommendations to administrators for new policies or changes in existing policy. For example, many schools have policies regarding the numbers of absences a student may have before their grades are lowered or they fail the course altogether. In such cases, student support personnel must ask, "Is this policy in the best interest of the students in this school?" and seize the opportunity to make their schools more user friendly by representing students in these matters. Additionally, when policies are in place that retard students' development, student support personnel must step into the advocacy role and act with students to make sure they are treated fairly by the school. An example of advocacy is when the counselor acts for students who are precluded from AP (advanced placement) and honors courses by restrictive policies. These policies often preclude talented students who have achieved at relatively low levels, but who are ready to improve their performance, from enrolling. Because AP and honors course are weighed heavily by college admissions officers in making admissions decisions, students who are denied access to them are disadvantaged in the college admissions process. (See Chapter 3 for a fuller discussion of the advocacy role.)

In the sections that follow, strategies that can improve the orientation of continuing and new students will be discussed. An in-service training program designed to heighten teachers' awareness of the importance of school climate and involve them in the process of improving the climate of the school will then be presented.

Influencing Student Perceptions by Facilitating Transitions

Students make transitions when they
- leave their families and enter school for the first time;
- move from elementary school to middle school;
- move from middle school to high school;
- transfer to a new school; and
- are moved from one school to another because of redistricting.

At each of these transition points students and their parents need to be welcomed to their new school and introduced to the faculty as well as the policies and procedures of the school. When transitions occur at typical times, as they do when students move from one level to another, letters should be sent to parents welcoming them to the school and inviting them to an open house. Because not all parents will come to an open house, essential information regarding the school should accompany the letter even when the information is provided at events such as kindergarten registration. For example, students entering school for the first time need to know who their teachers will be, the room number and location of their classroom in the school, health information including information regarding required immunizations, the school schedule, a list of required school supplies, lunch and breakfast arrangements including the cost of cafeteria food, information about after-school programs, how parents can make appointments to see teachers, policies regarding tardiness and absences, and, if the student is to ride a bus, his or her bus number and schedule. *The informational packet should also contain a letter from student support personnel explaining their roles in the school and how they can be contacted.*

Open houses for parents should include time for meetings with administrators, teachers, and school support personnel as well as opportunities to ask questions about the functioning of the school. School support personnel should take this opportunity to talk about their roles in the school and to invite parents to contact them. Soon after school begins, if the budget permits, a newsletter that describes the services provided by school support personnel should be sent to parents. Moreover, telephone calls to parents who did not attend the open house may facilitate the establishment of positive working relationships between school support personnel and parents. Parents must be fully informed about the workings of the school and must feel that school personnel care about their children. Just as importantly, the normal anxiety that students feel when they change schools must be allayed.

Continuing Student Orientation

Normally orientation activities occur in large groups, although group size should probably not exceed the enrollment in a typical classroom. Typical orientation activities include the following:

Spring - visits to feeder schools to discuss
- scheduling classes (high school). Student options should be explained, listings of courses provided, and schedule sheets sent home for parental approval;
- differences between new school and the school they are attending (e.g., moving from self-contained classrooms to clusters where several teachers work together, block scheduling, movement from class to class on a regular basis, the size of the schools, activities, etc.);
- services provided by student support personnel;
- Parent open house scheduled with students' present to answer questions about classes and policies at the new school. Follow-up telephone calls to parents who did not attend the open house should be made;
- Student trips to new schools that may include a tour of the facility, meetings with key people such as the principal and the assistant principal for the new class, subgroup meetings with sponsors of various activities, and talks by students who can provide a "student's eye" view of the school. Students may be broken into subgroups with student as leaders to get students' point of view regarding the nature of the new school and answers to their questions; and
- junior and seniors in high school or eighth graders in middle schools may be assigned to new students as their New School Friends. If this is to be done, these introductions may be made at the time of the visit to the new school and the purpose of the New School Friend Program explained–to provide newly

arriving students with a mentor who can answer questions and provide advice regarding the best ways to deal with problems that arise.

Fall

Training sessions with New School Friends held. These sessions should include

- walk-in-my-shoes sessions that put New School Friends in touch with their feelings when they entered new schools. The issues that should be addressed in these sessions include adapting to a new set of teachers, school being harder or easier, loneliness, keeping in touch with friends from their former schools, adapting to new policies regarding attendance, grading, qualifications to participate in activities, and so forth;
- information about school policies regarding attendance, tardiness,discipline,academic qualifications needed to participate in school activities, and graduation requirements.
- information about the counseling program including making appointments and scheduling classes;
- attending skills training. (listening and responding); and
- referral skills including guidelines for referring to counselors for help by highly anxious students, depressed students,discouraged students, discouraged students as well as newstudents who have been singled out for abuse by other students, new students who are not connecting, that is, not making friends and feeling comfortable,and new students who are too dependent on their New School Friend.
- Issue *Student Handbooks* and have these passed on to new students by their New School Friends.
- Reintroduce New School Friends at the beginning of school.
- Student support personnel visit every classroom that has sixth graders or ninth graders and welcomes them to the school and explain their roles in the school and how students can make appointments to see them.
- Brief (15 min.) conferences scheduled with individual or small groups of students as soon as possible for "get to know you sessions" and for determining if any problems have developed in the transition.
- Open house for parents to discuss the transitional problems being experienced by their students. Follow-up this meeting with telephone calls to parents who did not attend. Other approaches to involving parents will be discussed in Chapter 13.

Transfer Student Support Groups/Orientation

Groups should be organized throughout the year as the need arises. Normally transfer student groups consist of no fewer than 6 and no more than 10 students. The exact number of students involved in each group depends on two factors: the age of the students and the time available for the group. Generally speaking, when younger students are involved and when the time period available for the group the group is relatively short, fewer students should be included in the groups.

The first step in organizing new groups is to identify all newly enrolled students as early in the school year as possible. This information should be available in the principal's or registrar's office. Once a list of new students is identified, students should be contacted to determine their interest in participating in a support group. In order to save time, the initial contact may be made in a pregroup meeting, although individual contacts with individual students to determine interest are generally preferred. During the screening interview, the purposes of the new student group should be clearly explained. Additionally, information about the number and time of the group meetings should be provided. Students who volunteer should be included in the groups.

The second step in organizing new student groups is to identify students, preferably students who have transferred successfully to the school from another school, to serve as New School Friends to the transfer students. The role of these students is to be available to answer questions when the group is not in session, either in school or after school. These students should be positive role models who have a good reputation in school. They need not be honor students, but they should have a positive attitude toward school. They should be identified by direct solicitation in the classroom. An alternative approach is to ask the members of one of the service clubs in the school to assume the role of New School Friends.

A Note about English as a Second Language (ESL)Students

Baird (1997) pointed out that many schools receive transfer students who have limited proficiency with the English language. He suggested that student support personnel who are planning support groups work closely with (ESL) teachers so that an interpreter will be available to help these students make the transition to their new school. Additionally, if ESL students are included in new student support groups, students who have some proficiency with their languages should be involved, either in the role of coleader or as an interpreter. An outline for a series of sessions for transfer students follows.

Session 1 - Getting Acquainted

Objectives

- Outline the purposes of the new student group.
- Develop a safe environment in which students can express their concerns.
- Identify immediate concerns that students are experiencing.
- Build a supportive environment and help students develop new acquaintances.
- Help students understand the reasons they are in new schools (e.g., parents have accepted jobs that require moving the family from one location to another; family break ups; redistricting to achieve racial balance within the school district; choosing to attend a magnet school that offers a specialized curriculum).

Activities

1. Welcome students to group and reiterate purposes of group which are to

- Provide students with the support they need to make a satisfactory transition
- Provide needed information
- Identify specific problems and to solve them if possible
- Discuss the skills needed to make friends in this school

2. Have students get acquainted. This can be accomplished by having students tell about their former schools, the circumstances that led up to their move, their impressions of the new school, and some things about themselves such as hobbies, favorite songs or musical groups. Exercises such as What's in your purse or billfold? can also be used to help students get acquainted. In this exercise students select one item from their purses or billfolds, such as a picture of a friend, and tell the group the personal significance of that item.

If students from different cultures are in the group have them tell something about their culture including its history, traditions, and religion *if they feel comfortable sharing this information.* If students come from other countries have them share information about their countries *if they feel comfortable doing so.*

3. Have each student complete this statement: The problem I am having in this school right now is – and take notes for later action. Brainstorm solutions to problems and identify problems that need resolution (e.g., schedule changes) outside the group.

4. Set up a panel made up of transfer students to discuss – My Problems When I Transferred and What Happened to Them.

5. Ask students if they would like a New School Friend to help them with the transition. Explain that these students have agreed to provide assistance by answering questions when the group is not in session and after the group is over. Also, stress that the role of the New School Friend

ends after the first grading period.
Homework

Think about the concerns you have about the school and whether you would like a New School Friend

Session 2 - The Information You Need (I)
Objectives
- Provide students with the information about student support programs.
- Introduce students to key personnel in the school.
- Help students gain the information they need to function in their new school.

Activities

1. Provide information about the counseling program such as
   (a) how students are assigned to counselors,
   (b) how to make appointments to see counselors,
   (c) course scheduling, and
   (d) graduation requirements, etc.

2. Introduce key personnel. Bring in representatives from administration, health services, the attendance office, and other areas to discuss their roles and the types of assistance they can provide to new students.

3. Issue a *Student Handbook* to each student.

Homework

Generate questions for next week when the information you need to "survive" at your new school will be provided.

Session 3 - The Information You Need (II)
Objective
- Provide information about policies that govern students' participation in school.

Activities

1. Provide information about policies regarding discipline, attendance, tardiness, grading policies, gaining admission to clubs, activities (e.g., grade point average required), and services provided by the school (e.g., health services). This can be done by student support personnel, students (New Student Friends), or other staff members. Be sure to allow time for questions.

2. Ask students if they would like to have a New School Friend who they could contact to get day-to-day questions answered. Bring in New School Friends and make introductions.

3. Set up a panel of transfer students to discuss Getting Involved and Making Friends in This School.

Homework

Introduce yourself to someone you have not talked to before.

Session 4 - Making New Friends (I)

Objectives

- to provide the information need to establish new friendships.
- to develop active listening skills.

Activities

1. Have students complete handout 4-1, Am I a Good Friend?
2. Introduce the topic of listening.
   - What is listening?
   - How do I know when I'm being listened to by others?
     - (a) Eye contact; discuss the idea that in some cultures direct eye contact is not acceptable (e.g., Vietnam - direct eye contact may sign of aggression; In some American Indian tribes, direct eye contact is a sign of disrespect);
     - (b) body posture (open and facing speaker, forward leaning); and
     - (c) person paraphrases what I say.
   - Demonstrate good and bad listening in role-play.
   - Break students in dyads and have them practice active listening.
   - Ask, how many students said that you were good listeners on the self-assessment device? Do you still think that you are a good listener? Why or why not?
3. Explain that listening is the foundation of making friends, but other skills are needed as well.
4. Ask about friends in former school. Why did they become friends? What was it about them that you liked? Did they have any characteristics you did not like? Were they good listeners?
5. What are the characteristics of a good friend from your perspective? What would you add to the handout's list?
6. How have your efforts to meet new people, including the homework assignment from last week, paid off? Role-play meeting new people. Be sure to do this from their perspective – not an adult perspective.
7. Talk about meeting new people through school groups and activities as well as community activities.
8. Outline common mistakes in choosing people who might be your friend. Ask them to identify problems they have had. Some common errors include trying to be friends with the most popular person in the school, selecting a the friend in desperation, relying on a friend in another town for companionship and support, selecting a manipulative friend, selecting a domineering friend, having an "outlaw" friend, trying to break into cliques (discuss cliques and how they function), and trying to be friends with an individual who has none of your interests or values.
9. Talk about dealing with rejection.

Homework

Continue your efforts to meet new people. Try introducing yourself to five people this week.

Session 5 - Making New Friends (II)

Objective

Continue to build friendship skills focusing on listening and responding skills.

Activities

1. Use Handout 4-1, Am I a Good Friend? to help students identify weaknesses in their friendship skills.

2. Have students discuss their reactions to people who do not keep secrets, are disloyal, gossip, and generally fail to act in a trustworthy fashion.

3. Role-play situations that will help students develop new skills such as

- introducing one's self to another student;
- responding to a request for gossip (Have you heard?);
- responding to a request to be disloyal when a student says something negative about an acquaintance (Don't you think Jana is disgusting sometimes?); and
- student's attempt to make friends with another student is rejected.

When role-plays are concluded, ask students if they have specific skills they wish to improve.

4. Discuss maintaining friendships, focusing on what happens when friends fight. Introduce with a role- play with one of the students that involves a borrowed sweater or shirt that is not returned promptly and is dirty. Play the disgusted angry friend, then the assertive friend who stands up for her or his rights. Then lay out the following model for "fighting" with friends:

- Identify the problem: The sweater was returned late and dirty.
- Get the facts: Why was the sweater returned late and dirty? Are there legitimate reasons?
- Deal with negative emotion: If you feel yourself getting angry, frustrated, or disgusted take a deep breath and exhale very slowly, tell your self to stay calm because a friend is more important than a sweater, take time out or tell your friend that you are getting angry and need to stop the conversation for a minute or two.
- Stand up for your rights: You have the right not to loan clothing to others, but if you do, you have the right to have it returned on time and in good condition.
- Agree on a solution to the current problems and establish ground rules for the future: You may wish to take the sweater back as is and tell your friend that you will be unable to loan her/him clothing in the future; make him or her promise to get the sweater clean and back promptly as the basis for loaning clothing in the

future or have your friend clean the sweater and not loan him or her clothing in the future.

5. Have the group generate other conflicts that they have experienced and use this model to teach members how to deal with them.

Homework

Continue efforts to meet new people. Consider involving yourself in one of the school's activities as a way to meet more people.

Session 6 - Commitment to Provide Support and Wrap-Up

Objectives

- Develop an understanding of the need for social support when dealing with stress.
- Develop personal commitments so group members will have support.

Activities

1. Explain the importance of social support in dealing with stress.

2. Ask group members to commit to each other to provide support in the form of listening to the concerns of others.

3. Review active listening and model active listening for the group. Then have them role play the process if someone calls with a problem with a teacher, another student, homesickness, or other issues.

4. Tie up loose ends and terminate by having group members share one or two positive aspects of their group experience. Begin this good-bye activity by modeling the type of positive self-disclosures you wish the students to make.

Follow-Up

Schedule short conferences with each new student within 2 weeks to determine how they are adapting to new school. Evaluate the success of New School Friend relationships and remediate by assigning another New School Friend if necessary.

Heightening Teacher Awareness

Student Support Personnel can have a definite impact on the climate of a school as a result of the services they deliver. However, classroom teachers are probably a more pervasive influence on the climate of the school than student support personnel because of their day-to-day interactions with students. Unfortunately, most teacher training programs focus more attention on the delivery of subject matter material than they do on the importance to establishing a positive classroom climate. Because most teachers are required to participate in continuing education to earn credits (CEUs) to renew their licenses, student support personnel can influence their ability to create positive learning environments by delivering continuing education courses that will allow them to accumulate CEUs. Normally what is required is that the continuing education course be sanctioned by the school district's director of continuing education, and that the course of study be placed on file in the director's office. Because some school districts require that each continuing education course be offered for at least 10 hours (10 hours = 1 CEU), a 10- hour CEU course is outlined here. Portions of this outline can be used if a district allows courses to offered for less than one CEU. Although the outline provided is for five 2-hour sessions, the actual number of sessions may vary.

A Note about Skill and Knowledge

Some student support personnel are hesitant to offer in-service training to teachers because they doubt that they have the expertise needed to offer a 10-hour course. However, outside speakers from government agencies such as the department of social service, the community mental health agency, the state department of public instruction, and colleges and universities as well as offices inside the school district such as the central administrative offices can be included in courses that are offered. Moreover, student support personnel from schools throughout the district may wish to pool their expertise to develop an in-service training program for teachers and offer it at their schools.

Organizing the Class

Begin by getting approval from the building principal. Then proceed to get approval for the course at the district level. The next step in organizing the in-service unit is to recruit members. Send letters to all faculty members that state the purpose of the training, the number of CEUs that can be earned, where the class will meet, and the time of the class.

Session 1 - The Importance of School Environment
Activities
1. Provide an overview of the entire series of sessions including objectives:
- Identify aspects of the school that contribute to or do not foster achievement.
- Have teachers recognize their centrality in establishing a positive school environment.
- Start the empowerment process by getting teachers involved in improving the school climate through the utilization of their expertise to solve existing problems.

• Help teachers develop strategies for improving the climate in their own classrooms.
• Highlight the importance of multiculturalism.

2. Introduce an exercise that allows teachers in the class to become better acquainted. It is often the case that teachers function in relative isolation from each other and thus do not know each other very well. Hand out 4-2, Opening Exercise for In-Service Training of Teachers, can be used for this purpose. This exercise should be conducted in groups of 8 to 12 and will take from 45 to 60 minutes to complete. If the group membership is larger than 12, break it into smaller groups and then have people in each group share one new thing they learned about people in their group.

3. Give a mini-lecture on schools that foster achievement. Tell teachers that schools foster achievement when (1) the people in the school are perceived as warm, caring, and concerned by each other and students; (2) faculty, staff, and administrators see students as valuable and treat them with respect, even when they have misbehaved; (3) educational policies, including those affecting program admission, grading, promotion, and discipline, are designed and administered so they foster personal and educational development; (4) programs, including the curriculum, are designed to be inclusive (this means that programs and activities are designed to include students from all cultural/racial backgrounds as well as physically, mentally, and emotionally challenged students); and (5) students are recognized for their accomplishments and encouraged to fulfill their potential. Then have the teachers complete Handout 4-3, Rate the Achievement Climate of Your School.

4. Break the group into 5 subgroups to examine and evaluate each of the areas listed in Handout 4-2. The mission of the subgroup is to come to some general conclusions about each of the areas listed in Handout 4-2 and to identify some specific examples to support their case. Appoint a recorder for each subgroup and ask him or her to take notes and bring copies of those notes for each person in the class next time.

> Subgroup 1 - Are people in our school perceived as warm and caring? Why or why not?
>
> Subgroup 2 - Are all students seen as valuable? Which ones are not? Why or why not? Which ones do not?
>
> Subgroup 3 - Do our policies foster educational and personal development? Why or why not?
>
> Subgroup 4 - Are programs and activities, including the curricula, inclusive? Do minority students "see themselves" in the curricula and in the school? What is the racial cultural makeup of clubs such as the National Honor Society, athletic teams; and other clubs? If all students are not included, why is this so? Are there policies in place that amount to institutional racism, that is, they inadvertently preclude students of color

and others from access to all aspects of the school?

Subgroup 5 - Are all students encouraged to achieve to their potential? What types of things need to be done to encourage more students to achieve?

Session 2 - Does the Climate in Our School Encourage Achievement?

1. Review last week's activities.

2. Review the reports from each subgroup. Try to reach consensus on the strengths and weaknesses of the faculty, administration, and school policies with regard to fostering a school climate that encourages achievement. Then identify weaknesses that require remediation at this time and separate those that have to be attacked at the district level. Also separate problematic policies from people problems.

3. Outline strategies for attacking policy concerns. Examples include the following:

- Attendance policies unduly penalize students who miss school by lowering grades: find alternative means for punishing students who miss school such as in-school suspension, and after school study sessions.

- Departmental policies preclude some students from enrolling in advanced placement and honors courses. Identify ways to enroll students who are ready for these courses regardless of grades in other courses.

- Clubs and activities have preclusive policies (e.g., the National Honor Society has standards higher than guidelines laid down by national chartering group) that limit student access. Examine these policies and revise them to allow students freer access to these clubs and policies.

- Clubs are insufficient in number to meet the diverse interests of students. Lobby the district to increase funding for sponsors of clubs; organize community volunteers to support clubs.

- Participation in decision making by teachers and school support personnel is limited. Lobby the principal for more participation in the decision-making process using a rationale based on the teacher empowerment movement (e.g., Short & Greer (1997).

- Disciplinary policies place students in out-of school suspension for extended periods of time. Lobby to get more offenses punished with in-school suspension (ISS), or, if ISS not available,work to get an ISS program started.

- Multicultural activities are limited in time and scope. For example, African American History Week only focuses on one group and lasts for a relatively short period of time. One approach to emphasize this point is to bring in a panel of students from

different religious, racial, and ethnic backgrounds and have them discuss their reactions to the multicultural efforts in the school.
- Some activities preclude poor students because of the expense involved. Alternatives include scholarships for poor students from organizations such as the PTA, or having funds allocated by the school board so that the activities are free for all students.
- The curricula have a European American bias. Revise both curricula and materials/books used.

4. Assign groups to think about action-taking strategies for the next session.

Session 3 - Addressing the "People Problems" That Influence Classroom Climate

Activities

1. Examine the strengths and deficits identified in the subgroups, focusing on those related to classroom teachers.

2. Have groups reach a consensus on the problems that teachers have and identify collegial strategies for remediating problems. Examples of problems and potential solutions include

- A teacher is unmotivated and burned out: Discuss the possibility team teaching in departmental meetings; be more openly supportive of colleagues; schedule morale builders such as group luncheons on teacher work days; ask the principal to be supportive and encouraging during performance appraisal process; greater involvement in the decision-making process.
- Discipline is based solely on negative/aversive approaches such as open criticism, sarcastic threats, and taking away privileges: strategies include departmental or building-level meetings that outline positive approaches using innovative teaching approaches, the use of positive reinforcement and encouragement, individualizing instruction, welcoming students to class each day, reinforcing students when they have done their best, making books available on positive approaches to classroom management (e.g., Albert (1996), Walker & Shea (1995), giving a most positive teacher award every 9 weeks based on student motivation, changing performance evaluation to focus on positive approaches to discipline, not just control, and in-service training that teaches Adlerian, behavioral, and other positive approaches to discipline.
- The teacher has poor instructional skills: strategies include visits to the teacher-of-the-year's classroom, mentoring, supervision and support from department head, and paid leave to attend workshops.
- Some students feel as though the teacher does not care about them. Simple strategies such as welcoming each student to class,

using positive feedback, providing awards for greatest improvement, and encouraging students who are not working up to their potential can be used to remedy this problem.

4. Have subgroup recorders develop handouts for each class member that identify the problems and potential solutions suggested.

Session 4 - Action Taking To Improve Classroom Climate
Activities

1. Review the conclusions about problems that detract from the positive climate in the school and strategies developed to remediate them in the last two sessions.

2. Have the group as a whole prioritize the problems they believe are most serious using the nominal voting procedure. In this procedure the group is given a list of all the problems and asked to rate them in terms of their importance with 1 being the most important, 2 being the second most important, and so forth. The ballots are then tallied by averaging the ratings for each item. The item with the lowest score is the most important to be addressed by the group, and the item with the highest average score is seen as the least important. The averages should be posted and the group allowed to discuss them and make adjustments in the rankings by majority vote.

3. During the remainder of the session have small groups (these may be different than the original subgroups) examine as many of the highly ranked problems that are retarding the development of an atmosphere that fosters achievement as possible along with the strategies that have been identified to correct or ameliorate these problems. The groups should evaluate each of the remedial strategies in terms of the likelihood of it will work in their school. At the end of the session, each group should have drafted a preliminary plan to remediate one or more of the problems that have been identified.

4. Have one member of each small group take responsibility for making copies of the preliminary plan that has been drafted for each member by the next session.

Session 5 - Action Taking to Improve Classroom Climate
Activities

1. Have the entire class evaluate the likelihood of success of the activities that have been suggested in the preliminary plans drafted by the small groups. Using brainstorming techniques, identify ways to improve the strategies that seem most promising and then draft an action plan for each. The action plans should include:

• how each teacher intends to improve the climate in his/her classroom. For example through
(a) class meetings with students to get their perceptions of the classroom climate;

(b) baseline evaluation of students' perceptions of climate and periodic evaluations;

(c) Collaborative efforts with other teachers to observe each other and provide feedback; and

(d) listings of specific strategies that will be employed.

• plans for broadcasting their efforts to other teachers.

2. Summarize and end the class.

Summary

The climate of schools has been shown to be influential in promoting or retarding student achievement. In this chapter, two aspects of school climate have been addressed. One of these factors has to do with influencing the perceptions of students so that they will view schooling more positively and the second has to do with involving teachers in the process of improving school climate.

References

Albert, L. (1996). *Cooperative discipline.* Circle Pines, MN: American Guidance Services.

Baird, C. (1997). A systematic transition plan for new students. *Professional School Counselor, 1,* 69-70.

General Accounting Office (1992). *Educational issues.* Washington, DC: Author

MacGregor, R. R., Nelson, J. R., & Wesch, D. (1997). Creating positive learning environments: The school-wide student management program. *Professional School Counseling, 1,* 33-35.

Nelson, J. R., Covin, G., & Smith, D. (1996). The effects of setting clear limits on thesocial behaviors of students in the common areas of the school. *Journal for At-Risk Issues, 3,* 10-19.

Purkey, W. W., & Schmidt, J. J. (1996). *Invitational counseling.* Pacific Grove, CA: Brooks-Cole.

Short, P. M., & Greer, J. T. (1997). *Leadership in empowered schools.* Upper Saddle River, NJ: Merrill.

Walker, J. E., & Shea, T. (1995). *Behavioral management: A practical approach.* Englewood Cliffs, NJ: Prentice Hall.

Wilson, C. (1993). Providing support for high school transfer students. *The school counselor, 40,* 223-227.

Am I a Good Friend?

Think about your friendship skills. If the following statements are true and they describe you, write a T in the space provided. If they are false and they do not describe you, write in an F.

Friendship Skills

_____ 1. I will initiate contacts with people I do not know.

_____ 2. I can discuss a number of topics including sports, fashion, movies, television programs, events at school, and so forth.

_____ 3. I don't have to have my own way.

_____ 4. I can deal with rejection without getting angry.

_____ 5. I am cheerful and positive. I don't look for the negative.

_____ 6. I am willing to try new things.

_____ 7. I don't whine or complain.

_____ 8. I am a good listener.

_____ 9. I don't laugh when others make a mistake that embarrasses them.

_____ 10. I don't put others down.

_____ 11. I compliment others when they do something well.

_____ 12. I can share my friends with others. I don't have to "own" them.

_____ 13. I share. I'm not selfish.

_____ 14. I take turns. I don't have to be first.

Trust Building

_____ 15. I can keep a secret.

_____ 16. I always keep my word.

_____ 17. When I tell someone I will do something, I do it when I say I will do it.

_____ 18. When I borrow something, I return it on time.

_____ 19. I do not gossip.

_____ 20. I am loyal. I don't say bad things about my friends when they are not around.

_____ 21. I will go out of my way to help my friends.

Opening Exercise for In-Service Training of Teachers

The purpose of this exercise is to let other people know more about you by sharing things about your family history.

Fill in the following chart with the names of your grandparents and parents. If you did not grow up with your parents, use whatever parent figures you have:

Maternal Grandmother _____
Maternal Grandfather _____

Paternal Grandmother _____
Paternal Grandfather _____

Mother _____
Father _____

Share the following information about each of your relatives. It does not matter if this information was gained by direct experience with the person, or you learned it via indirect information from family members and others.

1. Where was he or she born and raised? What was her or his race or ethnic group?

2. What was her or his early life like? (e.g., How many family members were there?; What about early schooling?)

3. What were his or her outstanding characteristics?

4. What was her or his career like?

5. Can you trace any of your attitudes and /or behaviors to this person?

6. Do any of your family traditions (activities; foods; travel; holidays; etc.) come from her or him?

7. Which of these people are you most like? Why?

8. Did any of your family impact your educational philosophy? In what way?

Rate the Achievement Climate of Your School

Respond to each of the following statements by checking either True or False

True   False

A. Teachers are warm, caring and concerned.

___   ___   1. Almost all teachers in this building demonstrate that they
                care about students.
___   ___   2. Teachers regularly go out of their way to help students
                improve their achievement.
___   ___   3. Teachers keep in touch with parents, particularly when a
                student is having difficulties.
___   ___   4. Teachers regularly consult with other teachers and student
                support personnel about the problems students are having.
___   ___   5. Students of color are treated with respect in almost all of
                the classes.
___   ___   6. Teachers are sensitive to cultural differences and avoid
                remarks that might be interpreted as racist.
___   ___   7. Teachers avoid sexists remarks and have zero tolerance
                for sexual harassment.

B. Administrators treat students with respect.
___   ___   1. There is zero tolerance for racism by administrators.
___   ___   2. There is zero tolerance for sexism, including sexual
                harassment in this school.
___   ___   3. All school policies are administered fairly in this school.

C. Policies, including those affecting program admission, grading,
promotion, and discipline, are designed and administered so they will foster
personal and educational development.

___   ___   1. The membership of clubs in this school is characterized
                by diversity.
___   ___   2. Admission to programs for the academically gifted and
                advanced placement and honors courses are open to open
                to students who can do the work regardless of their past
                performance.
___   ___   3. All students are disciplined according to the same
                standards regardless of race of ethnicity.

D. Programs and curriculum are inclusive.

___   ___ 1. Texts and materials used provide an objective view of the contributions of women to American/World society.

___   ___ 2. Texts and materials used provide an objective view of the contributions of minorities to American/World society.

___   ___ 3. Texts and materials used provide an objective view of the historical treatment of women and minorities.

___   ___ 4. Major non-Christian holidays such as Ramadan are noted and students are given an opportunity to learn more about the beliefs of people who celebrate these events.

___   ___ 5. Providing information about the culture, values, and beliefs of minorities beyond discussions of holidays and religious celebrations.

E. Students are recognized for their accomplishments and encouraged to fulfill their potential.

___   ___ 1. There are many programs in place to recognize effort in this school.

___   ___ 2. Students at all levels of achievement are rewarded for exemplary work.

___   ___ 3. Parents are made aware of the accomplishments of their children at times and using means other than report cards.

___   ___ 4. There are special efforts in place to encourage achievement among minority students.

___   ___ 5. There are homework support programs in place to aid students.

___   ___ 6. Parents are regularly involved in helping students to do better in school.

___   ___ 7. Sessions aimed at helping parents assist their children to achieve at a higher level are offered periodically.

Chapter Five

A Study Skills Program

Although our schools are increasingly concerned with academic performance, few school districts require the teaching of study skills. The reasons for this oversight are twofold. First, many teachers and counselors assume that students have learned study skills, either from other teachers or from their parents. Second, school support personnel and teachers often are unacquainted with methods for teaching study skills. It is the primary purpose of this chapter to acquaint educators with the knowledge and skills needed for successful study.

Assessing Study Skills

The objective of study skills assessment is to determine specific weaknesses so that strategic interventions can be made. Study skills may be assessed by a number of methods. The one used most frequently is simply asking students to describe the approaches they use when studying and compare what they report to an idealized approach. A second method for assessing study skills is through the use of study skills inventories. An older but still useful inventory, the Survey of Study Habits and Attitudes (SSHA) can be used with middle and high school students to assess 7 areas deemed critical by the authors. These are (1) delay avoidance, (2) work methods, (3) study habits, (4) teacher approval, (5) education acceptance, (6) study attitudes, and (7) study orientation. When completing this inventory, students respond to 100 statements such as "I feel like skipping school whenever there is something I would rather do" by indicating whether it is rarely (0-15% of the time), sometimes (16-35% of the time, frequently (36-65% of the time), generally (66-85% of the time), or almost always (86-100% of the time) true of themselves. Students' scores on the 7 scales can be compared to the scores of students who received good grades.

Perhaps the most important aspect of the results of an inventory such as the SSHA is that school support personnel and teachers are provided with motivational information as well as information about study habits. The study skills inventories (Handouts 5-3, Study Skills Inventory – High School and Middle School and 5-4, Study Skills Inventory – Elementary School) included in this chapter provide the same type of information, but do not provide student support personnel, teachers, and students with the opportunity to compare scores to those of successful students.

A third method for assessing study skills is through student self-monitoring. The objective of student self-monitoring is to determine how much time is spent studying, what is studied, the nature of the study environment, students' motivational level when they start to study, and problems encountered as they study . The use of an assessment device such as the Weekly Study Log (Handout 5-1) yields a great deal of useful, direct information about study habits such as how well students are organized when they study. However, it is time consuming, and persuading students to keep good records about their studying can present a problem. The study skills inventories found at this end of this chapter, the weekly study log, and informal assessments such as asking the students to estimate their strengths and deficits in specific study habits can be employed to assess study skills. (If student support personnel and teachers wish to compare the study habits of students in their classes to those of successful students, they can ask successful students to complete both the weekly study log and a study skills inventory so that data that can be used for comparative purposes can be obtained).

A Study Skills Course for Middle and High School Students

The study skills course outlined in the subsequent section can be tailored to either middle school or high school students. The 6-session course covers all aspects of developing study skills from assessment to adopting new study strategies.

Session 1 - Assessment
Objectives
- Make students aware of the importance of study skills.
- Increase motivation by having students establish some initial goals to improve their study skills.
- Make students aware of the strengths and weaknesses of their study skills.

Activities
1. Give a minilecture on importance of study skills. Point out that students will be studying throughout their lives for examinations that relate to their jobs, such as civil service examinations and professional licensure examinations, and for credentialing courses such as automotive repair or auto tune up.

2. Ask students to record the average number of hours they study per week on slip of paper.

Record range and average of class as baseline information.

3. Introduce the idea of keeping a study portfolio. Pass out pocket

folders. Then ask students to consider how many hours they study at the present time and engage them in goal setting. They can decide to study more, study smarter (which means that they will use their study time more effectively), or both. Ask students to write down their personal study goal and place it in their study portfolio.

4. Administer and have students score Handout 5-2, Study Skills Inventory – High School/Middle School. Discuss each area on the inventory and have students place them in their portfolios.

5. Discuss and assign students to complete handout 5-1 Weekly Study Log .

Homework

Bring notebooks and portfolios to class next week.

Session 2 - Getting Organized

Objectives

- Help students recognize that efficient study depends on readiness to study.
- Help students to recognize that being organized requires that they write down assignments, take good class notes, organize class materials in notebooks as the class progresses, and have all books, notes, equipment (e.g., calculators), and assignment sheets available when they begin to study.
- Provide aids that will allow students to become better organized.

Activities

1. Review handout 5-1 (Weekly Study Log) and have students complete the assessment process. Then have them rewrite their goals for the course. "Last week you wrote whether you wanted to increase the amount of time you study, use the time you spend more effectively, or both. Now identify specific areas of your study skills that need to be improved and rewrite your goal." Give examples of goals:

- I want to use my study time more effectively by becoming better organized.
- I want to learn more during the time that I study by using better study strategies.
- I want to spend more time studying and I will give up 30 minutes of TV watching to make time to study.

2. Have students review their answers to Section 3 (Preparation and Organization of Material for Study) of the Study Skills Inventory – High School/Middle School and to look at the Problems Encountered column of their Weekly Study Logs (Handout 5-1) to determine whether they are well organized.

3. Determine how many people have problems remembering assignments.

4. Handout Two Week Assignment Sheet (Handout 5-3), which is to

69

be placed in the front of students' notebooks.

5. Divide the class into small groups, with some students who have identified themselves as disorganized and some students who are organized in each group. Have them look at each others' notebooks and share ideas about getting organized.

6. Engage the entire class in brainstorming exercise to identify better ways to organize for study time.

7. Give a mini-lecture on the role of motivation in being organized and studying effectively.

Homework

Bring notebooks with completed assignment sheets next week (Handout 5-3) and keep notes about times when it is hard for you to study and what you do, if anything, to increase your motivation.

Session 3 - Getting Motivated

Objectives

- Help students become aware that everyone faces motivational problems at times.
- Help students understand that motivation may be affected by organization prior to studying, the place where studying occurs, interruptions/distractions, lack of specific study goals, and lack of long-term educational and career goals.
- Help students adopt strategies to increase their motivation to study.

Activities

1. Review SSI (Handout 5-2, Section 2) results, Motivation Index on Weekly Study Log (Handout 5-1), and notes about motivation kept during the past week.

2. Have students identify their motivational problems by asking these questions:

- Which subjects cause you the greatest motivational problems? Are they too hard or just boring?
- Do you have specific goals when you study?
- Is there a time when you have the greatest difficulty getting motivated?
- Is the place where you are studying related to your motivational problems? Why?
- Distractions? Too comfortable (e.g., lying on a bed)? Too uncomfortable (e.g., hard chair?)
- Is your physical condition related to your lack of motivation? Too tired? Sleepy after a big meal? Is it possible you need glasses?
- Is your lack of organization related to your motivational problems?
- Do you have specific educational and career goals? If not, is this deficit related to your motivational problems?

3. Have students identify 1 to 5 factors that negatively influence their

motivation. Identify potential strategies for overcoming the problems they have identified. This can be done by identifying common problems and asking students in class to make suggestions for dealing with them. You may also wish to provide suggestions for techniques that can be used to overcome motivational problems such as rewarding one's self for getting down to work, punishing one's self (not doing something pleasurable) when failing to get school work done, and asking parents for rewards for completing homework.

4. Discuss the role of specific objectives in the study process. Remind students that if they do not know what they are trying to accomplish, they probably will be unsuccessful. Begin by checking homework assignment sheets and then establish goals for study sessions. Prioritize the list based on importance. It may be best to do homework that is least "interesting" first.

Show Overhead 5-1, Step Approach to Major Homework Assignments Completion:

- Read material and place main points on flash cards (preview).
- Identify and memorize main concepts in the lesson (mastery).
- Complete the 25 math problems assigned and check answers (assignment completion).
- Pick a topic for the term paper assigned in English (1).
- Develop an outline for the term paper that was assigned in English. (2).
- Write a draft version of the term paper assigned in English (3).
- Rewrite and edit the term paper assigned in English (4).

5. Get organized. Make sure all materials, books, and equipment needed to attain goals are available.

6. Select a comfortable study place free from distractions and interruptions. Stress individual differences. For example, some people can study with music and some cannot. Have students define what is ideal for him or her.

7. Impose a no-interruptions rule: no telephone and no talking.

8. Arrange to videotape favorite TV programs that may be missed. No studying with TV!

Homework

Work on factors that influence your motivation. If you do not have educational goals, contact your counselor and begin to set goals.

Session 4 - Taking Notes In Class

Objective
> • Increase students' ability to take notes during class lectures.

Activities

1. Give a mini-lecture on the importance of good note taking.
   • Note taking in class keeps you on task by making you listen.
   • Note taking keeps you alert and awake.
   • Note taking requires that you use your eyes, ears, and hands in the learning process. You hear, write down and see what is written. Then you write. Later, if you say the major points out loud, you have used 4 of your senses in the learning process. This will increase retention for most students and makes studying for tests easier.
   • Note taking makes boring classes pass more quickly because you are doing something.

2. Have students share techniques they now use and problems they encounter when notes get "cold.".

3. Outline note-taking procedure. Show Overhead 5-2, Rules for Note Taking and Overhead 5-3, A Shorthand System for Note Taking.
   • Get to class on time and look over the notes from the last class.
   • Be sure to use a heading that identifies the topic of the lecture.
   • Learn to abbreviate, but if you use shorthand or symbols, make notes about the meaning of the abbreviations or symbols so you will be able to decipher later. Use ink and write clearly.
   • Listen for cues that some topics are important.
      (a) If a teacher repeats something it is generally important.
      (b) Main points often come at the very beginning of a lecture.
      (c) Main points are also included in the teacher's summary of the topic in most cases.
      (d) Cue-words and phrases indicating that a topic may be important include:
      A. *First*
      B. *Remember*
      C. *Notice that*
      D. *A major issue is*
      E. *The main idea is*
      F. *For example* (examples are used to clarify main points)
      G. *In contrast* or, *on the other hand* (Illustrating importance of main point)
      H. *The fact is*
      I. *My last point is*
      J. *Finally*
      K. *To summarize*

L. Some cues are non-verbal (facial expressions, hand gestures)

• Anything written on the board or on overheads should be considered as important.

• Use a yellow or pink highlighter to mark important points such as dates, definitions, or places.

• Don't try to write down every word. Get the important points.

• If you do not understand a point, either ask a question or make a note to see the teacher later. Generally speaking if you do not understand something that is being said, others are having the same problem.

• Always write down mathematical formulas, definitions, and specific facts such as dates and places.

• Develop a buddy system so that if you miss class you can get the notes from another student.

• Keep your notes together in a section of your notebook or in a separate notebook.

• If students can, they should word process their notes as soon after class as possible. Not only will they be easier to read later, they will have conducted their first review of what they wrote.

• Review your notes regularly whether you have a test or not. If, when you are reviewing something is unclear, check with your teacher.

4. Give a minilecture on a topic of interest to students and test their note-taking ability. You may also get a teacher to give this lecture. Have students compare their notes.

Homework

Make a list of cue-words you hear in your lectures for the next week and add these to the list provided.

Sessions 5 - Study Strategies (I)

Objectives

• Introduce basic learning principles.
• Teach the SQ3RT method of studying.

Activities

1. Give a minilecture on learning principles:

  • You are more likely to remember the first things and the last things you study (primacy and recency principles).

  • Spaced learning sessions are superior to bunched or crammed learning sessions for retention.

  • Learning is enhanced when it occurs without distractions.

  • Learning is enhanced when the learner is alert. Get lots of sleep and take breaks to stay fresh.

  • Learning is enhanced when it occurs in pursuit of desired outcomes. For example, if better grades isn't one of students' desired outcomes, they need to learn to reward themselves for studying with food, going to a movie, or spending time on the telephone with a friend.

- Learning is enhanced when it involves the eyes, ears, touch (if possible), and the sixth sense (visualizations)

2. Introduce SQ3RT method using Overhead 5-4, SQ3RT Method of Studying

- *Scan:* Using your finger as a pointer, quickly scan the material that you are to learn. The purpose of this exercise is to get an overview of the material. (A long paragraph should be selected from material students are studying and this approach should be practiced at least once to clinch this point.
- *Question:* What are the main points? (topic sentences, new words, dates, important events, formulas)
- *Read:* Read one section at a time (notes or book) and then stop and question: What were the main points? Do I understand the major concepts? What can I do to remember this material?
- *Recite:* Look away from materials and ask yourself questions aloud. Answer aloud.
- *Review:* Go back over material, particularly material that is difficult. Retention requires that you review several times.
- *Test:* Make up your own test. Try to think as your teacher does while you do this. What would he or she want me to know? Make up true/false, multiple choice, and short answer questions.

3. Provide a lesson to be studied. Take the students through the lesson one step at a time. This will work best if the lesson is from one of their current classes. Repeat this step as time permits.

Homework

Use the SQ3RT method this week, and bring material that you need to learn next week.

Session 6 - Study Strategies (II)

Objective

- Provide students with techniques that will increase retention of material they must study.

Activities

1. Discuss the idea of mental mapping. Many things that are to be learned are related to each other. Drawing mental maps of these ideas can be very useful. For example, the process of photosynthesis can be mapped as follows: sunlight + carbon dioxide + water + chlorophyll in plants --> oxygen. This map might also be drawn with a picture of the sun, chemical symbols (CO^2 for carbon dioxide or H^2O for water), water, a plant, and an oxygen tank for oxygen. Illustrate this point to the class and have them try this approach.

2. Define anagrams and give them a series or list they need to memorize such as the elements needed for photosynthesis: chlorophyll, air, water, and sunlight [carbon dioxide] CAWS. Then have them identify lists that they need to memorize from their current classes and construct anagrams that will help them learn the lists.

3. Retention can also be improved if the sixth sense, (visualization) is used. Ask students to visualize sunlight and air with small black dots (CO_2) being absorbed into the plant's leaves; then have them visualize water coming in the roots and joining the sunlight in the leaves; see them mixing together and oxygen leaving in a sky-blue stream. Tell students that visualization can be particularly helpful when learning series of things such as how food moves into the body and is digested, a series of events that led up to an important event (the battle of Yorktown during the Revolutionary War), mathematics equations, or any other information that must be learned in a specific order.

3. Have each student identify where they could place notes that would serve as reminders of things they need to remember.

3. Remind students that it may be useful to review material that needs to be retained just before going to sleep or just before going into a test (recency). It may also be useful to record material and listen to it just as they are falling asleep.

4. Work on students' beliefs about their ability. Only about 10% of the brain's capacity is fully utilized. They need to challenge self-talk such as "I can't learn" with self-talk such as "I can learn, but I may need to get help."

5. Have students place bets with themselves about their ability to recall information needed for a test. "I'll bet you a million dollars you can remember how to work that equation." Have them continuously challenge themselves to learn and do better.

6. Give a minilecture on cooperative learning. Point out that when students help others they are in fact teaching themselves.

Homework

Use the techniques and strategies you have learned to improve your achievement and be prepared to give examples next week.

Additional Sessions

Other units in this book can be used to add lessons to the 6 sessions outlined above. For example, study skills units often contain one or two lessons on time management and test preparation.

Study Skills in Elementary School Students

Many of the elements included in the study skills program for middle and high school students can and should be incorporated into a program for elementary school students, although in a more rudimentary form. At least seven sessions are needed : defining study skills and assessment, habits that improve studying, listening, taking responsibility, note taking, setting goals for school and studying, and taking for tests.

Session 1 - Defining Study Skills and Assessing Study Habits
Objectives
- Develop an awareness of the need for good study habits
- Have students understand their own study habits.

Activities

1. Ask each student to take out a sheet of paper (or provide one). Then tell them to write the answers to the following questions.
- What is the capitol of Montana? (Helena)
- Who was the first man on the moon? (Neil Armstrong)
- Who invented the telephone? (Marconi)
- What is the square root of 9? (3)
- What is the chemical symbol for gold? (Au)

Then give them the answers and find out how many they got right. Assuming that some students are able to answer one or more of these questions, ask them why they remembered the answers. Then ask all students if they could get all of the answers right if you gave them the questions and answers and told them you were going to readminister the quiz the next day. Ask them if they would try harder if they knew they were going to be embarrassed if they did poorly or were going to get $1000 for getting them all correct. Summarize by indicating that studying would improve their scores on the quiz, and that they would study hard if they were motivated (define).

2. Define study skills as activities that increase what they learn and improve their grades in school. Point out that even straight A students do not learn everything they are taught and thus everyone can benefit from learning better study skills.

3. Administer Handout 5-4, Study Skills Inventory - Elementary (SSI-E). Point out the importance of eating a balanced diet and getting enough sleep (questions 1 and 2) to being alert in school and studying. Ask for students to tell what happened when they were very hungry in school and/or sleepy.

Then discuss motivation. Tell them that many students are not motivated to do work in school because they think school is unimportant. Ask for examples of people they know who have done well as a result of schooling.

Tie one of the strongest students to a heavy desk or a stationary item with a rope or cord around his or her waist. Have her or him try to pull the desk or object. Tell students that low motivation acts like a drag on learning and studying. So does lack of sleep or not eating well.

Review the answers to the remainder of Handout 5-4, Study Skills Inventory-Elementary School. Tell students that they need to be organized (questions 4 to 6), have good work habits (questions 7 to 9), have good study habits at home (questions 10 to 16) if they are to be successful students.

4. Review major points of the lesson. Ask each student to tell one thing they learned in this lesson.

Homework

Ask students to interview a student or adult to determine one thing that helps him or her learn better. Tell them that each of them will be asked to report to the class during the next session.

Session 2 - Habits That Improve Studying and Grades
Objective
- Help students understand that good work habits often are related to good study habits.

Activities

1. Compile and discuss the list of suggestions that grew out of the homework assignments (Compile a master list and develop a poster for later sessions.)

2. Introduce this section by writing on board or showing an overhead with the following work habits which will need to be carefully defined.
- Punctuality (being on time)
- Cooperation (working together without fighting, helping each other)
- Perseverance (sticking to the job, even when it is hard)
- Following directions (doing the things that you are told to do correctly)
- No procrastinating (getting down to work)
- Questioning (asking questions when you are unsure)
- Task oriented (you don't allow others to keep you from completing a job)
- Listening

3. Give students Handout 5-5, Work Habits Sheet, and have them complete it. Then engage the students in a role-play and have them demonstrate bad work habits. Then have the students act like teachers as they correct the errant students.
- Vignette 1: Student walks into class late or hands in homework after the due date.
- Vignette 2: Three students are working on an in-class assignment, and they get into an an argument. One person accuses another of not doing his or her share.
- Vignette 3: A student is sitting at home studying. The homework is hard and he or she throws the paper in a wastebasket and yells, "I quit!"

- Vignette 4: A student is sitting at a desk at home. He or she says aloud, "This is boring. I think I will watch TV."
- Vignette 5: A student is sitting at home and can't remember the homework assignment. He or she wonders out loud, " How could I have gotten this assignment ? "
- Vignette 6: A student is studying and the phone rings. Her or his friend asks her/him to play a game. He or she says, "This homework can wait. This sounds like fun."
- Vignette 7 - One student is trying to talk about school and the other keeps interrupting.

4. Review by pointing out that good work habits are important for success in school. Ask students to identify them.

Homework

Search for good work habits. Observe each other and identify good work habits. Who is on time? Who helps others? Who asks questions? Who listens to the teacher and others? Who is task oriented? Give them Handout 5-6, Work Habits Stars, which is a sheet to be used to nominate people who have good work habits. Have them report during the next session.

Session 3 - Listening

Objectives
- Have students understand the importance of listening in the learning process.
- Improve students' ability to listen to others.

Activities

1. Ask for a volunteer. Then tell the group they are to learn as much as they can while listening to information about the Internet. Tell them you are going to quiz them after the lecture. However, the volunteer will talk nonstop while they are learning about the Internet. The volunteer can talk about anything and they may talk to the class during the lecture regarding the Internet. When the volunteer starts talking read the following passage to them:

> The Internet is a communications system that carries information over a web of telephone lines. Millions of people use it everyday instead of the telephone to communicate with friends, relatives, and business associates using what is called electronic mail or e-mail. When e-mail is sent, it arrives almost instantaneously. People also use the Internet to buy and sell things. For example, you can buy stock in Coca-Cola or Pepsi on the Internet. You can also buy other products such as software. Software can help you do things like design greeting cards, balance your checkbook, or learn a new computer skill. One of the unique things about the Internet is that people and

companies can establish websites that can be visited by Internet surfers. You can get all types of information from websites such as sport scores, listings of job openings, and the latest news stories. You might even wish to build your own website.

Once you have stopped reading the story, ask the student to tell you as much as he or she can about the paragraph. Then reread the paragraph (without interruption) and have the students tell you as much as they can about what they heard.

2. Pass out Handout 5-7, Am I A Good Listener? Have the students answer all questions, then discuss each of the following questions:
   • Why is it important to look at the speaker?
   • Why is it important not to interrupt?
   • What might the teacher think if you fidget or move around when he or she teaches?
   • Why is it important to ask questions? What are the reasons why some students don't ask questions?
   • Why shouldn't you daydream when the teacher is teaching?
   • Why should you ignore people who want to get your attention when the teacher is teaching?
   • Why is listening for directions important? (Give students a model or complex problem without directions to break the discussion period.)
   • Why is important to listen from the beginning of the lesson to the end? (Tell them half a story and ask them how it ends.)
   • Why is important to listen for main points? (Tell them that they will learn how to do this better.)
   • Why is it important to listen to other students? (Make sure the ideas of respect and cooperation are involved in answering this discussion.)

3. Review what it means to be a good listener.
4. Look at the sheet from last week's homework assignment (Handout 5-6, Work Habits Stars) to see who has been identified as a good listener. Applaud each one.
Homework
Give students another copy of Handout 5-6, Work Habits Stars. Have them complete the entire form, but have them pay particular attention to listening this week.

Session 4 - Taking Responsibility for Yourself in School
Objectives
- Continue to demonstrate the importance of listening for school achievement.
- Have students understand that taking responsibility for one's own behavior means listening for directions (so they don't have to ask others), completing assignments on time (punctuality), and not blaming others when homework and/or seat work is not complete (honesty).

Activities
1. Introduce the word *responsibility* and have students brainstorm about its meaning. As this is done write (or have a class member write) each student's response on the board.

2. Before drafting a definition of responsibility, use some examples of not taking responsibility:
- A student does not listen to the teacher and fails to get the assignment. What would a responsible student do?
- A student blames a faulty alarm clock for being late to school when it was really the result of oversleeping. What would a responsible student do?
- A student blames another student for bothering him or her while they were studying? What would a responsible student do?
- A student hands in an assignment late. What would a responsible student do?

3. Ask the students, "Can we agree that taking responsibility for one's self in the classroom means listening to the teacher instead of relying on others to tell us what he or she said, getting to school on time and handing in our homework when it is due, and not blaming others when we have not completed our work?" The major components of taking responsibility (listening, punctuality or being on time, and honesty about who is responsible) should be put on the board, a poster, or on an overhead.)

4. Now I am going to tell you a story. When you hear that a student in the story is not taking responsibility, raise your hand. When you hear a student acting responsibly, snap your fingers (demonstrate). Tell students that responding to this story takes good listening skills.

Tom, Jamarcus, and Kwan are walking home from school. Tom says, "I forgot to write down my math assignment. Can I get it from you?" Jamarcus and Kwan shrug their shoulders. They didn't write down the assignment either. They see Tanya ahead and yell, "Did you write down the math assignment?" She yells back, "Yes I did." "Can we get it from you?" the boys say in unison. "Sure," Tanya replies.

The next day Kwan, Tom, and Jamarcus are on their way to school. Kwan is worried and says, "I didn't get my math homework done. I fell asleep while I was watching television and my parents let me sleep. It is their fault." Jamarcus chimes in, "I got mine done. Why don't you just copy the answers?" Kwan says, "That's cheating. I wouldn't want to do that, but what can I tell the teacher?" Tom says, "Tell her you lost it or some bullies tore it up. You're a good student. She will believe you." Kwan says, "I don't want to lie. I guess I'll just tell her that my parents didn't wake me up to do my homework, and it is their fault." The boys agree, and they go on to school.

5. Process the story with the students by going back through each interaction and identifying responsible behavior versus irresponsible behavior. Pay particular attention to Jamarcus' offer to share his homework.

6. Next have students fill out the Handout 5-8, Am I A Responsible Student? After they complete it, go over the answers. Don't embarrass the students by having them give their answers, but point out that questions 1 through 5 should be answered Yes if a student is acting responsibly and questions 6 through 8 should be answered No if a student is acting responsibly.

Homework

Give the students Handout 5-9, Responsible Students Nominations Forms. This form should have the names of all the students in the class in the right hand column. The categories of responsible school behavior are listed across the top. Ask the group to nominate students who are acting responsibly by placing an X in the appropriate column during the next week.

Session 5 - Note Taking
Objectives
> • Reinforce the importance of taking responsibility for one's own behavior in the classroom
> • Teach basic note-taking skills.

Activities

1. Collect Handout 5-9, Responsible Students Nominations Form from each student. Read aloud the names of the students who have Xs in the responsibility column. Then have students gives themselves a big round of applause for acting responsibly.

2. Introduce the importance of listening in good note taking. Tell students that teachers always tell them when to write something down, but they may do it indirectly by using signals. These signals should be seen as stop-and-take notes signals. Draw a stop sign on the board or have it predrawn on an overhead or poster. Show Overhead 5-1, Rules for Note Taking.

> • Stop and take notes when the teacher writes something on the board.
> • Stop and take notes when the teacher gives you a definition or date.

- Stop and take notes when the teacher uses her or his hands to make a point.
- Stop and take notes when the teacher gives you a list to remember.
- Stop and take notes when the teacher repeats a point.
- Stop and take notes when the teacher raises her or his voice.
- Stop and take notes when teachers say, "This is important."

3. Post these rules for note taking so all students in the room can see them. Then tell them that you are going to read them a story and they are to say STOP each time they should take notes. The story is as follows:

African Americans were first brought to this country as slaves in 1619 (STOP– date). (Raise your voice.) In all, nearly 8 million Africans were brought to this country and sold. Prior to the American Revolution, slaves were held in all colonies (STOP –Voice raised). The earliest Africans who arrived in this country were treated like indentured servants. An indentured servant is a person who works for a period of time to pay off debts and then becomes free (STOP – definition). However, by 1740 the slavery system was established, and it was assumed that Africans would not become free (STOP – definition). All Southern states passed laws intended to control slavery. Slaves did revolt because of their treatment. (Write on the board.) Three of these were revolts were (STOP – list):

Prosser and Bowler revolt	1800
Denmark Vesey	1822
Nat Turner	1831

The Civil War began in 1861 partly because some people in the North were against slavery (Stop – date) They were called abolitionists (STOP – definition). Other Northerners were not as concerned about slavery they as they were about the fact that the South could produce crops and goods cheaper than they could by using slave labor. It is important to remember that in 1862 African Americans were allowed to enlist in the Union Army, and 209,000 did (STOP – remember). They took part in over 200 battles and over 68,000 died in the war. Slavery started in this country in 1619 (STOP – repeated point). It ended officially at the end of the Civil War. However, discrimination against African Americans still continues.

4. Go back over the story. Point out the STOP points. Then have students tell what they would write in their notes at each point in the story.

Homework

Take notes on a lecture that the teacher gives (arrange with teacher) and bring your notes to group next week.

Session 6 - Setting Goals for Studying and School

Objectives
- Link good work habits, listening, and taking responsibility to study skills.
- Identify good study habits.

Activities

1. Give a minilecture that relates good listening, work habits, and taking responsibility for one's self to successful studying. Emphasize that these skills and attitudes are interrelated.

2. Have students brainstorm pros and cons of studying.

Pros	Cons
Get better grades	Takes time from friends
Promoted with your peers	Less time for TV
Pass end-of-grade tests	May be boring; not always fun
Learn some neat stuff	
Graduate from high school	
Prepare for life after school	
Avoid going for remedial work (e.g., summer school)	
Makes school more enjoyable	

3. Ask, "How many of you want to be promoted from this grade to the next? How many of you want to complete middle school? High school? College? Get a good job after high school instead of going to college? Did you know that you will be required to study, even on the job? For example auto mechanics, fire fighters, refrigerator repairers, teachers, counselors, and others have to return to school and study throughout their careers.

4. Have any of your parents gone to school lately? Get examples.

5. What are good study habits?
- Being organized. Have your assignments, notes, and books when you need them.
- Selecting a place to study that is free of distraction. No TV and no stereo.
- Avoiding interruptions. Do not take telephone calls.
- Having goals. (e.g., Tonight I will complete all my math problems and check the answers.)
- Getting help when you need it. This may involve calling a friend or an adult.
- Getting down to work. No delays.
- Studying to remember. (Preview: What do I need to learn? Review - After reading, quiz yourself by asking, "What were the main points in what I just read?")
- Involving your hearing. Repeat important points out loud. You will remember more.
- Using Post-it™ notes and flash cards to help you remember important materials.

Homework

Give students Handout 5-10, My Study Habits, and ask them to identify their good and bad study habits for the next 5 school days.

Session 7- Studying for and Taking Tests

Objectives

- Emphasize the importance of day-to-day studying in preparation for tests.
- Identify strategies that will help students prepare for tests.

Activities

1. Collect Handout 5-10, My Study Habits Sheets, from each student as they enter the room. Do a quick analysis of the results, checking for strengths as well as weaknesses. Provide feedback on how well students did.

2. Ask, How many of you like tests? Why or why not?

3. Discuss the purpose of tests (to determine how much students have learned).

4. Ask, How many of you get nervous before a test? Do any of you have trouble sleeping? Sweaty palms? Ask for other physical and mental symptoms of nervousness.

5. Explain test anxiety. When we approach an event such as a test that makes us afraid that we might fail or do badly our body and our mind react. Our mind may tell us that we are going to do poorly, that we are going to fail, that we will be embarrassed by the results of the test. Then our body reacts with some of the symptoms you just identified. Let's work on stopping those negative statements and your physical reactions to them.

6. You will not be so fearful of tests if we are prepared. Being prepared means

- studying the material that is to be covered by the test regularly, not just before the test;
- studying for mastery. Previewing, self-quizzing, using note cards, Post-it™ notes, getting help;
- using your ears as well as your eyes to take in information. (Saying important things out loud);
- getting a good night's sleep before the test;
- eating a good breakfast the morning of the test (if the test is after lunch, not eating a heavy meal);
- reviewing hard-to-remember material just before you go into the test;
- not panicking when you find a question you do not know;
- pacing yourself during the test so that you will be able to finish all parts of the test;
- asking questions during the test if you do not understand the directions or a question on the test; and

• doing your own work. Sometimes if we are panicking we may want to look at the answers others are giving. If the teacher catches you, you will be embarrassed and fail the test.

Wrap-Up

Summarize the 7 sessions and distribute the handout 5-11, The Rules for Test Taking. Ask students to post this handout in their study area or in the front of their notebooks.

Evaluating Study Skills Programs

There are several ways to evaluate the impact of a study skills program, the most obvious of which is to examine students' grades a few weeks after the program is completed. Students' perceptions of their study skills and the confidence with which they approach studying may be process indicators that the study skills program is having the desired effect. Teachers' records of change in factors such as punctuality in handing in homework, percentage of homework handed in, and percentage of homework completed correctly can also be used as indicators of the success of the program. Moreover, teachers' perceptions of students' use of class study time, percentage of students who are writing down class assignments, students' willingness to get to work when assignments are made, and readiness of students when they come to class may also be used as indicators of success. Finally, parents' perceptions of students' use of study time, degree to which student's study without distractions or interruptions, and students' willingness to study may also be used as indicators that the study skills program is having an impact.

Summary

Academic achievement is dependent on a number of factors, not the least of which is the amount of time students spend in the learning process. As students advance in the educational system, they are expected to spend increasing amounts of time studying on their own. However, if the time they spend studying is to be used efficiently they must have certain personal characteristics and academic skills. Student support personnel can improve the acquisition of knowledge by teaching responsibility-taking and basic study skills. In this chapter two course of study, one for high school and middle school students and one for elementary school students were presented.

Weekly Study Log

Dates Covered: From _____ To _____

    This log is to be completed each time you study, whether the studying occurs in school or out-of school. Provide the Following Information.

Date - Month and day (e.g., 11/3)
Time - Exact time in the morning (a.m.) or evening (p.m.) the studying started and ended.
Place - Write an S if the studying occurred at school or H if the studying occurred at Home. If your studying was not done at home or school, place an E (elsewhere).
Subject Studied - Math, Sci, Span, Lit, Civ, Eng, etc.
Conditions - List distractions such as students talking, TV on or stereo playing.
Motivation Index - On a 1 (very low) to 10 (very high) scale, rate your motivation when you started to study.
Problems Encountered - List any problems that you encountered during the study period such as interruptions, assignment information incomplete.

	Time					1 - 10	
Date	Start	End	Place	Subj.	Distractions	Mot/Ind.	Problems Encountered

Total Hours _____   **Average Motivation Index** _____

Study Skills Inventory - High School/Middle School

© 1998 Duane Brown

The questions that follow are designed to help you identify factors that may prevent you from studying effectively. However, if the results are to be useful, you must answer the questions as honestly as possible. Place a check by your answer to each question.

General Considerations
Agree Disagree
_____ _____ 1. Generally speaking, I eat a healthy diet.
_____ _____ 2. Generally speaking, I get a good night's sleep.
_____ _____ 3. I am in good physical health.
_____ _____ 4. I take no medications that would interfere with my concentration (make me sleepy).
_____ _____ 5. I avoid studying after eating a heavy meal.

Motivation to Study
Agree Disagree
_____ _____ 1. I like school.
_____ _____ 2. I can usually see value in the material assigned in class.
_____ _____ 3. I want to finish school no matter what it takes.

Preparation and Organization of Material for Study
Agree Disagree
_____ _____ 1. The notes I take in class are easily understood.
_____ _____ 2. The notes I take in class are thorough.
_____ _____ 3. I highlight the most important points teachers make in my notes.
_____ _____ 4. I review my notes before class.
_____ _____ 4. The material I need to study is easy to locate.
_____ _____ 5. The material I need to study is well organized and ready to be learned.
_____ _____ 6. I almost always write down class assignments.
_____ _____ 7. I keep a calendar that includes important dates such as when tests will be given

Time and Place to Study
Agree Disagree
_____ _____ 1. I have a regular place to study at home.
_____ _____ 2. I have a regular place to study at school.

____	____	3. The place where I study at school is free from distractions (e.g., people talking)
____	____	4. The place where I study at home is free from distractions (e.g., loud music or TV).
____	____	5. I have identified the time I am most alert and use this time to study.

Study Strategies
Agree Disagree

____	____	1. When it is time to study, I get to work immediately.
____	____	2. I review assignments before settling down to work to get a clear picture of what is expected.
____	____	3. I study the most difficult subjects first.
____	____	4. I have time to study all the subjects that need my attention.
____	____	5. When I am reading, I can identify the most important concepts in the material.
____	____	6. I highlight or place on note cards the most important concepts in the material that I am studying.
____	____	7. After I have read a section in a chapter, I review by quizzing myself or taking the quiz at the end of the chapter if one is available.
____	____	8. I review material that is not clear after a self-quiz or chapter quiz.
____	____	9. When I am studying, I take occasional short breaks.
____	____	10. I space my study sessions instead of "cramming" the night before a test.
____	____	11. I ask for explanations from teachers when I do not understand assignments or ideas discussed in class.
____	____	12. I involve at least two senses when I am trying to memorize material by reading or saying concepts and ideas aloud.
____	____	13. When I am having trouble remembering something, I review it just before dropping off to sleep.
____	____	14. I use Post-it™ notes on the mirror and other places to remind me of material I need to memorize.
____	____	15. I make up anagrams to help me remember groups of materials.
____	____	16. I reward myself for sticking to my study plan.
____	____	17. I use flash cards to help me remember important material.
____	____	18. I study until I master the material.

Two Week Assignment Sheet

Write in the subjects that you are taking at this time in the numbered slots. Each time you receive an assignment in one of your classes record it in the appropriate column. In the section at the bottom of the sheet write additional notes about assignment.

Subjects

Days	1. English	2. Math	3.	4.	5.	6.
October 1	_____	_____	_____	_____	_____	_____
October 2	_____	_____	_____	_____	_____	_____
October 3	_____	_____	_____	_____	_____	_____
October 4	_____	_____	_____	_____	_____	_____
October 5	_____	_____	_____	_____	_____	_____
October 8	_____	_____	_____	_____	_____	_____
October 9	_____	_____	_____	_____	_____	_____
October 10	_____	_____	_____	_____	_____	_____
October 11	_____	_____	_____	_____	_____	_____
October 12	_____	_____	_____	_____	_____	_____

Additional Notes (e.g., test in English on October 12 will emphasize grammar. Review pages 140 - 166 in book):

_____

_____

_____

Study Skills Inventory (Elementary)

Answer the following questions with a Yes or No.

	Yes or No
1. I eat breakfast almost every day.	_____
2. I get a good night's sleep during the school week.	_____
3. I try to do my best at school.	_____
4. I almost always have the supplies I need.	_____
5. I almost always write down assignments.	_____
6. I am ready to begin when the teacher is ready to start class.	_____
7. I know how to take good class notes.	_____
8. I have learned how to study for tests.	_____
9. When we have study time in class, I use it to get my work done.	_____
10. I have a quiet place to study.	_____
11. I study at the same time each day.	_____
12. I turn the TV and radio off when I study.	_____
13. When I get ready to study I know where my books and assignments sheets are.	_____
14. When it is time to study I get right to work.	_____
15. I complete my homework each night.	_____
16. I remember what I study.	_____

Work Habits Sheet

Answer the following questions with a Yes or No.

	Yes or No
1. I get my schoolwork done on time.	_____
2. I work well with others.	_____
3. I stick to a job until it is done	_____
4. I almost always follow the teacher's directions.	_____
5. When I have work to do I get right to work.	_____
6. I ask questions when I am unsure what to do.	_____
7. I work on a job until it is completed.	_____
8. I am a good listener.	_____

Work Habits Stars

Write down the names of students in your class who had good work habits this week.

1. Who was on time this week?

2. Who worked well with others this week?

3. Who stuck to a job even when it was hard this week?

4. Who followed directions this week?

5. Who got to work when the teacher made assignments?

6. Who asked questions this week?

7. Who did not allow others to complete their work this week?

8. Who listened to others this week?

Am I A Good Listener?

Check which statements are true about you.
_____ 1. I look at the teacher when he or she is speaking.
_____ 2. I never interrupt the teacher when he or she is speaking.
_____ 3. I don't fidget or move around in my seat when the teacher or others are speaking.
_____ 4. I ask questions to help me understand what the teacher is trying to teach.
_____ 5. I don't daydream when the teacher is speaking. I'm on task!
_____ 6. I ignore students who are not listening and want me to quit listening.
_____ 7. I almost always know the directions the teacher gives because I have listened to what he or she had to say.
_____ 8. When the teacher is talking, I listen to all that she or he has to say. I don't get distracted.
_____ 9. I listen for main points.
_____ 10. I listen to other students who have things to say during class.

If you checked all of the above statements, you are a good listener. If you did not check some of the statements, these are the things you need to work on to improve your listening.

Am I A Responsible Student?

Answer the following questions with a Yes or No
_____ 1. I write down assignments so I don't have to ask others what the teacher has assigned.
_____ 2. When I do **not** complete an assignment, I tell the teacher why the assignment is late.
_____ 3. I get to school on time unless my bus or carpool is late.
_____ 4. I complete my seatwork on time.
_____ 5. I hand in my homework on the day it is due.
_____ 6. Sometimes I blame others when I don't get my work done.
_____ 7. I often depend on others to write down the assignments the teacher makes.
_____ 8. I am often late in handing in assignments.

Responsible Students Nomination Form

Your job this week is to identify students who are acting responsibly. These are students who (1) listen to the teacher and write down assignments, (2) complete work on time, and (3) take responsibility for their own behavior. They do not make excuses when schoolwork is not completed. Place an X by the student's names each time they are responsible.

Student	Wrote Down Assignments	Did Work on Time	Took Responsibility
———	———	———	———
———	———	———	———
———	———	———	———
———	———	———	———
———	———	———	———
———	———	———	———
———	———	———	———
———	———	———	———
———	———	———	———
———	———	———	———

Handout 5-10

My Study Habits

Before you go to bed each night think about your study habits that day. Answer each of the following questions with a Yes or No.

During my study time:	1	2	3	4	5
1. I got right to work. I did not delay.	——	——	——	——	——
2. I studied in a quiet place. There were no distractions	——	——	——	——	——
3. I did not interrupt my studying to take telephone calls.	——	——	——	——	——

4. I had goals. I knew what
   I needed to complete when
   I studied.   ____ ____ ____ ____ ____
5. I took breaks to keep fresh. ____ ____ ____ ____ ____
6. I previewed what I was
   to learn.   ____ ____ ____ ____ ____
7. I quizzed myself over
   material that seemed
   important.   ____ ____ ____ ____ ____
8. I said the things I needed to
   learn out loud.   ____ ____ ____ ____ ____
9. I used memory aids such
   as Post-it™ notes to help
   me remember.   ____ ____ ____ ____ ____
10. I asked for help when I
    needed it.   ____ ____ ____ ____ ____

Handout 5-11

The 10 Rules for Test Taking

1. Be prepared. Studying a little each day is the best way to prepare for a test.

2. Involve your ears. Hearing and seeing information will improve your memory.

3. Use memory aids such as flash cards and Post-it™ notes to remind you of facts, definitions, or lists of things that you need to remember.

4. Get a good nights sleep.

5. Eat breakfast.

6. If the test is after lunch, don't overeat.

7. Pace yourself during the test so that you can finish it.

8. Don't panic if there is a question you cannot answer.

9. If there is anything you do not understand about the directions or the test questions, ask the teacher.

10. Never cheat.

Overhead 5-1

A Shorthand System for Taking Notes

Common Words	Dimensions	Measurements
@ = at	wd = width	"= inches
2 = to	ht = height	' = feet
2gthr = together	< = less than	yds = yards
4= for	< = greater than	mi = miles
bef = before	blw = below	k = kilometer
ex = example	abv = above	m = meters
info = information	mny = many	c = centimeters
p = page		l = liters
v = very		ml = milliliters
w/ = with		= = equal
u = you		
w/o = without		
thru = through		
thru/o = throughout		
----> = conclusion		
sum = in summary		

RULES FOR NOTE TAKING

• Stop and take notes when the teacher writes something on the board.

• Stop and take notes when the teacher gives you a definition or a date.

• Stop and take notes when the teacher uses her/his hands to make a point.

• Stop and take notes when the teacher gives you a list to remember.

• Stop and take notes when the teacher repeats a point.

• Stop and take notes when the teacher raises his or her voice.

• Stop and take notes when the teacher says, "This is important."

Overhead 5-3

Step Approach to Major Homework Assignment Completion

• Read material and place main points on flash cards (preview).
• Identify and memorize main concepts in the lesson (mastery).
• Complete the 25 math problems assigned and check answers (assignment completion).
• Pick a topic for the term paper assigned in English (1).
• Develop an outline for the term paper that was assigned in English (2).
• Write a draft version of the term paper assigned in English (3).
• Rewrite and edit the term paper assigned in English (4).

SQ3RT Method of Studying

• **Scan:** Using your finger as a pointer, quickly scan the material that you are to learn.

• **Question:** What are the main points (topic sentences, new words, dates, important events, formulas)?

• **Read:** Read one section at a time (notes or book) and then stop and question:
    What were the main points?
    Do I understand the major concepts?
    What can I do to remember this material?

• **Recite:** Look away from materials and ask yourself questions aloud.

• Answer aloud.

• **Review:** Go back over material, particularly material that is difficult. Retention requires that you review several times.

• **Test:** Make up your own test. Try to think as your teacher does while you do this. Make up true/false, multiple choice, and short answer questions.

Chapter Six

Improving Test-Taking Skills

The educational reform movement has put new emphasis on the importance of testing, and this emphasis is likely to increase in the future. When international test scores become available, they attract the attention of prestigious newspapers such as *The New York Times*. The results of statewide testing programs are heralded in the newspapers of every major city in a particular state. Why is this the case? Rightly or wrongly legislators, state school board members, and the general public have bought into the idea that tests scores are important indicators of the performance of today's schools. Fortunately, school counselors, psychologists, and social workers can improve test scores, including scores on college admissions tests, without teaching a lesson. They can either teach students *about tests* or coordinate efforts to do so.

There are many types of tests. It is therefore necessary to specify the types of tests being discussed in this chapter. Generally speaking this discussion focuses on the improvement of two types of achievement test scores: norm and criterion referenced tests. Norm-referenced tests, such as the California Achievement Test,are administered for the purpose of comparing students' performance to the performance of similar students. For example, a local school board might develop norms, which could consist of average scores of students at each level in the school district, and then compare the average scores of students at each grade level of XYZ School to the school district norms. The same thing can be, and often is, done on the state, national, and international level. However, this type of comparison can be meaningful only if the norm group to which the students at XYZ School is being compared is similar in makeup to the students at XYZ School. Thus, it is probably inappropriate to compare students from Alabama to students from Minnesota because of the differences in the socioeconomic levels of the residents of the two states. However, this does not preclude legislators and others from making these comparisons.

Increasingly, legislators and state boards of education are using criterion-referenced tests to evaluate the effectiveness of their schools. When criterion-referenced tests are used, students are compared to a pre-established standard. In the processing of establishing a standard or criterion, test developers take two factors into consideration: the curriculum being taught and the level of achievement deemed appropriate for students at various grade levels. For example, at what grade level should a student have mastered long division or acquire the ability to write a cohesive paragraph? What are the minimum academic competencies that a student should have prior to graduation from the third grade? High school? These standards are set by educational psychologist, educators, legislators, and others and used as the basis for determining the success or failure of individuals, individual schools, and entire school districts.

Approaches and Guidelines

Wilson (1986) reported that a humorous musical can be used to familiarize elementary school students with standardized tests. The play includes six characters, four students, a teacher, and a school counselor. Using rewritten folk songs such as *Oh, Susanna* and *On Top of Old Smoky* students were introduced to ideas such as guessing when they are unsure of their responses, the importance of tests in their lives, and the role tests play in developing self-understanding. Unfortunately, only anecdotal reports are provided to support the efficacy of this approach

An important issue in testing is the use of these devices with cultural and ethnic minorities. However, this is not a new issue. Over 20 years ago Berry and Lopez (1977) warned student support personnel to be aware of the testing problems raised by cultural variations and deficits in the use of the English language. Students who do not speak English or who have not developed a scholastic vocabulary (as opposed to a social vocabulary) should be tested in their first language. Moreover, test administrators should be aware that the technical language used and the analytical atmosphere in testing situations poses a problem for many minority students. Berry and Lopez (1977, pp. 267-268) developed a set of guidelines for testing Spanish-speaking students. These are rephrased in Figure 6-1 to include all English-as-a-Second-Language (ESL) students.

Figure 6-1

Testing Guidelines for ESL Students

Cultural Considerations
  - Do the items on the test correspond to the student's family values system?
  - Are items on the test arranged to minimize students' feelings of failure, that is, are they arranged from least difficult to most difficult?
  - Does the test take into consideration time orientation and motivation?

- Is the test culturally fair, that is, are the examples used include the cultural experiences of the students taking the test?
- Were representatives from the community of the ESL students used in the selection of the tests?

Language Considerations
- Are tests in the first language of the student?
- Are there opportunities for students who have English language deficiencies to ask questions to get clarifications that may be related to language?
- If the tests contain nonverbal content, are the symbols culturally relevant?
- Is the verbal content of the test culturally relevant?
- Are the tests at the reading level of the ESL students?

Norm Considerations
- Are there students in the norm group like the ESL students? Are the test norms representative?
- Are there local norms for the test? Statewide norms?
- Has consideration been given to using criterion-referenced tests versus norm-references tests in the assessment of ESL students?

Administration Considerations
- Will the test be given in an environment that is supportive of ESL students, that is, with native speakers if necessary?
- Is the test available in the native language of the student?
- If the test is to be administered in the language of the student, are regional differences in language taken into consideration in the choice of administrators?
- Will the test administrators be able to establish rapport with the ESL students?

Legal and Ethical Considerations
- Will the test results be used as nondiscriminative guides to the evaluation of ESL students?
- Are administrators aware of the cultural variables that may influence test performance and prepared to deal with them during the test administration?
- Are the tests being used culturally fair?
- Are professionals who use the test results fully versed in the cultural and psychometric issues that affect performance and how these may interact to influence the results?

Interpretation

- Will the interpretation of test results be done based on culturally relevant considerations?
- Will information other than test results be used when decisions such as retention are made regarding ESL students?

Although the recommendations made by Wilson (1986) and Berry and Lopez (1977) are useful, they do little to answer questions regarding the content or efficacy of programs designed to increase test scores. Rathvon (1991) and Wiggins (1992) reported conflicting information regarding the efficacy of programs to increase test scores. Wiggins found that efforts to increase Scholastic Aptitude Test (SAT) scores were successful, and Rathvon (1991) reported that efforts to increase students scores on teacher-made examinations were generally unsuccessful. These results are not surprising. Unlike teacher-made tests, standardized tests, such as the SAT, are administered and scored in identical fashion regardless of where they are administered or who administers them. Moreover, standardized tests are prepared with a certain testing philosophy in mind, a philosophy that can be taught to students. However, teachers have various philosophies and their testing procedures are far from standardized in most instances. Rathvon's results may have been attributable to the variability associated with the development, administration, and scoring of the teacher-made tests used to evaluate the success of the program. That is why the focus of this chapter is upon standardized tests. Data from a wide variety of sources—ranging from The Princeton Review, which specializes in preparing students for the SAT, to locally prepared and delivered courses—support that test preparation programs can increase standardized test scores.

The remaining question is, What should be the content of test preparation groups? Brown (1982), after a review of the literature, suggested that there are three aspects of test-wiseness programs. One of these components involves time use, which seems particularly appropriate for students who are not as oriented to time as most European American students. Time use involves familiarizing students with the structure of the test so that they can understand the (1) directions, (2) mark answers appropriately, (3) ask relevant questions, and (4) pace themselves so they can answer all questions and have time to check their answers. The second component identified by Brown, is error avoidance, which involves orienting students to the underlying concepts being tested. The third component involves allaying the anxiety relating to the test. For many students the anxiety is "normal" performance anxiety that can be handled using relaxation techniques. For others, the anxiety is a more serious component of the problem and involves responses that can be quite intense.

Michael and Edwards (1991) tried to answer the question of what should be included in test preparation programs by surveying 115 elementary, middle, and high school counselors. Counselors were asked to identify the essential elements of a test preparation program. At least 81% of the respondents to the survey identified the following components: following directions, reading questions carefully, understanding the vocabulary of the test, using time effectively, relaxation strategies, responding to various types of items, using separate answer sheets, and understanding the overall importance of tests.

Thus for obvious reasons, two types of course outlines are presented in this chapter. The first of these deals with orienting students who do not have phobic responses to tests. An overview of this type of unit can be found in Figure 6-2, Outline of an SAT Preparation Course. This course, which was developed by Agnew and Bell (1997) for use in high schools, illustrates many, but not all, of the principles that should be followed when designing courses and small group experiences to improve test scores. The major oversight appears to be that Agnew and Bell included nothing on dealing with anxiety in their outline. The second course outline, which is presented at the last section of this chapter, focuses on helping students overcome intense test anxiety.

Figure 6-2

Outline of an SAT Preparation Course

1. Background of a school planned and delivered SAT preparation course.
   - Agnew and Bell (1997) have developed a guide for this course.
   - The course is coordinated by student support personnel.
   - The course is delivered by math and English teachers.
   - Students pay a modest fee to cover cost ($100).
   - Scholarships are provided to needy students by school district, businesses, or Parent Teacher Association (PTSA).
2. Session outlines
   Session1 (all sessions 3 hours)
   - Set expectations, including attendance, assign homework for Session 2.
   - Administer pretest from Barron's *How to Prepare for SAT I* (scored in class).
   - Present Math and verbal strategies for taking the SAT.
   Session 2
   - Assign homework for Session 3.
   - Present Math strategies - divisibility rules, patterns for exponents.
   - Present verbal strategies - decoding words, analogy relationships.
   - Administer practice test (scored in class).
   Session 3
   - Assign homework for Session 4.

- Present Math stategies - right triangles, perimeter and no Pi problems.
- Present verbal strategies - analogy relationships.
- Administer practice test (scored in class).

Session 4
- Assign homework for session 5
- Present Math strategies - Venn diagrams, zero time, ratio problems.
- Present verbal strategies - sentence completion strategies and practice.
- Administer practice test (scored in class).

Session 5
- Assign homework for session 6.
- Present Math strategies - fractions, proportions.
- Present verbal strategies - reading comprehension strategies, questions.
- Administer practice test (scored in class).

Session 6
- Assign homework for session 7.
- Present Math strategies - exterior angle of a triangle, circle graphs.
- Present verbal strategies - Critical reading strategies and practice.
- Administer practice test (scored in class)

Session 7
- Give final reminders about test taking.
- Adminster final practice test (scored in class).

Preparing Students for Major Tests

All students should be taught test taking skills when they first encounter standardized tests. This training should be repeated on an abbreviated basis at each subsequent test administration for students who identify themselves as being in need of help. The course outlined here may be used in either large or small groups.

Session 1 - Introduction to Tests: Why Tests Are Important

Objectives
- Acquaint students with the purposes of tests.
- Increase students' motivation to do well on tests.

Activities
1. Bring copies of the exterior of the test booklets (these may be copies) and give one to each student.
2. Ask students if they understand (1) when the tests are to be given and (2) why tests are given?
3. Tell students when test are to be given and how much time they will take to complete.
4. Briefly go over the school district's reason for giving the test (e.g.,

to evaluate how well schools are doing as a result of a statewide mandate).

5. Outline why these tests are important to individuals. Depending on the test, some of these reasons might be to:
- compare your progress to that of other students like yourself (norm-referencetests);
- measure how much you have learned aour core subjects (criterion-referenced tests);
- decide if you have the academic competencies needed to graduate from high school (high school competency tests).
- decide if you will be promoted to the next grade (criterion-referenced end of course tests); and
- determine if you need extra help such as tutoring (criterion referenced tests).

6. Explain the testing process. Who: Will teachers or other proctors administer the tests? When: Tests are scheduled to begin early in the morning, and thus students need to get a good night's sleep and eat a healthy breakfast. If the testing is conducted after lunch, students should not eat a heavy meal to avoid sleepiness.

7. Answer questions and summarize.

Homework

Talk to a student who has taken this test in the past and learn all you can from a "student's eye view."

Session 2 - Taking Directions and Basic Testing Concepts

Objectives
- Familiarize students with the basic testing process.
- Develop students' confidence in their ability to follow directions.

Activities

1. Bring in copies of the directions for the test and the answer sheets that will be used. Give each student copies of these materials and review them as you would in an actual testing situations, and take students on a "dry run" through the beginning of the test. Encourage students to ask questions during this time.

2. Practice completing the answer sheet, working on columns and rows, filling in responses properly.

3. Review and define basic concepts that might appear on the test such as opposite, usual, similar, correct, matching, and so forth. If possible, use items from past tests to illustrate how these concepts might be used on the test that the students will take. At the very least, show how these concepts might be used in test items. *Take extra care to insure that ESL students understand these concepts.*

4. Without divulging the nature of the test, give students a vocabulary list of words that might appear on the test and review these with them. Have them use these words in sentences

5. Summarize and emphasize that students should ask questions if they do not know a word or understand a concept.

Homework

Ask students to look up the words on their vocabulary list and use them in a sentence. Give prizes for student who get them all right. Language arts/English teachers may also wish to make this list a part of a graded homework assignment.

Session 3 - Types of Test Items

Objective

Familiarize students with detail questions, context questions, and inference questions , as well as other types of questions.

Activities

1. If possible, take items from past examinations that illustrate the types of items used. Samples of these items should be given to students. Then, using several types of questions, illustrate how students should go about go about answering the questions.

2. Detail questions cover names, dates, and places. Students should read all answers before answering. Often there are two answers that are fairly similar, so jumping to conclusion is a poor test taking strategy.

3. Context questions ask students to read a paragraph and select an answer based on the information in the paragraph. Student should first look for words in the paragraph that are similar to those in the question. They should then eliminate answers that they are sure are wrong and then select their answers.

4. Inference questions ask students to draw conclusions based on information provided. In order to answer these questions, students should read the information provided carefully, identify the section that the conclusion is to be drawn from, and then select an answer.

5. In some instances, students are asked to select the best answer as opposed to the correct answer. This means that two or more of the answers provided have some correct information in them. These types of questions require that students pay very close attention to the question and then identify the answers that provide some correct information prior to answering the question.

6. Review other types of items that may be included on the test. Distribute Handout 6-1, Test-Taking Strategies to each student.

7. Summarize.

Homework

If possible give the students sample test items to work on for the next week. Have them review Handout 6-1, Test-Taking Strategies.

Session 4 - The Process of Test Taking

Objectives

- Familiarize students with the process of deciding whether or not to guess.
- Orient students to the importance of pacing when taking a test.
- Teach students how to relax during testing.

Activities

1. Ask students how many of them have guessed on a test before. Ask them if they think this is a good idea.

2. Some tests penalize students for careless guessing. For these tests, students should leave the item blank unless they can eliminate half of the distracters. If test scores are not corrected for guessing, then students should guess if they do not know the answer. The advice given to students should be based on the information from the technical manual of the test. At the end of this discussion, students should have a firm strategy for guessing in mind. Put test items on an overhead to illustrate the process of deciding whether to guess or not.

3. The topic of time usage is important for all students, but should be emphasized for students who (1) may have little experience with tests or (2) may be from cultural backgrounds that do not have a great deal of emphasis on timeliness. Emphasize that it is important to work fast enough that all items on the test are attempted. The rule here is do not get stuck on one item. If you do not know the answer, place an identifying mark by the question and move on to other items. After all items have been attempted, answers should be checked and skipped items attempted.

4. Give a minilecture on relaxing during the test. Many students get very tense during the process of taking the test. Show Overhead 6-1, The Escalating Panic Reaction to Tests and explain. Handout 6-2, My Symptoms may also be used at this point. The easiest way to relax yourself is to take several very deep breaths and exhale very slowly after filling the lungs completely. Start by filling the lungs completely. Then hold the air in the lungs while counting - 1001 -1002- 1003 - 1004 - 1005. The exhale should be very slow and should take at least 5 seconds: 1001----1002----1003----1004----1005. Repeat this process three or four times and the anxiety will dissipate.

5. Have students practice the breathing exercise outlined above.

6. Continue the lecture. Muscles also get tense during the test-taking process. In order to release this tension, identify the muscles that are tense and **increase** the tension in the muscle for 5 seconds; 1001 ----1002----1003----1004----1005. Then release the tension in the muscle and remind yourself to relax. Repeat this process three or four times or until the tense muscle is relaxed.

7. Summarize

Homework

Identify material that students can study that will help them do well on the forthcoming test. Ask them to complete it. Tell them that in the next sessions they will be tested.

Sessions 5 and 6 - Practice Tests

Objective

- Administer and score a test that is similar to the test that students will take.

Activities

1. In conjunction with a classroom teacher, administer a test that approximates the test that will be taken.
2. Score the test.
3. Arrange for tutoring or reteaching as needed.
4. Retest and rescore.
5. Continue tutoring to remediate weaknesses.

Helping Students Cope With Test Anxiety

As noted earlier, test anxiety is an intense phobia-like response. Test anxiety is generated by irrational, catastrophic thoughts about the outcomes of the testing situation. Typically students are afraid that they will fail the examination. However, failure may not mean the same thing for all students. Some students fear they will not achieve a score that is near the top of their class while others are concerned that their end-of-class test scores will not be sufficient to permit them to move to the next grade level with their classes. Regardless of the nature of the thoughts, persons having them exaggerates the consequences of failure as he or she imagines their failure.

Test anxiety has two components: the anxiety that occurs while the person is in the test and anticipatory anxiety. Anticipatory anxiety occur prior to the test and is a reaction that approximates or equals the response in the test. In some ways anticipatory anxiety is worse than the anxiety that occurs during the test because it occurs over a longer period of time. Tests last from 1 to 6 hours. Anticipatory anxiety may be experienced off and on over a period of several days or weeks. Programs that are designed to deal with test anxiety must deal with anticipatory anxiety and anxiety that occurs during the test. Fortunately, the techniques needed to deal with both problems are very similar.

It is important that anyone leading a test anxiety group understands the panic cycle (Wilson, 1987). The test is the stimulus that initiates the anxiety, and the result is fearful thoughts. As already indicated, the basis of these thoughts are exaggerated concerns about the consequences of failure. Fearful, anxiety-evoking thoughts give rise to certain physical symptoms including a racing heart, tense muscles, upset stomach, shortness of breath, dry mouth, and sweaty palms. In severe cases other symptoms developed including dizziness, overdilated pupils that hamper vision, chronic pains in the temporomandibular joint or TMJ (the muscle that fastens the lower jaw to the skull), vomiting, shaky hands, confusion, inability to concentrate, feeling of weakness in the extremities, numbness in lips, hands or feet, and/ or diarrhea. Unfortunately, students who experiences these physical symptoms often become more anxious because they can be quite disturbing. The panic cycle is displayed on Overhead 6-1, The Escalating Panic Reaction to Tests. The good news is that all of these symptoms can be stopped with the use of a few fairly simple, easily teachable techniques.

It is also important that leaders of test anxiety groups understand why the symptoms develop. As just noted, thoughts set off fear-evoking responses. At the millisecond that the fearful thought occurs, epinephrine from the adrenal gland is pumped into the blood stream, and the body goes into a fight-or-flight mode. The epinephrine increases the breathing rate so that the body will have additional oxygen to flee or fight. Unfortunately, because this excess oxygen is not being burned off by activity, the oxygen /carbon dioxide ratio in the bloodstream is altered, the pupils of the eye dilate, and dizziness can result. The epinephrine also precipitates a response in which blood flows from the extremities (feet and hands) to the central body cavity to bathe the vital organs in blood in case the student is wounded in her or his fight-or- flight. For this reason hands get cold. Additionally, because the brain begins to function in a more primitive area of the brain (the brain stem) instead of the cerebrum where information is stored, people often declare that they cannot "think straight." In this case, people have a great deal of difficulty recalling information during fight-or-flight response. Finally, the epinephrine causes the muscles to tense so that quick responses are possible. Unfortunately, one of the responses to this is muscle pain in the lower back, the TMJ, and other parts of the body. Again, the good news is that all of these physiological responses can either be stopped or reversed with the techniques that students will be taught. Prior to beginning the course, leaders should familiarize themselves with the physiological reactions and the resulting symptoms described here.

Delivery Format

Test anxiety training should be delivered using a small group format. Normally six 45-minute sessions will be sufficient to deal with this problem. Normally these groups should not exceed 10 students.

Recruiting Students

Recruiting for test anxiety groups may be a two-pronged process. First, the needs assessment devices listed in Chapter One may be used to identify potential group members. Second, a special needs assessment and request for referrals can be sent directly to teachers. The note included in Figure 6-3 can be used for this purpose.

Figure 6-3

Request for Referrals for Test Anxiety Group

To: All Teachers
From: Counseling Department

As a part of our ongoing effort to help students perform better on tests we are planning to run small groups for students who are unusually anxious about testing. These students may worry excessively about the outcome of their tests, even though they typically have high test scores. In other instances, anxious students complain that they actually studied hard and knew more than the test results revealed, but then they panicked during the test and forget some or much of what they learned. Still other students are noticeably uncomfortable during the testing process. They may perspire heavily, have to be dismissed to go to the bathroom, or simply appear to be uncomfortable.

If you have students in your classes who are unusually anxious about tests, please list their names on the bottom of this sheet and return it to the Counseling Office. A member of the Counseling Staff will contact them for a screening interview.

Thank you for your help with this important concern.

The following students might benefit from your group for students who are unusually anxious about tests:

_____   _____

_____   _____

_____   _____

_____   _____

_____   _____

_____   _____

Teacher's Signature _____

Best Time To Contact Students _____

Screening Group Members

All prospective group members should be individually screened. The following questions and assessment strategies are helpful in determining which students should be placed in the group.

- Do you worry before a test? How long before the test does this begin? Does worrying interfere with eating or sleeping?
- Estimate the intensity of your pre-test worrying using a 1 to 10 scale with a 1 being practically not at all and a 10 being extremely worried.
- What physical symptoms, if any, do you experience before and during a test?
- Have you ever totally panicked during a test and forgotten almost all you had learned in your preparation for a test?
- Do you often remember things that you should have known during the test after you leave the testing situation?
- Does your worrying before a test and your anxiety during a test lower your test score?

Students who have intense anticipatory anxiety, uncomfortable physical symptoms that go beyond those associated with normal test anxiety, and believe that their anxiety lowers their test scores should be included in the group if they want to be involved. Students who are candidates for the group should be asked if they wish to be in a group to help them reduce their anxiety about tests and improve their functioning on tests. They should be asked to state a preliminary goal that they hope to achieve in the group. Unmotivated students and students who have low levels of anxiety should not be included in the group. Students who are anxious but are not preparing for tests should not be included in these groups *unless* they are so anxious they cannot study.

Session 1 - Understanding and Measuring Test Anxiety
Objectives
- Have group members get acquainted.
- Have group members understand the cognitive, affective, and physical aspects of test anxiety.
- Teach students to assess their test anxiety.

Activities

1. Conduct an icebreaker: Divide students into dyads. In the dyads have students take turns introducing themselves. For five minutes student A will listen to student B, and then student B becomes the listener as student A tells about himself or herself. When they come back to the group Student A will introduce Student B and vice versa.

2. Reintroduce the purpose of the group as (1) helping members become

more comfortable with tests and (2) assisting students raise their test scores. Not all students will be pursuing both goals.

3. Do rounds. Each student should state their goal in terms of being more comfortable with tests, doing better on tests, or both.

4. Give a minilecture based on Handout 6-1, What Happens To The Body When You Are Anxious. The purpose of this minilecture is to help students understand the mechanics of their anxiety. After completing the minilecture, personalize by asking students to complete the Handout 6-2, My Symptoms Checklist. Explain that the techniques for controlling the symptoms will be taught in subsequent sessions.

5. Distribute Handout 6-4, Measuring My Test Anxiety. This is when students learn to measure their anxiety. Ask students to rate their anxiety the day before a big test, as they begin the test, and when they encounter the first question they cannot answer.

6. Process their answers by pointing out peak periods and then relate these to the symptoms. Ask students, "What symptoms do you experience at the point when your anxiety level is the highest?"

7. Summarize.

Homework

Practice measuring your test anxiety this week using the scale you have just learned. If your anxiety goes to a very high level this week, make a note regarding what caused it to escalate.

Session 2 - Learning to Stop Unwanted Thoughts

Objectives

• Reinforce students' ability to measure their anxiety.

• Teach thought-stopping skills.

Activities

1. Review homework assignment to determine whether students experienced difficulty in measuring their test anxiety throughout the last week. Reteach using handout 6-4, Measuring My Test Anxiety, as necessary.

2. Review the role of thoughts in anxiety. Handout 6-4 can be used to support this effort.

3. Give students Handout 6-5, Thought Stopping. Also give students a thick rubber band and show them how to place it over the palm of the hand. Never have students snap their wrists in this exercise because this is potentially damaging to the blood vessels in the wrist.

4. Ask students to write down the thoughts that they have that produce their test anxiety. Reassure them that they do not have to share these thoughts. However, if some of the students want to discuss their thoughts that they have, encourage them to do so.

5. Outline the process of thought stopping.

Thoughts >>>>Don't Want >>> Snap >>>>>"Yell" >>>>>>Reassure Self >>>>>Repeat		
Thoughts	STOP	I AM PREPARED!

6. Several rules regarding thought stopping should be outlined. These are:
   - The response to the thoughts about tests should be immediate. As soon as a student has a negative thought, he or she should respond with thought stopping.
   - The use of the rubber band is optional.
   - The STOP is subvocal. Yell STOP in your head.
   - The order to STOP thinking will be more effective if a stop sign is visualized too.
   - The reassurance statement (I AM PREPARED!)only works if the student has been preparing for the test. If he or she has not prepared he or she will need to work on study skills.
   - Thought stopping is not a technique that students have to practice forever. However, they must use it as long as their anxiety about tests lowers their scores.
7. Have students practice thought stopping.
8. Review the steps and summarize.

Homework

Practice using thought stopping to deal with negative thoughts about tests.

Session 3 - Controlling Breathing as a Relaxation Strategy
Objectives
- Review thought stopping and reteach as necessary.
- Teach students how to regulate their breathing when they become anxious.

Activities

1. Have students review their use of thought stopping. Also ask them about their ability to measure their anxiety.

2. Introduce the idea of controlling anxiety through the use of breathing strategies by revisiting Handout 6-2, My Symptoms. Shallow, thoracic breathing (from the upper chest) causes many of the symptoms students experience. By breathing with the large sheath-like muscle under the rib cage (the diaphragm) many of the symptoms listed on the My Symptoms handout will be eliminated.

3. Give students Handout 6-6, Controlling Your Breathing, and review it with them. Tell students this strategy should be used when their anxiety is high and they are experiencing some or all of the symptoms listed on the My Symptoms Checklist, particularly symptoms 1 through 13.

4. Begin the process of teaching the breathing strategy by asking students to count the number of breaths they take in a minute and recording the number of breaths taken on a sheet of paper.

5. Then have students place one hand on their stomachs and continue to breathe normally. If the hand rises and falls as they breathe, they are breathing normally.

6. Next, have the students sit up straight in their chairs and tighten their stomach muscles. Then have them place one hand on their upper chest and one on their stomach as before. Students should notice that the hand on the upper chest moves and the one on the stomach does not. This is what happens when they become anxious. They can self-diagnose to determine if they are breathing correctly by placing one hand on the stomach and one hand on the upper chest.

7. When they are breathing from the upper chest they can use the directions in Handout 6-6, Controlling Your Breathing, to calm their bodies and relieve many of the symptoms they are experiencing,

8. Practice and summarize.

Homework

Practice the breathing exercise along with thought stopping and measuring anxiety until the next group session

Session 4 - Learning to Control Tense Muscles

Objectives
- Review measuring anxiety, thought stopping, and controlling breathing, and reteach as necessary.
- Teach students how to relax the major muscle groups.

Activities

1. Ask students to discuss their successes or failures relating to the first three sessions: measuring anxiety, thought stopping, and controlling breathing.

2. Introduce relaxing tense muscles by reviewing Handout 6-2, My Symptoms. Have students note that symptoms 14 through 23 can best be handled using muscle relaxation. It may also be helpful to review information about the anxiety cycle, starting with the injection of epinephrine into the blood stream. This immediately cause muscles to tense. If students stay anxious for a fairly long period of time, tense, painful muscles will be one of the results.

3. Give students Handout 6-7, Relaxing Tense Muscles, and review the approach with them. Muscle relaxation involves three steps: TENSE>>> HOLD >>>RELEASE THE TENSION AND RELAX THE MUSCLE. However, because students are sitting in a confined space when they are taking a test, they need relaxation strategies that they can use sitting in their seats.

4. Using Handout 6-7, Relaxing Tense Muscles, as a guide, demonstrate what is to be done with each major muscle group. Then have students practice each exercise two or three times.

5. Remind students that they now have an understanding of their anxiety and how it effects their bodies. Also remind them that they have identified the physical symptoms they experience and have learned strategies that can be used to cope with their symptoms. Their task is to identify which of these techniques they will use when they become anxious.

6. Summarize.

Homework

Practice using the strategies you have learned to relax your tense muscles as well as the other techniques you have learned.

Consider which technique they will use to handle your test anxiety on an ongoing basis.

Session 5 - Developing a Plan to Cope with Test Anxiety

Objectives

- Review all of the techniques that have been taught in sessions 1 through 4.
- Have students consider which of these techniques they are likely to use most successfully to control their test anxiety and draft a plan for using them.

Activities

1. Ask students about their use of muscle relaxation strategies. Did students use them? Were they helpful? Reteach as necessary.

2. Give a minilecture on using techniques together. In this minilecture students should be told that most people have to use more than one technique to control their anxiety. For example, Anticipatory anxiety often causes muscle tension and thus the strategy for relaxing tense muscles can be used to deal with this problem. However, when panic occurs during a test, it is likely that both thought stopping and taking control of breathing will be needed. Therefore, students need to develop a plan to use the techniques they have learned to deal with their test anxiety.

3. Give students Handout 6-8, Plan for Coping With My Test Anxiety, and have them complete it.

4. Ask students to compare plans and provide their rationales for their plan. Make suggestions if students have oversights in their plans.

5. Summarize

Homework

Students should use their plans to cope with their test anxiety as needed.

Session 6 - Evaluation Plans to Control Test Anxiety
and Wrap Up

(To be held at least two weeks after session 5.)

Objective

• Help students evaluate the utility of their plans to cope with their test anxiety

Activities

1. Ask students about their progress toward coping successfully with their test anxiety.

2. Ask students for suggestions when a part or all of an individual's plan is not working as it should.

3. Ask students who are having trouble to rewrite parts of their plan.

4. Give a minilecture on backsliding. Eliminating or greatly diminishing test anxiety is not a totally smooth process. There may be times when some of the anxiety returns. Some students may believe that the techniques do not work. This is not the case. All that is required is that students continue to work on their anxiety using the techniques they have learned in the group.

5. Summarize the group's content. Note the progress students have made dealing with their anxiety.

Homework

1. All students who continue to have problems with test anxiety should make an individual appointment for additional work.

Summary

The school reform movement has placed renewed emphasis on testing. Legislators, school board members, and parents are anxious to get objective evidence about the performance of their schools. Some students, particularly ESL students, are disadvantaged in the test process because of language difficulties. and, in some instances, other variables that are common in the testing process. Most students can benefit from an orientation to the testing process. If the orientation to testing is combined with the use of diagnostic tests that can identify weaknesses in academic preparation, all students are likely to benefit.

References

Agnew, J., & Bell, K. (1997). *PACT student guide*. Chapel Hill, NC: Newbell.

Berry G. L., & Lopez, C. A. (1977). Testing programs and the Spanish-speaking child: Guidelines for the school counselor. *The School Counselor, 24*, 261-269.

Brown, D. (1982). Increasing test-wiseness in children. *Elementary School Guidance and Counseling, 16*, 172-179.

Michael, N., & Edwards, P. A. (1991). Test preparation programs: Counselors' views and involvement. *The School Counselor, 39*, 98-106.

Rathvon, N. W. (1991). Effects of a guidance unit in two formats on the examination performance of underachieving middle school students. *The School Counselor, 38*, 294-304.

Wiggins, J. D. (1992). Beating the SAT: Playing the game. *The School Counselor, 39*, 300-303.

Wilson, N. S. (1986). Meeting the challenge of standardized tests: A guidance musical. *The School Counselor, 33*, 338-344.

Wilson, R. R. (1987). *Breaking the panic cycle*. Rockville, MD: Anxiety Disorders Association of America.

Test-Taking Strategies

Multiple Choice Questions
- Cover answers as you read and try to answer the question without them.
- In many instances, your first impulse is correct. Put a mark by the answer that you first believe to be correct, but read all of the answers.
- Read all answers before deciding.
- Beware of answers that contain words such as *always, never, totally,* and *completely.* Try to remember if there are exceptions.
- Look for words such as *usually, sometimes,* and *frequently.*
- If two answers seem the same, one is probably correct. Study these carefully.
- Make calculated guesses after you have eliminated as many responses as possible.
- Make a mark by the answers that you are unsure of so you can check them later.
- You may get some clues from other test questions.

True/False Questions
- Look for words such as *always, never,* and *all.* These questions are often false. Questions with *usually and frequently* are more likely to be true.
- If the question contains two parts, read both as though they were one statement and remember if any part of a question is false, the entire question is false.
- Remember, double negatives in a sentence equal a positive. The statement, "George Washington was not unconcerned about the battle in Boston." means that he was concerned.
- Guess after you have done your best to recall the answer.
- Mark those answers that you are unsure of so you can come back to them later.
- Don't forget to check answers carefully after you have completed the entire test.

Matching Questions
- Read the directions very carefully to determine if items in the answer list can be used more than once.
- Read all questions and answers before you start.
- Look for words and phrases that provide clues to the answer.
- Answer the questions you are certain of first and as quickly as possible. If answers are to be used only once, cross them out as you use them.

Then answer the questions that you think you know.
- Guess wisely. After you have answered all the questions you are know the answers to, then guess.

Essay Questions
- Read the question and ask yourself, "What is the test maker looking for?"
- Always write out a brief outline before you write the answers to either short or long essay questions. This saves time and keeps you from forgetting information as you write.
- If there are several parts to the question, make sure you answer all parts.
- Write legibly and make your points easy to find (e.g., number them).
- Read your answer to make sure you have included everything you know.
- Do not include unneeded information. Individuals scoring the test are not impressed with information that is not related to the question, and they may actually deduct points from your answer.

MY SYMPTOMS

Check the symptoms you experience when you become anxious about tests.

____1. MY STOMACH FLUTTERS

____2. I FEEL NAUSEOUS

____3. MY HANDS GET COLD

____4. MY HANDS SWEAT

____5. MY HEAD ACHES

____6. MY FACE FLUSHES

____7. I GET DIZZY

____8. I HAVE TO GO TO THE BATHROOM OFTEN

____9. I HAVE TROUBLE EATING

____10. I BREATHE RAPIDLY AND SHALLOWLY

____11. I EAT AND EAT

____12. MY MOUTH GETS DRY

____13. MY HEART RACES

Symptoms 1-13 can be eliminated or reduced by controlling your breathing

____14. MY HANDS QUIVER

____15. I AM AWKWARD/SEEM UNCOORDINATED

____16. MY HEAD ACHES–USUALLY ON ONE SIDE

____17. THE MUSCLES IN MY NECK AND SHOULDERS ACHE

____18. MUSCLES IN MY LEGS, CALVES, OR ARMS GET TENSE

____19. I TAP MY FINGERS OR FEET

____20. I CLINCH MY TEETH OR GRIND THEM

____21. I STAMMER OR STUTTER

____22. MY MUSCLES IN MY CHEST ARE TIGHT

____23. MY TEMPOROMANDIBULAR JOINT ACHES (THIS IS THE JOINT AT THE HINGE OF THE JAW)

Symptoms 14-24 can be controlled by muscle relaxation

____24. I BITE MY NAILS

____25. I PICK AT THINGS LIKE LINT OR MY HAIR

____26. I KEEP FORGETTING THINGS

____27. I WANT TO RETREAT AND SLEEP, SAFE AT HOME

____28. I CANNOT CONCENTRATE

____29. I HAVE THE SAME THOUGHT RUNNING THROUGH MY HEAD REPEATEDLY

Symptoms 24-29 are the most resistant to change. To be successful you will have to stop your thoughts about tests, control your breathing, and relax your muscles.

You will be taught how to control all of these symptoms

What Happens to Your Body When You Get Anxious

A Test Is Assigned

You may begin to worry about the test days or even weeks in advance. This may produce a variety of physiological reactions including headaches, tense muscles, and an upset stomach. You may have minipanic reactions during this period. Also, you may not sleep well as you normally do and either under- or overeat.

For some students the anxiety does not kick in until the day of the test. What follows is an illustration of your anxiety reaction.

1. Thought: BIG TEST.
2. Epinephrine (adrenaline) is pumped into the bloodstream - to some degree this happens to everyone
   • oxygen level in blood increases;
   • carbon dioxide level decreases;
   • heart rate increases;
   • Muscles tense;
   • blood pools around vital organs;
   • blood sugar level increases; and
   • breathing becomes thoracic (upper chest).
3. Your body is ready for action
4. But, no physical activity burns the excess oxygen, and blood sugar.
5. Symptoms may increase and this may cause your anxiety level to go up, including
   • sweaty palms;
   • cold hands and feet;
   • dizziness;
   • irregular heartbeat;
   • can't "think";
   • legs weak;
   • numbness in lips, hands, and perhaps on the left side;
   • choking sensation; and
   • hyperventilating and passing out.
6. You may just hang on and finish the test.
7. Afterwards, self-criticism may occur because you knew more than the test showed.

Measuring Your Test Anxiety

100 _____	Extremely High
90 _____	Very High
80 _____	High
70 _____	Above Average
60 _____	Slighly Above Average
50 _____	Average
40 _____	Slightly Below Average
30 _____	Below Average
20 _____	Relaxed
10 _____	Very Relaxed
0 _____	Anxiety Free

Handout 6-5

Thought Stopping

As you now know, your scary thoughts produce bodily reactions that may increase your anxiety. It is a vicious cycle that you can stop. One important way to do this is to stop the fearful thoughts. The steps for doing this are as follows:

Step 1: Identify the automatic thoughts that are making you anxious such as

• I'll fail;

• I'll make a low grade, I'll be embarrassed; and

• I'll let my parents down.

Write your scary thought(s) here (you will not be asked to share these with others in the group):

_____

_____

Step 2: Decide you do not want these thoughts any more .

Step 3: Snap your palm with a thick rubber band. It is important that you give yourself a good snap! This produces pain which interrupts the scary thought for a moment.

or

Subvocally yell, STOP!!! Also it will help if you visualize a stop sign at this point.

It will also help if you can get angry at your anxiety (not at yourself) at this point.

Step 5: Tell yourself to "get a grip." Then remind yourself that you are prepared for this test.

Repeat this process as often as you need to get control of the anxiety. Although the use of the rubber band is optional, "big" snappers are usually successful in stopping their thoughts.

Handout 6-6

Controlling Your Breathing

When you control your breathing, you signal your body to relax. Controlling your breathing involves

- breathing no more than 16 times per minute;
- controlling the exhale by pursing your lips; and
- breathing diaphragmatically (from beneath the rib cage)

You can control your breathing using simple techniques. One of these is to count as you breathe as follows:

• As you inhale	1001--1002--1003
• Hold your breath	1001--1002--1003
• Exhale (purse lips)	1001--1002--1003
• Rest (don't breathe)	1001--1002--1003

The result is that you are breathing approximately 5 to 7 times per minute, you are filling your lungs from the bottom, and you are controlling the exhale.

Repeating this process for 5 -7 minutes will eliminate a racing heart, light headedness, most muscle tension, sweaty, palms, etc.

Why does this work? Because, when you breathe slowly, the liver processes the epinephrine (adrenaline) that comes into your blood-stream when you become anxious.

Relaxing Tense Muscles

Introduction

Muscle tension is a normal part of the response to anxiety. In some instances the tension is so intense students feel as though they must get out of their seats and move around. You need to learn to control your muscle tension, not only to give you a sense of control over your body, but also to make you comfortable when you are taking tests

Relaxing Tense Muscles

Step 1: Identify the muscle that is tense.

Step 2: Increase the tension in that muscle and hold the tension for five seconds: 1001----1002----1003----1004----1005.

If you get tension in the following muscle groups you can relax them by using the procedure that was just described. If you get tension in the **TMJ:** Stretch your lower jaw until your lower teeth extend further that your upper teeth.

Throat: Place your tongue in the roof of your mouth and push against the roof of your mouth hard as you can.

Chest: Pull your shoulders back and try to get your shoulder blades to touch.

Upper back: Put your elbows together just over your stomach.

Muscle under rib cage : Tuck the loose skin on your stomach (even if you do not have any) under your rib cage (this will cause very mild discomfort)

Legs: push your feet out in front of you and raise them a few inches above the floor. Then point your toes away from you. After 5 seconds, rotate your toes and feet and try to point them at your chin. If it is difficult to raise both feet at once this exercise may be done one leg at time.

Step 3: Release the tension while saying subvocally (in your head)– RELAX

Step 4: Repeat the process until tense muscles are relaxed.

Plan for Coping with My Test Anxiety

Pretest plan - anticipatory anxiety

Prior to a test I have the following symptoms:

_____

_____

_____

I plan to deal with these symptoms using the following techniques:

_____

_____

During the test

During tests I have the following symptoms:

_____

_____

I plan to deal with these symptoms by using these techniques:

_____

_____

_____

Evaluating my plan

I will know if my plan works if my anxiety score is lower or my grades go up

_____

_____

_____

The Escalating Panic Reaction To Tests

Hyperventilation

Chest pains

Normal Anxiety   Dizziness

Fearful   Sweaty Palms   Blurred Vision
Thoughts About >>>>> Dry Mouth >>>>>>>>>Nausea
Testing   Heart Rate Up   Hands Shake
                                                     Can't Think
                                                     Choking Feeling
                                                     Numbness

Chapter Seven

Time Management: An Essential Habit for Students

A well known economist is reported to have said, "The most precious commodity of all is time." Lakein (1973), author of the classic, *How to Get Control of Your Time and Your Life,* puts it this way, "Time is life. It is irreversible and irreplaceable. To waste your time is to waste your life, but to master your time is to master your life and make the most of it" (p. 11). Covey (1989,) in his best selling book *The 7 Habits of Highly Effective People*, indicated that one of the 7 habits of effective people is "putting first things first". He defines the habit of putting first things first as the ability to set priorities and act on them after they are established. Interestingly, students and other people treat time as though each person is allocated a different amount. All of us have heard people say, "You have more time than I do," which may mean many things. However, the fact is that all of us have exactly 168 hours in a week, and how we use our waking hours determines whether we will be successful as students, workers, or in other life roles. This chapter addresses the issue of time management.

Understanding Perceptions of Time

We know that some people manage their time better than others do, and the obvious question is, "Why does this occur?" The easy answer to this is that many people have never acquired the habits necessary to manage their time effectively. Managing time effectively requires more than the ability to organize a notebook or maintain an appointment book. Covey asserted that students must acquire two prerequisite skills if they are to be good time managers. These habits are proactive and start with the end in mind. Covey equated proactivity with accepting responsibility for one's actions and not being reactive. Many students blame others for their underachievement. One student told his mother, "If you stayed home and helped me with my work instead of working, I would be a good student." Another blamed her teachers charging them with being prejudiced against her. Accepting responsibility for one's self is defined as not blaming others for failures. Beginning with the end in mind means that students need to have a vision of their future. Locke and Latham (1990) detailed the role of goals in motivation, and the idea that goals are needed has been emphasized throughout this book. Visions of the future must be operationalized into specific objectives if they are to be helpful to students.

Covey (1989) suggested that all of us are confronted with four types of activities each day. These are urgent-important activities, nonurgent-important activities, urgent-unimportant activities, and non-urgent-unimportant activities. Crises growing out of procrastination regarding studying and completion of projects with tight deadlines qualify as urgent / important activities in students' lives. These students are not proactive, and thus their lives are chaotic. They do not plan and go from one crisis to another. They are **Reactors.** Students who do their homework regularly, study for mastery even when a test is not imminent, anticipate quizzes, complete projects and papers ahead of time so they can review them carefully, ask teachers about future assignments, and take SAT or ACT preparation course before they get low scores, are working on nonurgent-important matters. These students have accepted responsibility for their lives and are proactive. They are the **Visionaries.** Students who engage in urgent-unimportant activities allow telephone calls to interrupt their study time, put club and athletic activities ahead of studying, and cave in to the demands of their peers to engage in social activities. Students who allow urgent-unimportant activities to dominate their time are out of control. They are the **Unfocused.** Students who allow unimportant- non-urgent activities such as watching television, "hanging out," and time-wasting telephone calls to dominate their lives are **Trivializers.**

In order for students to become Visionaries, they must manage their time based on priorities. However, students must first identify their values, that is, their beliefs about what brings meaning to their lives. Individual values are the basis of students' visions of the future (Brown, 1996; Covey, 1989; Rokeach, 1973). Students already know that some of the activities they engage in are more satisfying than others, although they often do not understand why this is the case. However, many students have not crystallized their values, and they either are acting on the expectations of others (usually parents) extrinsically motivated, or they are unmotivated. In order to put first things first, as Covey (1989) suggested, students must crystallize their values so they can set goals and prioritize how they will spend their time to attain those goals.

Putting first things first should be the golden rule of time management; but Covey (1989) failed to recognize there are other personal and cultural factors that contribute both positively and negatively to the ability of students to manage their time. One the most important of these personal factors is students' personalities. Some students (and adults) have different perspectives on the importance of time based on certain personality traits. Millions of people have taken the Myers-Briggs Type Indicator (MBTI) (Briggs & McCaulley, 1992) and are familiar with the 16 personality types the instrument yields. Two of the dimensions of the MBTI, Judgment and Perception appear to be related to some degree to the manner in which people deal with time. Perceiving types, or what Briggs and McCaulley labeled the perceptive attitude, are open to incoming data and want to miss nothing in their outer worlds. Consequently, they may be more attuned to the collection of data than they are to the passage of time, and deadlines for assignments may be ignored, missed, or met in a flurry of activity at the last moment. In fact, even after Perceiving types have reached conclusions, they may want to reconsider the decision. On the other hand, Judging types (in the judgment attitude) are concerned about making decisions, meeting deadlines, and generally bringing closure to their endeavors. In the best of all personalities, there is a balance between these two attitudes. However, if Perceiving types have a deficit of judgment, procrastination is likely to be the outcome. If Judging types have a deficit of perception, the result may be timely, but ill advised decisions or poor quality work (Briggs & McCaulley, 1992).

Cultural values are also important determinants of perceptions about time. In Chapter 2 the traditional values of the major cultural groups in this country were presented. Figure 7-1 provides a list of the traditional values of the major cultural groups in the United States regarding time. People with a future time orientation, who are typically European Americans, believe that planning for the future is important, and that individuals need to manage their time as they prepare for the future. Individuals with a past/future orientation share the belief that planning for the future is important, but believe that the events and traditions of the past should not be forgotten. Although this is a value that has been associated with Asian Americans, individuals from all groups may hold this time orientation value. People with a present time orientation value believe that it is what is occurring in the present that is important, and, by default, the future is less important. Although this time orientation value has often been associated with Hispanic Americans, others subscribe to it as well. For people who hold a circular time orientation, the passage of time is measured by natural events, as opposed to time as measured by watches and calendars. Some American Indians, particularly those from western tribes, report that they cannot recall seeing calendars or watches in their homes when they were growing up.

Covey's (1989) ideas about time management are based in Eurocentric values in that they involve anticipating the future. Although it is probably necessary that students who do not hold Eurocentric values adopt a future orientation if they are to be successful in school, one questions that needs to be answered is, "How can future-oriented time management procedures be taught to students who have different perceptions of time?"

Figure 7-1
Traditional Time Orientation Values of Major Cultural Groups

Cultural Groups	European American	Hispanic American	American Indian	African American	Asian American
	Future	Present	Circular	Present	Past/Present

In summary, perceptions of time are influenced by cultural values, personality factors, and of course, situational demands. The time management course presented in the next section attempts to take all of these factors into consideration.

Taking Control of Your Time

Time management groups can be conducted most effectively with middle school and high school students. Either small groups or classroom size groups may be used to develop time management skills. This unit takes approximately six 30-to-45 minute sessions. If a small group approach is used, students must be recruited. Recruitment of students for time management groups should be done directly with students using the assessment device in Figure 7-2.

Figure 7-2

Survey Instrument for Identifying Students for
Time Measurement Groups

Time Management Survey

The Counseling Staff is offering time management groups to students who want to improve the way they manage their time. To see if you will benefit from these groups, answer the following statements by using True or False.

1. Sometimes I think there just aren't enough hours in the day to do all of my work._____

2. Like the rabbit in Alice in Wonderland, I'm always late for a very important date._____

3. My motto is, "Never do today what you can postpone until tomorrow."_____

4. I don't have enough time to do fun things._____

5. I don't seem to be able to set priorities._____

6. I'm burned out, and my schoolwork is suffering._____

7. I get my work done, but it seems as if I go from crisis to crisis. I'm always on the run._____

8. I'm constantly being distracted by others and don't get my work done._____

9. I have no system for manageing my time._____

10. I often hand in assignments after the due date._____

11. My life is out of control._____

12. It is difficult for me to set priorities for using my time._____

If you answered True to one or more of the above statements, you might benefit from a time management group. If you are interested, sign your name on the line below and tell us when during the school day would be best to contact you.

Yes. I'm interested in a time management group.
Signature_____
The best time to schedule a brief conference to discuss the group further would be (list time, day of the week, your location in the building, and your teacher's name during the period you wish to be contacted).

_____

Session 1 - Introduction to Time Management
Objectives
- Define time management and tell why it is important.
- Communicate the idea that time management is more than a series of techniques.
- Communicate the idea that, by managing their time, students are managing their lives.
- Begin the assessment of students' time management style.
- Introduce visualization as a planning strategy.

Activities

1. Ask students to relax in their chairs and close their eyes. Then ask them to take three deep breaths and exhale very slowly. After the students are relaxed, have them visualize themselves at age 30. Where will they be living? What jobs will they hold? Will they be married? Will they have children? What leisure activities will they enjoy?

Process the imagery. Many students will be unable to visualize their future. Have those students who are able to do so tell about their visualizations first. Then ask the other students if they have ideas about why they cannot visualize their future. Brainstorm reasons. Then suggest that one of the reasons that people do not have a vision of the future is that they are not in touch with their values, and explain that some of the sessions will be devoted to helping students identify their values. Have them record their visualizations on the Handout 7-1, Visions of My Future. Collect these and keep them in a folder. Each group meeting will begin with this exercise, and future visualizations will be recorded on the same sheet. Each week these should be checked to determine student progress.

2. Give a minilecture on time management based on Overhead 7-1, Time Management. Explain that time management

- involves taking control of your time and your life;
- results in greater success and less stress;
- doesn't mean living by a rigid schedule;
- may provide more time for fun;
- will make you more effective;
- requires students to determine what they want from school and life;
- may have different meanings in different cultures;
- involves priority setting; and
- most importantly, involves putting first things first.

3. Have students in the group share one of their time management problems (e.g., too little time to study, distractibility). If this is a classroom group have students who do not have a time management problem share one time management strategy that works for them.

4. Have students complete Handout 7-2, My Time Management Style. Discuss the results. Determine if the inventory is an accurate assessment of their style. If this is a small group have students share their results.

5. Begin the administration of the Life Values Inventory* to high school students (Crace & Brown, 1996). If the students are in middle school construct a values card sort using Handout 7- 3, Values Card Sort. Have students sort the values in the card sort into very important to me, important to me, and not important to me stacks. The results should be recorded and brought to Session 2.

6. Summarize session content.

*Available from Life Values Resources, 620 Bayberry Drive, Chapel Hill, NC 27514

Note: If there are students in the group who do not have a future or past-future time orientation, be sure to stress that there are roles that they fill where time may not be important and what they need to do is determine when time is important and when it is unimportant. However, in school and in the workplace later in life, time management will be important. If you are unsure of the values you may use Handout 2-1, Your Cultural Values, to assess their cultural values.

Homework

Complete work on the Life Values Inventory or the card sort and bring results to next meeting.

Session 2 - Values, Priorities, and Time Management
Objectives

- Have students prioritize their values based on the life values inventory and have them understand the links between values, goals, and motivation.
- Have students identify activities that will satisfy their values.
- Illustrate linkage between schools and future activities that will satisfy values.
- Have students commit to becoming more effective time managers.

Activities

1. Repeat the visualization exercise that was used in the first session. This exercise may be varied in that students can be asked to visualize their lives at different ages. Have them share their images and write them on Handout 7-1, Images of My Life.

2. Review results of the Life Values Inventory/Values Card Sort.

3. Discuss values as standards of behavior and sources of motivation and satisfaction, Show Overhead 7-2, The Importance of Values. Provide examples such as the following:

- Some people value health and physical activity. They exercise, eat healthy food, and learn to manage their health.
- Some people value wealth. They spend a lot of time thinking about and engaging in activities that allows them to make and accumulate money.

4. Ask students to give examples of times when they have acted on their values. Ask them how it felt to act on their values. Also ask students if they have ever failed to act on their values, that is, done something that did not correspond to their beliefs.

5. Discuss why school may not be motivating and be a high priority. Students often do not see how school will help them act on their values. Ask how many can see links between school and how they will spend their future.

6. Identify ways that school may help students act on their values now and later in life.

- Wealth: The subject most associated with high income is math. Why?
- Helping Others: What subjects are associated with our ability to help others?
- Being creative: What subjects are most likely to help you be creative?
- Responsibility: What subjects are most likely to help us act responsibly?

7. Do a series of three rounds (each student takes a turn) in which each student responds to the following stimulus: **If I am to act on my most important values either now or after I finish school, I must prioritize what types of activities?**

8. Ask if their time management style allows them to set priorities? Are they Visionaries?

9. Summarize. Point out that we tend to orient ourselves to activities that will satisfy our values and that when we have not decided what we really believe, we may allow others to set our priorities for us. Almost all students want to get a good job after school, but being accepted by others may be more important so we hang out. Also individuals' time management styles may not allow them to act on their values even when they have identified them.

Homework

Continue to think about priority setting. Identify times when you act or fail to act on the priorities associated with your values. For example, a test is coming up tomorrow that is very important, but you hang out with your friends instead of studying.

Session 3 -Time Management Habits (I)

Objectives

- Increase students' understanding of their time management habits.
- Have students commit to stop drifting or drowning and decide to budget their time.

Activities

1. Begin with the future visualization and have students record their images of their future on Handout 7-1, Visions of My Future.

2. Have students complete Handout 7-4, My Important and Unimportant Activities. Then have students share what they have rated as important and unimportant activities. Ask if they agree on what is important and unimportant. Ask them to share how much time they spend each week on important and unimportant activities. Is the amount of time spent on

important and unimportant activities related to their time management style?

3. Tell students there are three ways that people make decisions regarding their use of time:

- Decisions dictated by other people or events that occur in their live. (no control) - reactor unfocused trivializer.
- They decide (individual control) - visionary.
- They decide with others (mutual control) - visionary.

4. When people allow others to decide, they are adrift, they have no control over their lives. In the other approaches, they have control, although they may give up some of it to make harmonious decisions.

> Note: If you have Asian Americans, American Indians, or Hispanic Americans in your group they are likely to have a collective social value. If they have this value they are likely to subscribe to a shared approach to decision-making. This does not mean that they are out of control. Be sure to acknowledge the legitimacy of this perspective. Having a collective value in no way negates the need to use time more wisely, however.

5. Some people are out of control because

- they have not set priorities and thus they have no direction.
- they are non-assertive and cannot say no (Assertion is a decidedly Eurocentric concept and may not be appropriate in all cultures. Make note of that in your discussion. However, giving in to the demands of others can result in loss of self-esteem and can bring shame to one's family. This idea may be more important to Asian Americans and others who hold collective social values.)

6. The beginning of taking control is to develop priorities. The next step is determining how much of your time is spent in unimportant (low priority) activities. An unimportant (low priority) activity is one that doesn't need to be done to get the job done at school. The third step is getting organized. The fourth step is replacing those activities with important activities. The fifth step is staying focused and not backsliding.

7. Summarize the session.

Homework

Identify the strategies you use to manage your time.

Session 4 - Time Management Habits (II)

Objectives

- Have students identify their time management habits.
- Have students adopt new (or additional) time management habits.

Activities

1. Repeat the visualization exercise and have students record their

images on Handout 7-1, Visions of My Future.

2. Ask if anyone has changed the way they see themselves in the future.

3. Have students complete Handout 7-5, My Time Management Habits.

4. Process by asking people to share their habits and how well they work.

5. Ask which habits will help them become a Visionary time manager.

6. Ask students to adopt one new time management habit for 1 week. The list in Handout 7-5, My Time Management Habits, may be used as the basis for this selection.

7. Introduce Handout 7-6, Time Management Record, and have students write a vision statement.

Homework

Finish filling out Handout 7-6,Time Management Record, and try to follow it for the next week.

Use the newly adopted time management skill throughout the week.

Session 5 - Time Management Habits (III)

Objective

• Have students continue to work on adopting time management habits

Activities

1. Repeat the futures visualization and have students record their current vision on the Handout 7-1, My Vision of the Future.

2. Process visualization by asking students if "future" is getting clearer.

3. Follow up on the goal to adopt a new time management strategy and determine how students did in this area.

4. Follow up on the homework assignment regarding Handout 7-6, Time Management Record. Did the students complete the form and use it? Why or why not?

5. Using Overhead 7-4, Time Management Record, explain that the purposes of the Time Management Record are to

• give them a time management aid;

• encourage them to engage in priority setting that is in keeping with their values;

• encourage them to become Visionaries - to look ahead and anticipate the future; and

• encourage them to work continuously on their time management habits.

6. Give students another copy of Handout 7-6, Time Management Record, and have them complete it for the next week.

7. Discuss the resolutions section of Handout 7-6, Time Management Record. Use the analogy of a New Years resolution, which is a promise to yourself that you will improve your behavior. In the resolutions section of

the Time Management Record, have students promise themselves that they will improve some aspect of their time management such as staying with their priorities, improving their goal setting, or using a newly adopted time management strategy. Emphasize that this is the way habits develop.

8. Have students fill out their Time Management Record for the next week.

Homework

Use Handout 7-6, Time Management Record, to enhance your time management for the next week.

Session 6 - Time Management Habits (IV)

Objectives

- Review students' use of the Handout 7-6, Time Management Record.
- Encourage continued use of the Time Management Record.

Activities

1. Begin with the visualization exercise and have students record their visions on Handout 7-1, My Vision of the Future.

2. Process the visualization exercise by asking students if their images of their futures have become clearer. Encourage them to keep working on visualizations as a part of their Time Management Record Sheet and to keep trying to visualize their futures.

3. Review Handout 7-6,Time Management Record, to determine how the students followed through. Have students circle areas that were problematic and encourage them to keep trying. Did they backslide? Why?

4. Have students fill out a Time Management Record for next week.

5. Summarize by emphasizing the relationships among values, priorities, goals, and habits. Also remind students that even though they have made progress they can backslide.

Homework

Continue to use Handout 7-6, Time Management Record.

Optional Sessions

Additional sessions can be scheduled to reinforce use of the Time Management Record if theleader feels that they are necessary to insure its continued use. If additional sessions are scheduled, they should be scheduled 2 weeks apart and should follow the same outline as session 6.

References

Briggs, I. B., & McCaulley, M. H. (1992). *Manual: A guide to the development and use of the Myers-Briggs Type Indicator.* Palo Alto, CA: Consulting Psychologist Press.

Brown, D. (1996). Brown's values-based-holistic model of career and life role choices and satisfaction. In D. Brown, L. Brooks, & Associates, *Career choice and development* (pp. 337-372). San Francisco: Jossey-Bass.

Covey, S. R. (1989). *The 7 habits of highly effective people.* New York: Simon & Schuster.

Crace, R. K., & Brown, D. (1996). *Life values inventory,* Chapel Hill, NC : Life Values Resources.

Lakein, A. (1973). *How to get control of your time and your life.* New York: Signet.

Locke, E. A., & Latham, G . P. (1990). *A theory of goal setting and task performance.* Englewood Cliffs, NJ: Prentice-Hall.

Rokeach, M. (1973). *The nature of human values.* New York: Free Press.

Visions of My Future

Before each of the group sessions you will be asked to visualize your life at different ages. Record what you visualize on this sheet.

Visualization One

_____

_____

Visualization Two

_____

Visualization Three

_____

Visualization Four

_____

Visualization Five

_____

Visualization Six

_____

_____

Additional Visualizations

_____

_____

Handout 7-2

My Time Management Style
Check all of the following statements that describe you.

Section I
_____ 1. I don't waste time on unimportant things, but my life seems to be one crisis after another.
_____ 2. I'm always rushing to meet deadlines.
_____ 3. I never get caught up.
_____ 4. I don't have time to plan ahead.
_____ 5. I often cram for tests.
_____ 6. Sometimes I am surprised by the assignments teachers make.

Section II

_____ 1. I organize my time around important things. I put first things first.

_____ 2. I often finish assignments ahead of time.

_____ 3. I don't like to be caught by surprise so I complete my assignments every day.

_____ 4. When I go to class, I usually feel prepared for anything.

_____ 5. I don't have to cram for tests because I have studied regularly.

_____ 6. At the end of most school days, I have a plan for completing my schoolwork.

Section III

_____ 1. I worry too much about the wrong things, and lose a lot of time I should be using on important things.

_____ 2. Sometimes I wonder why I spend so much time on some things.

_____ 3. I often allow distractions, such as telephone calls from friends, to take me away from studying.

_____ 4. My life is out of control.

_____ 5. Every time I set priorities, something happens to keep me from acting on the ones that are most important.

_____ 6. Sometimes schoolwork gets done and sometimes it doesn't, but when it is done it is rarely my best work.

Section IV

_____ 1. Unimportant things such as watching television come first in my life.

_____ 2. It doesn't take much to keep me from doing schoolwork.

_____ 3. Sometimes I get others to do my schoolwork.

_____ 4. I know my life is out of control, but it doesn't bother me.

_____ 5. I don't worry about setting priorities in my life. Things will take care of themselves.

_____ 6. Sometimes, when I look back on a day, I'm not sure what I did with all my time.

Now tally your score for each section of the inventory.

Scores for:

Section I _____   Section III _____

Section II _____   Section IV _____

Students who have their highest scores in Section I are Reactors. They cannot manage their time because they are involved in crises after crisis. Because they are up to their backsides in alligators they cannot worry about draining the swamp. They feel overwhelmed and out of control. These students are playing Jeopardy ®. They may win, but they feel as if they may lose it all at any time.

Students who have their highest scores in Section II are called Visionaries because they look ahead, anticipate the future, and act to prevent crisis. They feel as though they are in control of their lives and are self-confident about their future. Life is not full of surprises for these students, and even if a surprise occurs they are ready. These students are playing the game of Monopoly ® and are likely to win.

Students who have their highest scores in Section III may also feel out of control and overwhelmed, but for the wrong reasons. These students are the Unfocused. They cannot set priorities, and thus they are always rushing out to do the wrong thing. They are involved in the Un Game ®. This is a game with no winner, because their activities lack meaning except for the moment.

Students who have their highest scores in Section IV fill their lives with activities and events that are relatively unimportant. This does not mean that these activities are not enjoyable, only that they have no long-term pay off for the student. These students are the Trivializers because their life is an ongoing game of Trivial Pursuit ®.

No student has a single time management style. For example, most people use a Visionary style from time-to-time, but they do not use it often enough to be good time managers. In the spaces provided below estimate the percentage of time you use each of the four styles to manage your time.

_____ % of the time I use the Reactor time management style.

_____ % of the time I use the Visionary time management style.

_____ % of the time I use the Unfocused time management style.

_____ % of the time I use the Trivializer time management style.

Values Card Sort

Construct several values card sorts by placing the following values on a 3" by 5" cards.

If you are using a word processor, you can use the address function in your letter wizard to imprint the cards. You can also use one of the address programs and print the names of the values on adhesive labels that can then be placed on cards. (Note: These should be type set so that there six on a page.)

Wealth	Caring for Others
Being Challenged	Being Healthy
Being Physically Active	Being humble (not letting others know about accomplishments)
Nature (the Environment)	Scientific Problem Solving
Being Responsible	Being Creative
Independence	Being Accepted by Peers
Variety in Life	Security
Being in Charge	Spirituality
Loyalty to My Family	Truthfulness

Have students sort the cards into three stacks:
1. very important to me; 2. important to me; 3. not important to me

Students should record the results by making a list of each value placed in each category.

My Important and Unimportant Activities

Important Activities   Unimportant Activities

_____   _____
_____   _____
_____   _____
_____   _____
_____   _____
_____   _____
_____   _____
_____   _____
_____   _____
_____   _____
_____   _____
_____   _____
_____   _____
_____   _____
_____   _____
_____   _____
_____   _____
_____   _____
_____   _____
_____   _____
_____   _____
_____   _____
_____   _____
_____   _____
_____   _____

Hours spent per week_____   Hours spent per week_____

My Time Management Habits

Check Yes or No as you respond to the following questions. Your answers should be based on how you usually act, your typical behavior.

I. Goals

Yes   No

___   ___   1. I have goals that I wish to accomplish each day.

___   ___   2. I have goals that I wish to accomplish each week

___   ___   3. I set goals for each grading period.

___   ___   4. I have long term-goals, a vision for my future.

II. Deadlines

Yes   No

___   ___   5. I meet almost all deadlines comfortably.

___   ___   6. I meet most deadlines, but I have to scramble to do it.

III. Priority Setting

Yes   No

___   ___   7. I set priorities and stick to them.

IV. Control

Yes   No

___   ___   8. I sometimes waste time to please others.

___   ___   9. I allow big events such as big games, favorite TV programs to determine how I use my time.

___   ___   10. I often allow the wishes of others to interfere with how I use my time.

V. Use of Time Management Aids

Yes   No

___   ___   11. I wear a watch so that I can keep track of the time.

___   ___   12. I keep a daily/weekly/monthly planner so that I can keep track of assignments and other deadlines.

___   ___   13. I limit the amount of time I spend on activities such as telephone calls.

___   ___   14. I have a daily routine divided between school-related and other activities.

___   ___   15. I keep an ongoing "things to do" list.

___   ___   16. I use notes to remind me of what I need to do each day.

Time Management Record

Weekly Planner for Week of: _____

My vision statement for this week. On friday afternoon I want to be able to say:

_____

_____

My top priorities for this week in order of importance: Related Values
1._____
2._____
3._____
4._____
5._____
6._____
7._____
8._____

Homework assignments due:
Monday_____
Tuesday_____
Wednesday_____
Thursday_____
Friday_____

Tests and quizzes expected (insert dates):

_____

Possible surprises (quizzes, assignments) this week (insert dates):

_____

This week's important activities other than school (insert dates):

_____

This week's resolutions regarding time management habits:

_____

TIME MANAGEMENT

• Involves taking control of your time and your life

• Results in greater success and less stress

• Doesn't mean living by a rigid schedule

• May provide more time for fun

• Will make you more effective

• Requires students to determine what they want from
school and life

• May have different meaning in different cultures.

• Involves priority setting.

• Most importantly, it involves putting first things first

Overhead 7- 2

The Importance of Values

• Values are beliefs that serve as standards by which we judge
ourselves.

• Values are the basis for satisfaction in our lives. When we act on
our values we are satisfied.

• Values are the basis of our life goals. Students who cannot
identify their values are directionless.

• Values are the basis for how we evaluate others. Often we judge
others who do not share our values as "deficient" in some way.

• Because students do not have much practice identifying their
values, some have trouble in this area.

Steps To Taking Control Of Your Time

1. Set priorities.
2. Determine the amount of time spent on low priority activities.
3. Get organized.
4. Replace unimportant activities with important activities.
5. Stay focused by using good time management habits.
6. Don't backslide.

Time Management Record

• Is a time management aid.

• Encourages priority setting that is in keeping with their values.

• Encourages visionary thinking - looking ahead to anticipate the future.

• Encourages continuing work on time management habits.

Chapter Eight

Behavioral Contracting and Encouragement

The strategies for improving achievement discussed in this chapter, contracting and encouragement, are selected from two disparate theoretical positions: Behaviorism (Skinner, 1974; Watson, 1930) and the Individual Psychology of Alfred Adler (Ansbacher & Ansbacher, 1967). Student support personnel and others who identify ideologically with either of these positions may be uncomfortable with this pairing. Modern Adlerians such as Sweeney (1989) believe, as Adler did, that reinforcing behavior contributes to the overall discouragement of students because the emphasis in reinforcement is on performance, not the worth of the student. Conversely, modern Behaviorists (e.g., Alberto & Troutman, 1995) still subscribe to the idea that attention, regardless of its purpose, may inadvertently reinforce the wrong behavior, thus interfering with the student's development. However, the melding of these two approaches is not a new idea. Wielkiewicz (1986) also borrowed from Adler's ideas in his book on behavior management in the school.

Encouragement is a process that separates the students from his or her behavior and involves expressing faith in students' inherent potential to achieve, function appropriately in social situations, and generally make positive contributions. Reinforcement involves recognizing a job well done by praising the student's accomplishments or providing a more tangible reward (see Figure 8-3). In behavioral contracting, reinforcement occurs when students achieve the goals that they have established for themselves. They should receive encouragement during the contracting process, particularly when they fail to reach their goals. Responses that some believe differentiate between these two approaches are

- reinforcement: You really did an excellent *job* on this test.
- encouragement: This shows that you really put a lot of *effort* into preparing for this test.

Sweeney (1989) suggested that one of the fundamental differences between reinforcement and encouragement is the emphasis on effort instead of the product of that effort. However, Alberto and Troutman (1995) provided several suggestions on ways to *reinforce* effort, and they would classify the example of encouragement provided above as reinforcement. Although some of the differences between reinforcement and encouragement are more semantic than real, there are differences. One difference between the two processes is that encouragement often precedes the act or deed while reinforcement follows the action. A student who comes to the teacher and expresses a concern about a forthcoming math test might hear, "I have confidence in your ability to do well on the examination." A behavioral interpretation of this interaction might conclude that the teacher is reinforcing expressions of worrying about tests because he or she paid attention to the student, thus providing a social reinforcer. Another behavioral interpretation might be that the teacher is providing a non-contingent reinforcer, with the result being that the teacher's verbalizations will have little impact on behavior. One alternative to responding to encouragement, ignoring students when they are anxious about the tests, is unacceptable to most educators. Encouragement or noncontingent responses are preferred to ignoring by most educators, regardless of its label. It is also the case that encouragement in the classroom and the educational process is as much an attitude as it is a technique. Teachers who value their students and believe in their potential express these attitudes through encouragement. Almost all of us have heard a student say, "I did it because he or she believed that I could."

The obvious question (to the author at least) is, Why should students receive only positive reinforcement for their performance, or have their feedback be limited to encouragement, when they can benefit from both? Students who need to improve their school performance benefit from positive feedback about their performance in much the same way that counselors, psychologists, and social workers benefit by being paid to perform their jobs. These students also need to hear that they are valued and that teachers, student support personnel, and others believe in their potential as students and human beings. In this chapter the primary focus is on behavioral contracts and reinforcement, but throughout the chapter examples of how encouragement can be used in this process are presented.

Using Behavioral Contracts

Most teachers, counselors, school psychologists, and social workers have used behavioral contracts. Professionals who consult with teachers often hear, "Oh, I tried contracting several times. It worked for a while, but then it stopped working. I don't use it anymore." Behavioral contracts are so conceptually simple that many individuals underestimate the complexity of the contracting process.

The steps in the contacting process are (1) identify students who wish to improve some aspect of their behavior, (2) select the most appropriate type of contract, (3) determine their current level of performance (baselines) in the areas that they wish to improve, (4) have students establish goals/ objectives for improvement in their behavior that can be measured quantitatively, (5) establish target dates for improvements in achievement to occur, (6) select reinforcers that will be provided to students if their objectives are attained, (7) monitor the contract on a periodic basis, providing reinforcers when targets are met, and (8) resetting goals as needed.

Rules for Success

Contracts fail when the basic rules of contracting are not followed. Alberto and Troutman (1995) identified several rules that must be followed if contracts are to be successful. These are paraphrased and extended in the following list.

1. Although contracts are designed to determine an ultimate or terminal behavioral objective, the initial goal should be a small approximation of the terminal goal. Setting initial goals too high results in failure and retards the contracting process.
2. Reinforcers should be provided immediately after the target behavior is performed.
3. Small reinforcers should be provided frequently, as opposed to large reinforcers on an infrequent basis.
4. Contracts that suggest that the student is simply being obedient (e.g., following the rules by doing what he or she is told) should be avoided. Focus on accomplishment. Focusing on obedience can and does engender resistance; moreover, when a student fails to attain an objective related to obedience the result can be punishment, thus making the contracting situation aversive.
5. A logical relationship between the reward and the behavior that is to be performed as judged by both the student and the teacher is essential. Contracts should be fair.
6. The terms of the contract must be clearly set forth. Ambiguity can lead to disputes, and these can make the contract aversive for all parties.
7. Contracting should be voluntary on the part of the student. Imposing a contract on a student makes it aversive.
8. Generally speaking, contracts should be positive. Adding aversive consequences if the student does not perform the target behavior should be avoided.
9. Once the procedures for the contract are established they must be followed *consistently*. For example, if contract review sessions are scheduled for Friday, they should occur on Friday.

Four other rules should be added to those provided by Alberto and Troutman. These are:

10. All behavioral principles should be followed during the

contracting process. For example, reinforcers, even edible ones, sometimes lose their reinforcing properties and must often be changed during the contracting process. Also, as already suggested, any aspect of the contract that is aversive to students may result in avoidance of the contracting situations or "dropping out" of the contract.

11. Contracts become aversive to teachers when they require inordinate amounts of work. The result is that teachers will not follow through and the contracts will fail. One implication of this is that, when possible, teachers should not be placed in the role of contract manager. Student support personnel and teacher's aides should be looked to first to fulfill this role.

12. Contracts should be culturally appropriate. Individual behavioral contracts are based on Eurocentric values such as individualism, future time orientation, and a doing activity orientation. Many cultural groups such as American Indians, Asian Americans, and Hispanic Americans may not subscribe to all of these values. The result is that in many instances group contracts are preferred to individual contracts for students who do not hold Eurocentric values.

13. Encouragement should be included in the contracting process. For example, at the outset it is important to express confidence in students' ability to improve their behavior. These types of expressions should continue throughout the contracting process. Perhaps more importantly, when students fail to reach their objectives is important to continue to express confidence in their ability to succeed. The attitude that students are worthwhile regardless of their classroom performance may prevent the contracting situation from becoming aversive whenever students fail to perform the target behaviors.

Types of Contracts

Contracts can be classified in a variety of ways, group or individual, contingent or noncontingent. Kazdin (1977) designed a sophisticated system for classifying behavioral interventions that can be applied to contracts (Alberto & Troutman, 1995). Kazdin's system, and a literature review conducted by Alberto and Troutman, concluded that the following types of contracts are possible:

1. *Individual contracts with individualized reinforcers:* If Yolanda hands in 100% of her homework this week, she will receive 15 minutes of free time under the supervision of the aide. Figure 8-1 shows a contract with all the basic components in place. Figure 8-2 contains examples of

simple contracts with individuals.

Figure 8-1

**Sample Behavioral Contract — Individual With
Individualized Reinforcer**

Date _____ Effective Dates: From _____ to _____
Student's Name _____
What is the student's level of performance of the target behavior at this
time? _____
_____

What behavior is the student to exhibit?_____
_____

What criteria will be used to measure success? (e.g., rate, accuracy, and
response time)
_____

Where is the behavior to occur? (e.g., classroom, gym, or cafeteria)
_____

Who will evaluate the behavior? (e.g., student, teacher, aide, other
student, or counselor)
_____

How will the student be rewarded if he or she is successful? (e.g., free
time, privileges extended, or money)
_____

Who is responsible for providing the reward? (e.g., teacher, parent, or
other)
_____

Signed (all involved persons should sign):
Student_____
Counselor _____
Teacher _____
Aide _____
Parent _____

Figure 8-2

Samples of Individual Contracts

• If Jorge completes all his in-class math assignments this week (insert dates) with 80% accuracy, he can take the gerbils home with him for the weekend.

Jorge _____

Teacher _____

• If YoKenda attends all of her Spanish classes this week (insert dates), she will receive a coupon from the counselor that allows her to take two of her friends to the cafeteria for free desserts on a day of her choosing.

YoKenda _____

Counselor _____

Cafeteria Manager _____

Date _____

• If Darryl passes his Civics test with a score of 75% or better on October 17, he will be placed on the students' team for the student-faculty basketball game.

Darryl _____

Coach of Students' Team _____

Counselor _____

Date _____

2. *Individualized contracts with class (entire group) with identical, individually administered reinforcers:* If any student (in this class) hands in all homework this week he or she will receive 15 minutes of free time under the supervision of the aide. A generic group contract is shown in Figure 8-3.

Figure 8-3

Sample Generic Behavioral Group Contract

Date _____

Students' names _____

_____

I. What is the target behavior for the students in the group? (Check one)
_____ 1. It is the same for all students, (specify behavior and time

154

period): _____

_____

_____ 2. It varies by student (specify):
          Derald _____
          Ebony _____
          Juan _____
          Laretha _____

II. How will the success of the students in the group be evaluated?
(Check one)

      _____ 1. Each student will be evaluated individually and reinforced individually.

      _____ 2. Every student in the group must perform the target behavior. The reward will be given to the group.

      _____ 3. All individuals who perform the target behavior will receive a group reinforcer.

      _____ 4. Individuals (specify) must perform the target behavior. The group will be rewarded.

      _____ 5. All students must perform the target behavior if students are to be reinforced. Reinforcers will be given to individuals in the group.

      _____ 6. If all students perform the target behavior at least at an 80% rate, all students will receive the reinforcer individually.

III. When and where is this behavior to occur?

_____

_____

IV. Who will evaluate the behavior? (E.g., students, teachers, counselors)

_____

_____

V. How will the students be rewarded if they are successful? (Check one)

      _____ 1. Each student in the group will be given the same reward at a time of his or her choice.

      _____ 2. The same rewards will be given to the group at the same time.

      _____ 3. Each student may select a reinforcer from the following list.
          15 minutes of free supervised time
          15 minutes on the computer
          Leave school 15 minutes early with parental permission

VI. Who is responsible for providing reward? (E.g., teacher, parent, counselor, or school psychologist.)
Signed (all persons involved should sign):
Student 1 _____
Student 2 _____
Student 3 _____
Student 4 _____
Teacher _____
Counselor _____
Other _____

3. *Contract with a subgroup of students with individualized reinforcers:* All boys who hand in 100% of their homework this week (I-1; II-1) will receive 15 minutes of supervised free time or 15 minutes of time on the computer (V-3).

4. *Contract that makes the receipt of a simultaneously administered reinforcer to the entire group contingent on individualized behaviors of all group members:* If Jamarcus hands in 100% of his homework, Latisha hands in 90% of her homework, Laura hands in 85% of her homework, and Jeremy hands in 75% of his homework (I-2) the group as whole (II-2) will receive 15 minutes of free time under the supervision of the aide (V-2).

5. *Contract with the same target behavior for each member of a group and allows all who perform it to be reinforced as a group:* All students in class who turn in 100% of their homework this week ((I-1) may join the aide for 15 minutes of free time Friday at 2:30 (V-2).

6. *Contract with a target behavior to be accomplished by the group as a whole, and the reinforcer is delivered to the group:* Class, I'd like for you to work together on your science homework. If all of you answer the questions with 100% accuracy (I-1), the class will get 15 minutes of free time with the aide Friday at 2:30 (II-2, V-2).

7. *Contract with a target behavior for an individual in a group that provides for group reinforcement if the target behavior is achieved:* Roberto, if you hand in 100% of your homework this week (I-2; II-3), the class (as a group) will receive 15 minutes of free time under the supervision of the aide (V-2).

8. *Contract that establishes a minimum level of performance for the group and makes the possibility of reinforcement for the entire group contingent upon group average achievement at the level established:* If the class average for completing homework is at least 80% (I-2; write in class), all student will be permitted to have 20 minutes of free time Friday at 2:30 (II-4; V-2). The teacher evaluates the behavior in this contract (IV) and provides the reinforcer (VI).

Which Type Is Best?

The answer to the question of which contract to use is, "It depends." Choosing the right contract for the situation depends on the cultural background of the student or students involved, the willingness of people in the school to assume roles in the contracting process, and the goals of the contracting process. Individual contracts with individualized reinforcers are probably the easiest contracts to manage, but they may not be the most effective. Establishing group contracts that stimulate peer pressure can be highly effective. However, there may be negative consequences of group contracts if pressure is brought to bear through aversive means (such as threats, verbal abuse, and isolation) when some students do not perform the target behaviors and, in failing to do so, prevent other students from receiving reinforcers.

Group contracts also have other problems, particularly if the target behaviors and/or reinforcers are not individualized. First, by adopting a single target behavior, the principle of successive approximations may be violated. A very low criterion for the target behavior can be established, but there is some likelihood that, even if the criterion for success is low, it will be too high for some students. If criterion for success is established at a high level (every student must complete 100% of his or her homework with 100% accuracy), failure for some students is virtually guaranteed. Second, if reinforcers are not individualized, there is increased risk of failure because it is unlikely that every student will view reinforcers in the same manner. Free time, time on the computer, a supervised game, or other reinforcers that might be viewed as highly attractive reinforcers/incentives by some, will not be incentives for other students. The problem of the reinforcer not being attractive, and thus failing to serve as an incentive, is reduced to some degree when reinforcers are delivered to the group because many students see group activities as highly desirable.

Group contracts have the probable advantage of being more attractive to students who prefer cooperative (as opposed to competitive) relationships. The students who are most likely to value cooperative relationships are Mexican Americans, Asian Americans, and some American Indians (Sue & Sue, 1990). However, it is mistake to assume that students have certain types of relationships and values because they belong to a particular ethnic group. The only sure way to determine which type of contract is most appropriate is to negotiate with the student(s) involved.

The Contracting Process

Earlier an eight step contracting process was outlined that can be used with a variety of behaviors and in a number of situations. Each of these steps, plus one additional one, identifying problems, will be discussed in

157

detail at this time.

Which Problem to Address? Although behavioral contracts can be used with a wide variety of problems, the focus here is on changing behaviors associated with student academic achievement. In a sense, academic achievement problems are the easiest to address with contracting because one of the most difficult problems in contracting is often eliminated. Behavioral contracting begins with establishing a baseline of performance. Most teachers keep records of test and quiz results; grading period; semester; and year-end grades; homework assignments handed in; the accuracy of homework assignments; attendance; and tardiness. These should be the primary targets of contracting. Certainly other behaviors, such as participation in class and attentiveness as measured by variables such as talking to neighbors and being out of seat, are related to academic achievement, but they are harder to measure because there is no system in place for determining their incidence. Unless teachers want to focus on these related behaviors, it is suggested that the focus of contracting be on those areas that are included in the normal record keeping in the classroom.

Identify Students Who Wish to Improve Their Academic Performance: The process of identifying students who may benefit from contracting should begin by surveying teachers and asking them to nominate students. Self-referrals from students can also be solicited from all but the youngest students. After a list is compiled, students should be contacted individually to ascertain whether they wish to work to improve their academic performance. During the interview with students, the voluntary nature of the behavioral contracts should be stressed to avoid establishing a coercive atmosphere.

Select The Most Appropriate Type of Contract: When students are contacted for the first time they should be asked if they would prefer to work on their problem alone or would feel more comfortable working on their problem in a group. A follow-up contact with teachers may help clarify which approach should be used. Generally speaking, if there are several students in the same classroom who have the same problem, group contracting should be considered simply for efficiency. This may also be the case if there are several students from different classrooms who have the same problem, but this situation may generate management problems such as those associates with the delivery of reinforcers. Moreover, if students come from cultural backgrounds that value cooperative relationships, and it can be discerned that the students place group concerns ahead of their own concerns, a group contract should probably be used.

Determine A Baseline Of Behavior: As has already been suggested, teachers keep certain records such as quiz and test grades that can be used as baseline information. A detailed description of the strategies used to gather baseline data regarding behaviors related to classroom achievement such as class participation is beyond the scope of this chapter. However there are dozens of behavior modification books such as the one by Martin & Pear (1996) that describe this process in detail. However, a simple three-step process for generating baseline information follows:

1. Define the problem behavior (the one that occurs too frequently or not frequently enough) in observable terms. This is the WHAT in assessment. Reciting without being called on is observable; having a poor attitude is not. Being highly motivated is not observable; handing in one's homework and participating frequently in class are observable. In this process ask "Can I see the behavior?" and " Will others see the same behavior if they observe the student?"

2. Define time and place where the problematic behavior is most likely to occur. This is the WHEN and WHERE of assessment.

3. Devise an approach to measure the rate at which the behavior occurs. This is the HOW OFTEN of assessment. Typically the how often question is answered through observations of students in blocks of time or time samples. An aide may be asked to observe a student during science for a week and from the data generated, the HOW OFTEN question can be answered. The aide may also be asked to set the alarm on her watch to go off every 15 minutes and, at the time the alarm goes off, observe the student to determine if he/she is performing the behavior being assessed. In some instances measurement in the third stage looks at DURATION, INTENSITY, or LATENCY OF RESPONSE instead of HOW OFTEN the behavior occurs. For example, teachers may be interested in the amount of time it takes students to get down to work after directions are given (latency of response), or the length of time a student spends on an assigned task (duration). In some instances teachers may also be interested in the having a shy student speak louder so that she or he can be heard by other students (intensity), but the major focus of assessment academic behavior will be on the number of responses (e.g., How many algebra problems were attempted? How many were correct? How many times did the student participate in class?).

Help Students Establish Goals and Dates for Their Attainment: At this time in the process it is a good idea to remember that one of the major reasons behavioral contracts fail is because initial goals are set too high, and students become frustrated by their inability to achieve them. Students and their teachers should be advised that it is better to set initial goals that are too low than too high. If a group of students is involved, it is possible that each student in the group have a different goal, but it is desirable from the point of view of managing the contract that the goals be the same. However, the generic group contract shown in Figure 8-3 provides an option that allows students to set individualized goals.

Establish Target Dates: The target date for attaining the goal that has been established becomes the anniversary date for the contract. This is the point in time when the contract is reviewed and reinforcers provided for goal attainment. For middle and high school students anniversary dates are typically 1 week apart. For students who are enrolled in primary elementary school grades (K-2), anniversary dates may be more often, perhaps as often as every other day.

Select Reinforcers: As noted earlier, a critical factor in the success of behavioral contracts is the selection of an appropriate reinforcer. It is suggested that a menu of reinforcers such as those shown in Figure 8-4 should be provided to students, and they should be allowed to select a reinforcer from the list. If groups of individual are to be given options regarding reinforcers, a similar strategy can be used. However, when groups of students are involved, single reinforcers may be selected by the group and provided to all members simultaneously.

Figure 8-4

Examples of Reinforcers

Social Reinforcers:
  verbal praise
  smiles and winks
  hugs
  pats on the back
  notes citing achievements
  certificates
  bumper stickers (great students)

Activity Reinforcers:

supervised sports	bird watching
computer games	trips and outings (e.g., zoo)
parties with snacks	movies
school landscaping	coloring or drawing
working on hobbies	dancing
computer time	reading favorite books
watching television	free time
walks	

Toy Reinforcers

balloons	marbles
puzzles	kites
whistles	stickers

Monetary Reinforcers
  gift certificates to fast food restaurants
  coupons to use at school store
  cash awards

Social Reinforcers
verbal praise	secret handshakes
notes citing achievements	notes
smiles, winks	certificates
hugs	time with special adults
pats on the back	bumper stickers
"high fives"	patches for clothing

Food Reinforcers
dried fruit (e.g., raisins)	potato chips
popcorn	candy/gum

As noted earlier, the use of single reinforcers provided in a group activity is desirable from a contract management point of view, as well as from the point of view of involving peer pressure as a force in the process of promoting goal attainment. The ongoing management of contracts is discussed in a later section, but it is never too early to anticipate that reinforcers sometimes lose their reinforcing properties after the novelty wears off. One way to counteract this is to allow students to include several reinforcers in the contract, although this makes management of the contract more difficult. It is probably better from a contract management perspective to renegotiate the reinforcer at each step in the behavioral contracting process.

Two final points should be made about reinforcers. First, DeRisi and Butz (1975), in their classic book on behavioral contracting, suggested the addition of bonus clauses to contracts to increase incentives for students to perform above the established goal. For example, if a student is to receive 15 minutes of free time when he or she reaches the contractual goal of participating in science class one time per day, an additional 15 minutes of free time can be added in a bonus clause for giving the correct answer 80% of the time (see Figure 8-5 for an example). This has the obvious advantage of providing incentives for quantity and quality of classroom performance. Second, another possibility for varying reinforcement when target behaviors students are making steady progress toward their goals is to provide "surprise" reinforcers. Surprise reinforcers may be presented in the form of verbal praise (I've noticed how well you are doing.), most improved student awards (see Chapter 9), notes to parents, public announcements, and coupons from fast food restaurants. When surprise reinforcers are used, students should be told that these types of reinforcers are not predictable, and they may never receive another one or they may receive another surprise shortly. The use of surprise reinforcers allows the contract manager to establish a pattern of intermittent reinforcers like those students receive in the classroom and elsewhere.

Figure 8-5

Sample Individual Contract with Incentive Clause

Student's Name: Kristina Smith
Effective Dates of Contract:____from March 25 to April 1_____

I. Kristina agrees to do the following each day:

    1. Come to math class on time each day.

    2. Bring all needed material (notebooks, text, pencils or pens) to class.

    3. Be in her seat with her book open ready for class to begin at the time the teacher begins the class.

II. Mr. Johnson agrees to keep records regarding Kristina's behavior by placing checks on a record-keeping form provided by Ms. Brown.

III. If Kristina fulfills her part of the contract as listed in I-3 above, Ms. Brown agrees to provide Kristina with a coupon good for a free meal at MacDonalds on April 1.

IV. Bonus

    If Kristina hands in her math homework on time 80% of the time this week, she will receive an additional coupon good for a meal at MacDonalds.

    Signed:

    Kristina _____

    Ms. Brown _____

    Mr. Johnson _____

Monitor and Troubleshoot as Needed:

    1. Meet with students on the anniversary of the contract.

    2. Evaluate goal attainment, and if the goal has been attained, arrange for reinforcement. Consider new goals and evaluate the incentive power of the reinforcer. Change both the goals and the reinforcer if appropriate.

    3. If the goal has not been attained, provide encouragement and investigate the possible reason using the troubleshooting guide in Figure 8-6.

Figure 8-6

Troubleshooting Guide for Monitoring Behavioral Contracts

If target behaviors are not being attained ask the following:

1. Is the target behavior clearly defined? Is it observable and measurable?
2. Are goals set too high? If it is a group contract, do goals need to be individualized?
3. Has the reinforcer retained its reinforcing properties? If it is a group contract, is there a need to individualize the reinforcer?
4. Are social reinforcers and encouragement provided along with the reinforcer that is specified in the contract?
5. Is the contract culturally appropriate: Is it individually-oriented for students from cultures who value individualism or group-oriented for students who value collateral relationships?
6. Is the amount and /or type of reinforcer appropriate for the amount of effort students must expend to achieve goal? Is the contract fair?
7. Has the relationship between the student, counselor, and teacher(s) been maintained throughout? the use of social reinforcers and encouragement? If it is a group contract, has peer pressure become aversive?
8. Is the reinforcer being presented immediately after the target behavior is achieved?
9. During the time between anniversary dates, is the student receiving positive reinforcers when approximations of the target behavior are achieved?
10. Was the contract negotiated or does the student see the contract as punishment that must be obeyed?
11. Is the contract being managed consistently, that is, are contract-monitoring meetings are held on time?
12. Are agreements being kept by all parties?
13. Are failures to attain goals attributable to life events (e.g., divorce in the family) that are not a part of the contract?
14. Is the contract still positive? Is the behavior of one or more peopleinvolved in the contract being interpreted as punishment?

When troubleshooting is required, it may be simplified by examining one aspect of the contracting process at a time (DeRisi & Butz, 1975; Wielkiewicz, 1986). These aspects are:

- the contract itself (Items 1, 2, 14)
- the nature of the reinforcer (Items 3,4, 6, & 8)
- the management of the contract (Items 9, 10, & 12)
- the human elements of the contracting process (Items 5, 7,10)
- Other (Item 13)

Renegotiating the Contract: Troubleshooting using the guidelines provided above occurs whenever students fail to meet their goals. In many instances the reasons for the failure may be easily identified and the problems resolved through simple renegotiation of the goals, reinforcers used, or by correcting or modifying some aspect of the contracting process. However, in some instances individual contracts may have to be substituted for group contracts, the person providing the reinforcers may have to be changed, or additional people such as parents included in the process. In the cases that require major changes in the contracting procedure, the contract should be totally renegotiated and rewritten using the guidelines that have been provided.

Termination: There are at least two times when a contract should be terminated. One of these is when the contract does not and cannot provide sufficient incentives to motivate a student. One-fourth grader wanted a $20 toy and refused to agree to alter his behavior unless he received it. Some high school students may see the incentives that are available to people in schools as insufficient to justify their efforts to succeed. When this occurs, the contract should be terminated.

The other time to terminate a contract is when the students involved reach their terminal objective and maintain their behavior for several weeks. Once this occurs, the contract manager should fade the contract (Martin & Pear, 1996), which simply means that the contract should be slowly withdrawn as an incentive. The first step in the fading process is to negotiate the removal of the contract with the students involved. Once students agree that they can maintain their behavior without the contract, several approaches to fading the contract may be used. One approach is to schedule contract-monitoring sessions further apart. A second approach is to remove the reinforcer but continue to have periodic monitoring sessions in which social reinforcers are provided. Regardless of the approach used in the fading process, it may be best to begin to fade the contract prior to natural breaks in the school calendar. These natural breaks coincide with holidays, semester breaks, and, of course, the end of the school year. Year-around schools provide other natural breaks because they operate on a quarter system that involves periodic breaks four times per year.

Once the contract is faded, it is probably a good idea to continue to monitor students' progress with informal checks with teachers. It is also advisable to provide surprise reinforcers that may consist of periodic meetings with students to compliment them on how well they are doing. Surprise notes to parents to students who have been on contracts can also serve as reinforcers to help students maintain their behavioral gains (see Figure 8-7, Sample Notes to Parents).

Figure 8-7

Sample Notes To Parents

Dear Parents:
We want to call your attention to a happy event. Ronaldo has handed in all of his homework for the past 2 weeks. He has also improved the quality of his in-class work. I'm very proud of Ronaldo's progress, and I hope you will share this note with him.

I'm sure that the two of you played a very important role in Renaldo's academic improvement, and I want to thank you for your effort. When teachers and parents work together, the results are always positive.

Sincerely,
Janice Laremy
Fourth Grade Teacher

Dear Mrs. Alston:
I want you to be the first to know that Larry will make the B honor role for the first time when the report cards come out next week. This is a tremendous accomplishment and shows how hard Larry has worked to improve his academic work. We are very proud of Larry, but we know that few students turn their academic performance around without the help of supportive parents. Thank you for your support.

Please congratulate Larry on this milestone. He has worked very hard.

Sincerely,
Jay Harris
Ninth Grade Counselor

Summary

Many individuals, sometimes with limited success, have used behavioral contracts. For the most part contracts are unsuccessful because the principles of contracting are violated. If the learning principles underpinning contracts are followed, relationships among the parties involved maintained, and contracts monitored carefully, contracts can be a powerful tool in the effort to improve student achievement.

References

Alberto, P. A., & Troutman, A. C. (1995). *Applied behavior analysis* (4th ed.). Englewood Cliffs, NJ: Prentice Hall.

Ansbacher, H. L., & Ansbacher, R. R. (1967). *The individual psychology of Alfred Adler.* New York: Harper

DeRisi, W. J., & Butz, G. (1975). *Writing behavioral contracts.* Champaign, IL: Research Press.

Kazdin, A. E. (1977). The token economy: A review and evaluation. New York: Plenum.

Martin, G., & Pear, J. (1996). *Behavior modification: What it is and how to do it.* Boston: Allyn & Bacon.

Skinner, B. F. (1974) *About behaviorism.* New York: Knopf.

Sue, D. W., & Sue, D. (1990). *Counseling the culturally different* (2nd ed.). New York: Wiley.

Sweeney, T. J. (1989). *Adlerian counseling: A practical approach for a new decade.* Muncie, IN: Accelerated Development.

Watson, J. B. (1930). *Behaviorism* (rev. ed.). Chicago: University of Chicago Press.

Wielkiewicz, R. M. (1986). *Behavior management in the schools.* New York: Pergamon.

Chapter Nine

Techniques for Establishing an Environment That Encourages Academic Success

Who are the most admired people in our schools? Are they the achievers, the students who study hard and make good grades? Sometimes they are. However, it is more likely that the students held in the highest esteem in most schools are the athletes, particularly the students who participate in major sports, because of the recognition they receive. Not only do athletes who play major sports perform before large audiences, but they are also highlighted in print and telephoto media, praised at assemblies and pep rallies, and often deferred to by faculty members. Many middle and most public high schools have established an environment of success — for athletes. In order to foster an environment that promotes academic success, educators must create an academic climate in schools that recognizes academic achievement.

The twin foci of efforts to stimulate academic achievement must be effort and performance. Just as there are super stars in the athletic arena, there are a few extraordinary young scholars who also deserve the label of super star. These outstanding scholars regularly make the A or A/B honor role, always pass end-of- grade and academic competency tests, and have high scores on the Preliminary Scholastic Aptitude Test (PSAT) and Scholastic Aptitude Test (SAT). However, most students, like most athletes, are not stars, but they may achieve at a high level in relationship to their ability. The students who have high levels of academic achievement in relationship to their ability exert effort and have demonstrable success. They are the performers. The remaining students can be classified as underperformers, which means that they are not achieving academically at a level commensurate with their ability, often because of too little effort. In order to turn these students into performers, we need to first recognize effort and progress. Underperformers will be the primary beneficiaries of an environment designed to encourage success.

Although the idea of creating an environment in which success is recognized and encouraged is intuitively attractive to most counselors, social workers, and psychologists, there are a number of barriers to implementing strategies to achieve this end. One of these barriers is that many teachers and administrators believe that students "ought to do the right thing" without recognition or encouragement. Fortunately, the educational reform movement has put a great deal of pressure on all professionals who work in schools. Some people have resisted incentive programs, changes in teaching strategies, and other innovations are now amenable to trying new strategies to improve students' achievement. Another source of resistance to efforts to promote improved achievement has come from the students themselves. Although students are bombarded with information that academic achievement is prerequisite to success in life, many students have chosen to ignore the message. Again, education reform innovations that demand that students pass end-of-grade tests before being promoted, or make it impossible to get a driver's license before the age of 18 for high school dropouts, have changed some students' attitudes about achievement. Not all sources of resistance to the establishment of a success environment have been overcome and are they unlikely to be overcome in the future. However, in many ways this is the best time in educational history to initiate changes that will lead to this end.

This chapter outlines a series of techniques for recognizing efforts and performance. In all instances they are based in the classroom, but as is shown, it is anticipated that student support personnel will be involved in their development and implementation.

Strategies That Recognize Effort and Performance

The Academic Extra Effort Award. Every school has students who go above and beyond what teachers assign in their efforts to be good students. The purpose of the Academic Extra Effort Award is to identify and recognize these students. This program can be initiated with two simple forms: an Academic Extra Effort Award nomination form (see Figure 9-1) and an Academic Extra Effort Award certificate. (Figure 9-7). In order to solicit nominees, nomination forms should be sent to every teacher in the school to solicit nominees for this award.

Figure 9-1

Academic Extra Effort Award Nomination Form

Dear Teacher:

The counseling staff is initiating an Academic Extra Effort Award to recognize students who go above and beyond the call of duty in their efforts to be good students. In order to be considered for the Academic Extra Effort Award students must (1) vigorously pursue academic achievement on their own behalf and (2) promote the academic achievement of their classmates by encouraging them to do well and by actively assisting them in their efforts. Nominees need not be straight A students, but they should have demonstrated an enthusiasm for learning, as well as a willingness to help others achieve. Award winners will be recognized during a school- wide Achievers' Assembly on June 6. A committee made up of counselors and teachers has been formed to select award winners.

Award winners will receive a certificate of recognition, a note will be sent home to their parents telling them of the award and inviting them to the recognition ceremony on June 6, and a notation will be placed on the students' permanent records that they received the Academic Extra Effort Award. Feel free to nominate all students that you believe deserve this award. However, please place each nomination on a separate nomination form. Nominations should be sent to the Counseling Office and are due by May 5.

Student Being Nominated _____

Please give a few examples of extra academic efforts made by this student that show that she or he is worthy of this award. These examples should include efforts on the student's own behalf such as exemplary class projects, term papers, or extra credit assignments as well as efforts to help other students do better in school. In order to determine which individuals in your class are most supportive and helpful to others, you may wish to have the students identify classmates who have encouraged and helped them achieve academically.

_____   _____
Teacher's Signature   Date of Nomination

For Use by the Committee:

Student's GPA _____

Class Rank If H.S. Student_____

PSAT/ACT/SAT Scores If H. S. Student_____

Other Information_____

Decision: Yes No   Parent Letter Sent: Yes No

Date Mailed _____

Figure 9-2 contains a sample letter that can be sent to parents of Extra Effort Academic Achievement Award winners. These letters need not be long, but they should provide enough information to allow parents to understand the basis for the award. As already noted, Figure 9-3 contains a sample certificate. If possible, plaques or monetary awards should also be given. Achievers' Assemblies are the ideal time to give these awards, but if it is to have the maximum effect on other students, announcements regarding the award should be made in classes, homerooms, the school newspaper (if there is one), local newspapers, and on radio and television public service announcements. It is also a good idea to give students and their parents bumper stickers that read, "Academic Extra Effort Award Winner On Board."

Figure 9-2

Sample Letter to Parents

Dear Mr. and Mrs. Jasper:

I am pleased to inform you that your student, Monir, has been selected as an Academic Extra Effort Award Winner for 2002. These awards goes annually to students who have vigorously pursued academic excellence, consistently exceeded the expectations set by their teachers, and have actively engaged in helping others in their academic efforts. The selection committee was impressed by Monir's efforts on her own behalf and on the behalf of her classmates. Both of you and Monir are to be congratulated on this accomplishment.

You are invited to attend the Achievers Award Ceremony on June 6 in the auditorium of the high school. The ceremony will begin at 7:00 PM and should be completed by 9:00 PM. We hope you can be in attendance on June 6.

Sincerely,
Janella Jackson, Chair

Academic Extra Effort Awards Committee

Figure 9-3

Sample Academic Extra Effort Award Certificate

𝔄thens 𝔇ive 𝔥igh 𝔖chool
𝔄cademic 𝔈xtra 𝔈ffort 𝔄ward

Awarded annually to students who have consistently gone beyond the
call of duty in their own pursuit of academic excellence and the promotion
of academic excellence in others.

Awarded this 6th day of June 2002

to

𝔐onir 𝔍asper

For the faculty_____

Marylyn L. Brown, Principal

Most Improved Student Group Award: Most Improved Student Awards
can be given for weekly, monthly, or yearly improvement in academic
performance. These awards, as the name suggests, are for progress based
on relative improvement in achievement in one or more subjects. For
example, in a middle school the mathematics, language arts, science, and
all social studies teachers could give a most improved student award each
month. These awards allow students who are functioning at a very low
level to be recognized for improvement. Look at the following example:

Month 1	Science Average	Month 2	Science Average	Gain
Student A	80%		90%	12.5%
Student B	70%		80%	14.3%
Student C	60%		70%	16.7%

All students in this group increased their scores by 10 percentage points,
but the relative increase is highest for Student C. Importantly, Most Improved
Student Awards do not have to be given based on the criterion of relative

improvement. All students who increase their average achievement by 10 or more percentage points could be given this award. Moreover, this type of award does not have to made on an individual basis. Groups of students assigned in a manner that equalizes their average test scores or the average number who complete homework assignments can compete for the award and be known as the Most Improved Group. As noted elsewhere, some students may feel more comfortable competing as members of a group than as individuals because they value collective relationships (Sue & Sue, 1990).

The first step in establishing a Most Improved Student/Group Award is to determine whether it will be oriented to individuals or groups. Group approaches have the advantage of stimulating peer pressure to increase academic achievement, but this can and does get out of hand. If a group approach is used, one of the rules of the competition is that students in the groups may help other students in the same group, but they may not verbally or physically tease, harass, or abuse other students who may not be contributing fully to the group's efforts to improve the average achievement of the group. Harassment of other members of the group should result in disqualification of the group.

The second step is to determine how the winner will be selected. If the focus is upon individuals, this is relatively simple: the student who makes the greatest amount of progress in relation to his or her baseline wins. In group approaches, the use of relative improvement of the group's average on test scores in a specific subject is probably the best and easiest way to determine the winner. If relative improvement in achievement is used as the criterion for determining the winner, groups of students that have the same average score on the criterion variable (e.g., average test score in algebra) should be formed.

The third step in setting up Most Improved Groups Awards is to discuss the importance of cooperation, particularly if the basic approach used in the classroom has been focused on competition. In competitive approaches, a student "wins" if he or she focuses on their own efforts and outperforms all other students. In cooperative approaches, the group wins the Most Improved Group Award if all students improve their achievement. The following example may be used to explain this concept to students:

Groups A and B are competing to improve their performance. They begin the competition with the following scores:

Group A	Average Test Scores	Group B	Average Test Scores
Student 1	90		90
Student 2	80		80
Student 3	70		70
Student 4	60		60
Group Average	75		75

At the end of the month (competition) the individual and group averages areas follows:

Group A	Average Test Scores	Group B	Average Tests Scores
Student 1	92		98
Student 2	85		88
Student 3	78		70
Student 4	72		60
Group Average	81.75		79.0

Point out that the students with the highest average test scores in Group B improved their scores, but the students with the lowest scores did not. In Group A all students made progress and won the Most Improved Group Award. The moral is that in order to win the award students must focus on their own achievement, and they must help other students in their group.

Although the example illustrates the advantage of cooperation, it does not illustrate what students are to do as they cooperate. It may be a good idea to tell students what cooperation *is* and *is not*.

Cooperation is not
- cheating by allowing others to copy homework or look over your shoulder during a test;
- doing other students' work; or
- threatening or using other coercive strategies in an attempt to stimulate achievement

Cooperation is
- making sure that all the students in the group understand the assignment;
- helping other students in the group learn the skills they need to do well on tests through tutoring;
- studying together to make sure that all students are studying the material that will be covered on the test;
- making sure that the group is on task in the classroom as opposed to talking or engaging in other activities that waste time;
- encouraging others in the group when they get discouraged;
- Helping the group and individuals in the group stay organized; and
- Monitoring the progress of other individuals in a supportive manner.

The fourth step is to establish a mechanism that will allow individuals or groups of students to monitor their progress. Designating a space on the classroom bulletin board as the Most Improved Student or Group Award section can do this. Each week the progress as computed based on relative improvement percentage (do not report individual test score averages or percentage of homework completed) should be posted. When the last week of competition is completed, the highest relative percentage of improvement score posted is the winner.

The fifth and final step in establishing a Most Improved Student/Group Award is the award ceremony. This ceremony should be held in the classroom, and students should be given award certificates (see Figure 9-4), applauded by other students, and allowed to explain to the class the nature of their approach to winning. At the end of this presentation, the teacher or counselor should identify the key cooperative strategies used by the group and reemphasize these. Then the competition should be restarted, perhaps with a different objective. If the emphasis has been on test scores, it may be shifted to focus on homework. If the students are in an elementary school classroom, the teacher may wish to shift from one subject to another (e.g., math to language arts).

Figure 9-4
Sample Most Improved Group Certificate

Brownsville Middle School
Most Improved Group Award

given to

GROUP A

Carlotta, Charlotte, Jeremy and Chan

For outstanding cooperation and dedication to improving their math test scores

June 6, 2002

Willis L. James, Teacher

Successful Alumni. Every elementary, middle, and high school has alumni who have done well at the next educational level and in their careers. Alumni can often provide inspirational advice regarding the importance of achievement to students, and alumni often have more credibility with students than student support personnel and teachers. Ideas for using alumni to motivate higher levels of achievement include the following:

  • Middle school students and high school students can talk to small and class-size groups in elementary and middle schools respectively, about the academic skills needed to succeed at the next educational level.
  • High school graduates can discuss the academic skills and study habits needed to survive in post-secondary educational programs.
  • Students who have gone directly to work can discuss the academic skills that they needed to survive in the work force. They can also discuss the idea that businesses expect workers to be lifelong learners.

Establishing an alumni seminar series involves identifying successful alumni (make sure that the alumni represent both genders and come from diverse cultural and racial backgrounds), deciding on the format (small groups, classroom groups, or school-wide assemblies), orienting and scheduling the alumni, scheduling the activities, and evaluating each session.

Alumni should be selected based on the likelihood that current students will identify with them, particularly students who are underachievers. Perhaps more to the point, alumni should be selected who are most like the students who are currently underperforming. It is very hard for a low-achieving student with 3 Cs, a D, and a F to identify with an alumni who had straight As, or who genuinely liked every aspect of school.

Scholars' Club. Isaacs and Duffus (1995) suggested that the dominant issues confronting educators who wish to stimulate higher levels of achievement among minority students are that these students are often unmotivated, and that they receive little support from their peers to do better in school. They suggested that a Scholars' Club, designed partially to create peer support for achievement, may be one means of resolving these issues and stimulating higher achievement among minority students. The Scholar's Club, an honor society, also strives to motivate students by providing public recognition of, and tangible rewards for, their efforts. Although the rationale for the Scholar's Club is sound, it is in all likelihood illegal because it uses minority status as the basis of selecting members. Court cases have consistently held that race or ethnicity cannot be used as the sole selection criterion for any club or organization. However, some of the ideas advanced by Isaacs and Duffus (1995) show how they can be broadened to include all students.

Isaacs and Duffus (1995) suggest that the first step in the process of establishing a Scholars' Club is the appointment of a faculty sponsor who will facilitate its development. The next step is to establish the general purpose for the club and prerequisites for membership. The club's general purpose should be to promote academic achievement and to provide service to the school and community. The specifics of the club's mission statement should be developed by a small group of founding members who are interested in establishing a Scholars' Club. The Scholars' Club should be open to all students who

- are dedicated to the improvement of their academic standing.
- will set as their goal to achieve a grade point average of 2.5 or above beginning the first full semester after their initiation and set goals to increase their GPA each semester thereafter.
- agree to support others in their efforts to become better students.
- provide 2 to 3 hours per week of public service to the school and community.

Once the purposes of the club and prerequisites for membership are established, the club may wish to initiate fundraising projects to produce revenue to support their activities and awards program. Isaacs and Duffus (1995) suggested that a Most Outstanding Scholar Award and Most Improved Scholar Award be given annually. They also suggested that students in each grade and subject receive awards for improvement and overall scholarship, and that these, and the other awards mentioned, be given at awards ceremonies.

Random Letters and Notes of Congratulation. Students and parents typically receive grade reports four times per year. Other communications with the home occur at teacher conferences which are usually held twice per year and through calls or letters home when a student is in some sort of difficulty. Letters and notes home can do much to do away with the stereotype that a note from a teacher or counselor is bad news. Types of notes that may be sent to parents from student support personnel include the following (A sample note can be found in Figure 9-5):

- congratulations on making the A honor role;
- congratulations on making the A/B honor role;
- congratulations on your progress/improvement;
- congratulations on passing the end-of-grade/course tests; and
- congratulations on passing the minimum competency test.

Teachers have many opportunities to communicate with students and parents. These include:

- congratulations on your great science or other project;
- congratulations on your marvelous essay;
- congratulations on your near miss (missed the A/B honor roll by one grade);
- congratulations on your perfect attendance;
- congratulations on handing in 100% of your homework; and

• congratulations on your improvement in _____
(subject specified).

Figure 9-5

Sample Letter to Parents of High School Students – A Near Miss

Dear Ms. Johnson

    As you know, your daughter Tracey received two As, three Bs, and one C at the end of the last grading period. Unfortunately, our school only recognizes two groups of students, those who get all As and those who get all As and Bs. Tracey is what I call a near miss, and she deserves our recognition because of her hard work. If the C she made in History had been a B, she would have made the A/B honor roll. I congratulated Tracey at school during a brief conference and encouraged her to keep up the good work. I hope that you will also congratulate Tracey for her academic accomplishments.

    It is a pleasure for me to work as Tracey's counselor. If I can be of assistance to you please do not hesitate to contact me.

Sincerely,
Diane Brown
Ninth Grade Counselor

As already noted, communications to the parents of middle school and high school students can be in the form of letters, but the notes to the parents of elementary schools students may include cartoons, pictures of animals, and other figures. One elementary school counselor sent Bat-Grams complete with drawings of Batman and the Batmobile to announce good news to parents. The note in Figure 9-6, Sample Note to Parents of an Elementary School Student, illustrates a note with a cartoon. This note was produced using Power Point, a software package that is readily available for use on most personal computers. Clip art software can also be used to produce notes with cartoon figures, animals, and other designs. Once the basic design is established, making a note becomes a matter of editing the content and printing a new note. If a color printer is available, these notes can be designed and produced in multiple colors.

Sample Note to Parents of an Elementary School Student

Alisha J Stedman

- Got a 100 on her test today
- Was nice to all students
- Helped other students with her homework
- Deserves our thanks and appreciation!

Success Bulletin Boards

This activity, which is most appropriate for elementary or middle schools students, requires that each classroom have access to a camera, a film budget, and a bulletin board. It can be done as a separate activity or as an extension of one of the strategies already discussed in this chapter. For example, all members of the most improved group can have their pictures taken and posted on the classroom bulletin board until another winning group is selected. However, a Success Bulletin Board can also be used to recognize people who do outstanding things on a day-to-day basis. For example the students who hand in the best homework, do the best projects, get 100s on their spelling tests, and are most helpful to others can have their pictures taken and posted for a week under a "These Are Our Achievers" banner. For this type of activity to be successful, it must be ongoing and accompanied by in-class award ceremonies.

Motivational Group Counseling

The National Standards for School Counseling Programs (Campbell & Dahir, 1997) set forth guidelines for school counseling programs and included the competencies that students should develop at each level. For example, at the elementary school level students should be able to understand the relationship between classroom performance and overall success in school. A competency identified for middle school students is that they demonstrating the ability to achieve at a level commensurate with their potential. High school students should be able to be able to use their decision-making skills to assess their progress toward educational goals according to these standards. The standards also suggested ways to develop competencies in students. One of these approaches is called motivational group counseling (Campbell & Myrick, 1990), which consists of five sessions. An outline of these sessions with modifications, plus an outline for a sixth session, are presented here. Although Campbell and Dahir (1997) suggested that the approach outlined here be used as an approach in the middle school, it can easily be adapted for use in grades 3 through 10. The outline that follows was designed for low-achieving students.

Session 1 — Getting Started
1. Have students get acquainted by sharing what they like to do when they are not in school. Then ask students to share what they would do if they had $1000 ($10,000 if older students are in the group).
2. Have students identify thoughts and memories of school as a pleasant place.
3. Have all students brainstorm behaviors needed to be successful in school, and have each student identify behaviors that he or she needs to improve.

Session 2 — Taking Responsibility
1. Generate statements and ask students to indicate whether the student depicted in the statement is assuming responsibility for himself or herself (statements should reflect ages of students).
- I lost my homework
- My homework simply disappeared.
- The teacher wasn't fair. She put things on the test that were unimportant.
- I forgot my homework assignment.
- My dog ate my homework assignment.
- I studied, but I studied the wrong things.
- I'm lazy
- The teacher doesn't motivate me.
- My mother couldn't help me with my homework last night, so I didn't get it done.

2. Process responses.

Session 3 - Identifying Times When Students Fail to Take Responsibility

1. Have students identify what their cop-out phrases, that is, statements they use to make excuses when a task is not completed. (If younger students are in the group, several examples will have to be provided to get them started. Substituting excuses for cop-out phrase for younger students may be a good idea.

2. Have students reword their cop-out phrases (excuses) to be responsibility-taking phrases.

3. Role-play situations (perhaps taken from session 2) in which practice taking responsibility.

Session 4 - The Positive Self

1. Introduce the term self-concept and discuss the impact of negative thinking (I can't statements; it's not important statements).

2. Ask students to rate their academic self-concepts. Do they have negative thinking about school?

3. Introduce the idea of using positive self-statements to substitute for negative thoughts.

4. Have students write down their negative thoughts about school. Then they should write down positive substitutes for their negative thoughts. These positive thoughts should be read aloud and then practiced subvocally. For example, the negative thought, "I can not do math." can be replaced by "I may not be able to get all As in math, but I can learn it." This new statement would be read aloud to the group and then practiced repeated subvocally.

5. Encourage students to visualize themselves being successful in areas of importance such as math and doing their homework. Third graders and up can do this with ease, but all students may need some introduction and practice. Start by having students visualize familiar things such as animals or fruit.

Session 5 - Planning for Success

1. Have students set short-and long-term goals. (These should be written down and copies made for the counselor's file).

2. Ask students to pair up to work together on their goals.

3. In dyads, ask students to draw up a mutual assistance contract and specify what each will do to help the other.

Session 6 – Follow-up (2 to 3 Weeks Later)

1. Ask students to share how they are progressing toward their goals. Use the goals from the file on the group to remind students what their goals were. Do their goals need to be reset?

2. Ask students to share how their buddy contract is working.

3. Ask students to report any objective data regarding their success. Applause please!

4. Determine if there is a need for another follow-up session.

Summary

The educational reform movement has set the stage for a number of strategies that can be used to establish an atmosphere that is supportive of success. For the most part these strategies focus on recognizing and rewarding effort and performance. Although teachers and student support personnel can be instrumental in rewarding success, it is also important to initiate strategies that will provide peer support for students who wish to improve their achievement.

References

Campbell, C. A., & Dahir, C. A. (1997). *The national standards for school counseling programs.* Alexandria, VA: American School Counseling Association.

Campbell, C. A., & Myrick, R. D. (1990). Motivational group counseling for low performing students. *Journal for Specialists in Group Work, 15,* 42-50.

Isaacs, M. L., & Duffus, L. R. (1995). Scholars' club: A culture of achievement among minority students. *The School Counselor, 42,* 204-210.

Sue, D., & Sue, D. (1990). *Counseling the culturally different* (2nd ed.). New York: Wiley.

Figure 9-7
Blank Academic Extra Effort
Award Certificate

𝔄cademic 𝔈xtra 𝔈ffort 𝔄ward

Awarded annually to students who have consistently gone beyond
the call of duty in their own pursuit of academic excellence
and the promotion of academic excellence in others.

Awarded this   day of

to

_____

For the faculty_____

Figure 9-8
Blank Most improved Group Award Certificate

Most Improved Group Award

given to
The Group

*for outstanding cooperation and dedication
to improving their math test scores*

Teacher   date

Chapter Ten

Using Peers and Adult Volunteers as Tutors

The idea of using people other than teachers or aides to tutor students is not new. Peer tutors have been a part of the educational process throughout the history of education (Anderson, 1976; Downe, Altmann, & Nysetvold, 1986). Moreover, the validity of the practice of using peer tutors has been supported empirically. After a literature review of the efficacy of peer tutoring, Gartner and Riessman (1995) concluded, "Research on peer tutoring indicates that the intervention (peer tutoring) is relatively effective in improving both tutees' and tutors' academic and social development." (p. 43). However, Gartner and Riessman's conclusions about the value of peer tutoring program should not be interpreted as an unequivocal endorsement of all peer-tutoring programs. In order to be successful, peer tutoring programs must have the support of administrators and teachers (Gartner & Riessman, 1995), and the tutors must be carefully trained and supervised (Tyndall & Foster, n.d.).

Importantly, tutoring programs can be successful at all educational levels and with all populations. Dineen, Clark, and Risley (1977), Greenwood, Terry, Utley, Montagna, and Walker (1993) and Gartner and Riessman (1995) described the educational benefits of a peer tutoring program in elementary schools, and Lazerson, Foster, Brown, & Hummel (1988) and Vacc and Cannon (1991) provided a similar description for middle and junior high school tutoring programs. What is particularly encouraging about some of these descriptions is that they involve successful efforts to improve the academic performance of students who are learning disabled (e.g., Lazerson, 1988) and mentally challenged (e.g., Vacc & Cannon, 1991). Further, as noted earlier, tutors seem to benefit academically and or socially as a result of filling the tutorial role (Azcoitia, 1988; Lazerson, 1988; Vacc & Cannon, 1991). Descriptions of the use of adults as tutors are less plentiful, although many school districts have tutoring programs staffed by adult volunteers in place.

Several descriptions of peer tutoring programs developed by student support personnel have appeared in the professional literature. For example, Corn and Moore (1992) and Lynn (1986) described the operation of peer tutoring programs in two comprehensive high schools. Lynn's (1986) report regarding the program at Randallstown High School is particularly enlightening. Her description suggested how a dynamic tutoring program can be used to improving achievement. The Randallstown High School Peer Resource Center was staffed by at least two high achieving seniors five periods per day. Each year tutors made more than 1,500 contacts with tutees. Additionally, the tutors spent over 400 hours acting as classroom aides. Importantly, Randallstown High School used its peer-tutoring program to deal with a dilemma common in many schools: an influx of immigrant students. Lynn reported that immigrant students with little or no proficiency in English were given the option of going to their regular English classes or receiving one-on-one assistance from peer tutors. Many students chose to spend time with peer tutors who spoke their language. The tutors provided instruction in English as well as tutoring in the immigrant students' other subjects. Not surprisingly, teachers responded very positively to this type of assistance.

Peer tutoring programs can take many forms and the model adopted will be dependent on many factors. Lynn (1986) described one model that involved three components: a peer resource center staffed by volunteer students, a classroom assistance component, and a long-term tutoring program. All of these components involved one-on-one assignments. In another example, Gartner and Riessman (1995) identified one high school that used an entire class of 500 students to tutor other classes. A fourth example, a program in operation in Wake County, N.C., transported low-achieving high school students from an alternative high school to an elementary school to provide tutoring as a means of improving the high school students' self-esteem and academic performance.

The amount of time peer tutors spend with tutees can ranges from 1 to 5 hours per week, depending on the needs of the tutee and the availability of the tutor. The contacts made to provide short term, ad hoc tutoring may last from a few minutes to an hour, depending on the amount of time students and tutees can spend away from their classes. Research reported by Morgan (1992)) suggested that that the greatest increase in achievement comes after 20 to 29 hours of tutoring, with some additional benefits coming with 15 additional hours of tutoring. However, his study needs several replications before final conclusions regarding the amount of time needed to make an impact on academic improvement can be drawn.

Tutoring programs using volunteers operate in much the same way as peer-tutoring programs do. Adult tutors may staff a volunteer tutoring service during the school day, provide assistance in classrooms, or be assigned to tutor students on a long-term basis. It is not unusual for volunteer tutors to offer tutorial services before and after school as well. In both peer and adult volunteer tutoring programs, tutors must be recruited, trained, assigned, and monitored. However, the first step in offering a tutoring program is to design the program. The remainder of this chapter focuses on the these processes, beginning with the design of a tutorial program.

Designing the Tutorial Program: the Who, What and Where Issues

As has already been demonstrated, tutoring programs can be complex entities. Although student support personnel can take the lead in the design phase, others must be involved if the program is to be successful. Building-level principals should appoint steering committees made up of administrators, parents, teachers, students, and student support personnel to design and monitor their tutoring programs. The task of this committee is to

(1) determine the need for the program,
(2) design the program,
(3) design and implement a training program for the tutors,
(4) publicize the program to students and parents, and
(5) evaluate the program on an ongoing basis.

A needs assessment device that can be used as one tool for determining the need for a peer-tutoring program is shown in Figure 10-1. This needs assessment instrument provides part of the information needed to design a peer tutoring program. Additional suggestions follow Figure 10-1.

Figure 10-1

Determining the Need for Tutorial Services

To: All Teachers
From: Tutoring Program Steering Committee

The purpose of this survey is to get a preliminary estimate of the number of students in our school who could benefit from a tutoring program. Assuming that some students will benefit from a tutoring program, we also wish to ascertain the types of tutorial services that would be most useful. Please take a few minutes from your busy schedule and answer the following questions.

Name_____

Grade Level You Teach _____ (For high schools, this should also include subject taught)

Room Number _____

1. At this time, how many students in your class(es) need individual tutoring? _____

2. If tutoring could be made available to these students, in what areas do they need assistance (e.g., math, language arts)?

3. Tutoring services can be provided using same age peers from their classroom who are trained in tutoring skills, older peers (cross grade tutoring) who are trained in tutoring skills, and adult volunteers who are trained in tutoring skills. Which of these approaches would you prefer?

(Check one) ☐ Peers from my classroom ☐ Older peers ☐ Adults ☐ No preference

4. Tutoring services can be offered in the classroom and in out-of-classroom situations. Considering your own situation, where would you prefer tutoring to occur?

☐ Out-of-classroom ☐ In the classroom ☐ No Preference

Thank you for your help. Please return this questionnaire to the principal's office by september 10.

The Who Question: The needs assessment questionnaire provides clues to teachers' preferences regarding who should provide tutoring services. However, when answering the who question, it is suggested here that, if possible, both adults and peers should be included in the tutoring program. The extensive need for tutors in most schools is unlikely to be met using only one group of tutors. The amount of time students can spend as tutors is increasingly restricted by demands from teachers that students attend to their own studies when class is in session. Also, some parents will be reluctant to allow their students to participate in tutoring programs because they fear that the time spent on tutoring will lower their children's achievement level. Moreover, adults will be hard to recruit in some communities and when adults are available to provide tutoring, scheduling and coordinating their efforts require an extensive amount of time. Peer tutoring programs are much easier to manage because students are easily contacted, their schedules are known, and their knowledge and background are easily evaluated. Students can be recruited from clubs, honor societies, athletic teams, and through self- and teacher referral. In order to recruit adults, senior citizens groups, service clubs, churches, businesses, and parent groups must be contacted.

When and where to offer tutoring services are two other important questions. Quite simply, tutoring services should be offered when students are available for help in a place that allows the tutoring process to proceed on an uninterrupted basis. When determining the time and place to offer tutoring services, the following questions must be answered:

- What are the school's policies regarding students missing a portion of class to be tutored?
- What are teachers' preferences regarding releasing students so that they can receive tutoring?

- Would they prefer that it be done in class or out of class in a tutoring resource center?
- Are facilities available that can be used as a tutoring resource centers?
- What are the preferences of the tutors?
- Are there practical considerations that argue for one approach over another? For example, if a tutor goes to the class room is it possible to work with several students at one time because of space considerations?
- Which tutoring option provides the best opportunities for supervision?
- Who will identify the material to be taught to students? The teacher may wish to meet briefly with the tutor to explain what is to be taught, particularly when young children are involved. Older students may be able to identify their weaknesses without assistance from their teachers. If the teacher is to be involved, is it simpler to provide the service in the classroom?
- Will in-class tutoring disrupt the instructional process?

Recruiting Peer Tutors

Notices such as the one in Figure 10-2 should be sent to all teachers when recruiting peer tutors. However, if one objective of the peer-tutoring program is to involve a specific group of students, such as students with learning disabilities to help other students with learning disabilities, the note included in Figure 10-2 needs to be altered to take this into account.

Figure 10-2

Sample Note to Teachers: Peer Tutor Recruitment

To: All Faculty Members, Coaches, and Club Sponsors
From: Tutoring Program Steering Committee

The purpose of this note is to ask for your assistance in identifying students who can serve as peer tutors. We are looking for students who (1) are above average in achievement, (2) are responsible, (3) punctual, (4) have good communication skills, (5) are interested in helping others, and (6) are sensitive to the unique problems confronted by physically and mentally challenged students and students who come from cultural backgrounds different from their own.

After we receive your nominations, we will contact the students who are nominated to ascertain their interest, get parental permission to participate in the program for the student who volunteers to participate in the program, and provide a 10-hour training program to prepare students for the tutoring role. Once peer tutors are trained, we will be establishing a Peer Tutoring Center, offering individualized tutoring services before and after school, and providing tutoring in classrooms if teachers request the service.

Thank you for your assistance.

Name of Teacher _____

I wish to nominate the following students for the peer-tutoring program:

Students' Names   Areas of Expertise (e.g., could tutor in Algebra I)

Students' Names	Areas of Expertise
_____	_____
_____	_____
_____	_____
_____	_____
_____	_____

It may also be necessary to recruit students directly to make sure that students with an array of academic skills are included as tutors. This recruitment can be done through brief classroom visits.

Once teacher and self-nominations are received, students should be contacted and the purposes of the program explained to them. During the screening interview, students should be asked to make two commitments: The first of these is to complete 10 to15 hours of training that will be offered in three afterschool sessions. The second is to provide 1 to 2 hours of tutoring per week for the remainder of the school year. Students who volunteer should be given a parental permission slip such as the one displayed in Figure 10-3.

Figure 10-3

Sample Parental Permission Note for Peer Tutors

To: Parents of Volunteer Tutors
From: Tutoring Program Steering Committee

We are establishing a peer-tutoring program at XYX School. The purpose of this program is to help students who are having difficulty in one or more of their subjects improve their academic performance. Based on research at other schools, we also believe that the academic performance of the tutors will be enhanced, and that they will become more sensitive to the problems experienced by other students. Your student has been nominated by the faculty to serve as a peer tutor because of her or his academic performance and personal characteristics. More importantly, he or she has volunteered to participate in the peer-tutoring program. However, students cannot participate in the program without their parents' permission.

If your student is allowed to participate in the peer tutoring program, he or she will be asked to (1) complete a 10 to15 hour training program that will be offered after school, and (2) spend 1 to 2 hours a week tutoring other students for the remainder of the school year. No tutoring sessions will be scheduled that interfere with your student's classes or other academic pursuits.

If you have questions about the program that you wish to have answered before giving your permission, please call Janette Thompson at 666-999.

I give my permission for (student's name)_____
to participate in the peer tutoring program.
Signature of Parent or Guardian
_____ Date _____

Recruiting Adult Volunteers

Recruiting volunteers to serve as tutors requires some personal contact with parent groups, service clubs, church groups, and senior citizen organizations, as well as media attention. Because most newspapers and television stations have educational reporters, the surest way to get a story published about the peer-tutoring program is to contact these reporters. Additionally, advertisements in the newspaper, public service announcements on radio and cable television, solicitations placed on the school's website, and notices in the school newsletters can be used to identify adult volunteers. Public service notices will of necessity be brief. They should include a call for adult tutors and provide a telephone number where interested people can get more information. Person-to-person and media recruitment efforts should outline the purposes of the program and the nature of the commitment tutors must make in order to qualify for the program. A notice such as the one in Figure 10-4 may be sufficient.

Figure 10-4

Sample Notice of Need for Adult Tutors

XYZ School Districts needs adults who can spend a minimum of 1 to 2 hours per week tutoring students. All volunteers will receive 10 to 15 hours of training to prepare them as tutors. After training, tutors will be assigned to students at schools throughout the school district based upon their preferences and their academic skills. Although volunteers who can tutor at all levels and for all subjects are needed, the demand for tutors who speak Spanish and other foreign languages is particularly acute. If you are interested in becoming a volunteer tutor, call Jack Sliverman at 888-2121.

Training for Tutors

Recommendations for length of programs for training tutors range from 10 to 30 hours (Corn & Moore, 1992; Lynn, 1986). A 10 to 15 hour training time was arbitrarily adopted for this chapter, but the length of the training program should be based on its content. At a minimum, tutors need instruction in basic communication skills, study skills, and tutoring skills. The course outlined in this section can serve as a guide for a tutor training course. Additional resources that can be used in the design of a course for peer tutors are listed at the end of the outline.

The training program outlined here is designed to prepare tutors to work with typical students who are underachieving. If tutors are expected to work with physically or mentally challenged students, training beyond that suggested here will be required and should be provided by a special education teacher. Some of the topics that should be covered in this extended training are mentioned in session 6.

Session 1 — Overview and Introduction to Communication Skills

Objectives
- Provide an overview of the training program.
- Introduce and define communications skills as they relate to tutor-tutee relationships.

Activities

1. Have tutors introduce themselves and tell why they want to be tutors

2. Provide an overview of training program. Tell tutors they will learn the basic communications skills needed by tutors and the study skills that they (if they are students) and the students they are tutoring can use to improve their academic performance. If the tutors are expected to work with physically and mentally challenged students, the overview should outline what they will learn about these students as well.

3. Demonstrate the importance of communication skills. Ask one of the participants to try to convince you (the leader) that learning math is important. In this demonstration do not look at the speaker, and do not respond verbally. Let the demonstration continue until the speaker is frustrated. Then have the group analyze what transpired. In this analysis ask, "What could (should) the speaker have done to improve the situation?"

4. Give a minilecture explaining that communication is a two-way process that requires a sender and a receiver. In the situation they just witnessed, there was one-way communication. The speaker paid no attention to the nonverbal behavior of the listener, who really wasn't listening at all. Another important aspect of communication is that it takes place in two channels: verbal and nonverbal. Moreover, the verbal behavior can be broken down into 2 components, the words or content of the communication, and the affective or emotional component, which can be inferred by the way that the words are spoken. Let's begin by looking at the nonverbal dimension of communication.

5. Good communicators "attend" or orient themselves to the person to whom they are speaking nonverbally. They maintain eye contact. However, remember there are different standards for eye contact based on cultural membership. Among European Americans it is a sign or disrespect not to maintain eye contact. Among many Asian Americans and some Native Americans, making eye contact may be a sign of disrespect. Intense eye

contact may be interpreted as a sign of aggression among Asian Americans, particularly Vietnamese. Further, some African Americans look at you when they are talking and look away when they are listening. It is important not to misconstrue non-eye contact as a sign of disrespect.

6. If there are participants from different cultures, have them talk about eye contact and nonverbal behavior in their cultures. If not, try to get representatives from different cultures to discuss nonverbal communication in their cultures. If possible, ask representatives from other cultural groups to observe and react to the next exercise.

7. Divide the group into same-sex dyads. If there are participants from different cultures pair them in dyads. Then have the dyads talk about any topic for 5 minutes, establishing eye contact as they would normally. After the "conversation," ask the trainees to react to what they experienced. If participants from minority cultures (Asian, Hispanic, African American, and American Indian) are involved, ask them for their reactions to the exercise. If you use a panel of adults or students from different cultures, have them react to what they observed in the dyads. Specifically, Was there too much or too little eye contact for their cultural group?

8. Give a minilecture regarding body language. A major concern when communicating has to do with establishing a suitable interaction distance between the speakers. Among male European Americans, the preferred distance is 42 inches. European American women and Hispanic Americans seem to be more comfortable with closer interaction distances. People from some Middle Eastern countries may be comfortable with communication distances of less than 12 inches. Importantly, when an individual moves away from the speaker, it often means that he or she is uncomfortable with the interaction distance. The speaker is moving into his or her personal space. When tutoring, an across-the-desk (42") interaction distance is a safe place to start.

9. Pair up the group into same-sex dyads. Have them position themselves (standing) 4 feet apart (a tape measure will be required) and carry on a conversation regarding their families from that distance. Tell them that when you say "freeze" they are to maintain their place and body position. After 3 minutes say "freeze". Then ask, how many of you have moved closer together? How many of you have adjusted your body posture by leaning to close the gap in the dyad. Now reposition the dyads two feet apart and have them carry on their conversation until you say "freeze." After three minutes "freeze" the dyads. Determine how many have moved away from each other and how many have adjusted their body by leaning backwards to establish a greater distance between the speakers. Process the exercise, focusing on their reactions to the physical distances.

10. Give a minilecture on other types of nonverbal behavior such as facial reactions that need to be attended to. Again point out cultural differences in this area. Hispanic Americans and European Americans are

more likely to smile, nod, grimace, and display other nonverbal behavior than Asian Americans and Native Americans. When speakers are not displaying these cues, listeners may mistakenly conclude that they are not listening or that they are disinterested. Reemphasize that cultural differences in communication are important.

10. Summarize.

Homework

Observe the nonverbal behavior of people you meet this week. If you have friends from different cultural groups, talk to them about nonverbal behavior in our culture that disturbs them.

Session 2 — Verbal Behavior

Objectives

- Develop an awareness of the content and affective dimensions of verbal behavior.
- Define and teach the art of making interchangeable responses and learn when they are appropriate.
- Develop the skills needed to reply to major categories of nonverbal behavior.

Activities

1. Get reports on the homework assignment. What did they learn about nonverbal behavior? Were they more aware of their own nonverbal behavior? What if anything needs to be retaught or explored further?

2. Give a minilecture on both verbal and nonverbal communication. The focus of this lesson is on both verbal and nonverbal communication. No matter how skillfully you attend to nonverbal behavior and communicate verbally, unless you are able to listen and communicate to students that you heard what was said, you may fail as a tutor. Hearing an individual means that you understand what is said verbally and nonverbally. That's right! In fact, some linguists claim that 80% of all communication occurs nonverbally. We do not have to ask if a friend is sad if they are sobbing uncontrollably. In fact, our friend is likely to think that we are not very sensitive if we ask such a question. How would you interpret the following nonverbal communications? A student comes in for tutoring and

　　a. tears are running down his face;
　　b. slumps down in the chair and looks down at the floor;
　　c. slams her books on the desk;
　　d. sits down and lets out a deep sigh;
　　e. sits down in the chair and grips the arms tightly; or
　　f. smiles.

In these cases it is likely that the student is (a) sad, (b) discouraged or depressed, (c) angry, (d) frustrated, (e) tense, and (f) relaxed. Although tutors are not therapists, they can help other students by recognizing some common types of nonverbal behavior and responding to it. A tutor might respond to the nonverbal behavior just listed follows:

    a. It must have been a bad day to get you so upset.

    b. It looks like school been pretty depressing to day.

    c. School's got you pretty angry.

    d. You seem really frustrated.

    e. You seem pretty tense today.

    f. You're in a good mood.

There are exceptions to the rule that it is a good idea to respond to the nonverbal behavior. Some Asian Americans and Native Americans do not want to show their feelings. In these cases, tutors should respond to verbal content only. If the tutees are Hispanics, European Americans, or African Americans tutors do not need to recognize the emotions that those students commonly experience and respond to them. Why? Trying to tutor a person who is angry, sad, depressed, or frustrated is at best difficult. Sometimes, when you recognize the feeling and communicate that you understand what the student is experiencing, you give them permission to vent their feelings. This may be all that is needed to get them ready to learn. Recognizing the feelings of students who come for tutoring also increases the likelihood of that tutoring will be successful in another way. Students are likely to think that tutors are people who care. Too often students who need tutoring believe that nobody cares. To summarize, you need to be able to recognize and respond to sadness, happiness, frustration, depression, tension, and anger when students come for tutoring.

Verbal communications occurs in two channels–verbal content and feeling/affective content–although not necessarily at the same time. Emotion is communicated verbally by rapidity of speech (excitement, anger, frustration = rapid, often louder speech); (sadness and depression = slower, often softer speech and stuttering, stammering, and inability to communicate as coherently as usual may indicate anxiety). In order to be a good communicator, individuals must be able to hear both the verbal content and recognize the affective or feeling component of the communication and respond to both channels with interchangeable responses. Interchangeable responses are responses that mirror the verbal and emotional content of what has been communicated.

3. Write responses to the following communications that show tutees that you "heard" both the content of what they said and their feeling (Give participants Handout 10-A, Responding to Verbal Content and Feelings of Tutees).

Student:

    a. Leaning back with a smile: "That was easier than I thought it would be."

Response

---

    b. "Geometry is so stupid. I'll never use it in real life." Drops head to break off eye contact.

Response

---

    c. Fist clenched: "If I had my way Ms. Smith would be fired. She is a terrible teacher."

Response

---

    d. Speaking slowly and softly, head down: "I really thought I would pass that test. I was so confident."

Response

---

    e. Speaking rapidly and louder than usual: "I just gotta get this stuff. If I don't pass I can't accept an athletic scholarship."

Response

---

    f. Slumped in chair: "I don't know why I keep coming to you. I'm still failing."

Response

---

    g. Head up, speaking rapidly: "I'm actually learning this stuff. It's great!"

Response

For answers see Handout 10-1B, Sample Answers to Handout 10-1A

4. Divide group into triads and have them take turns role-playing communicating the types of content and affect that students might communicate. The groups should consist of a tutor, tutee, and a rater. The rater's responsibility is to give feedback to the tutor about the interchangeability of her or his responses. In other words, raters should determine whether the tutees responses mirror both the content and affect communicated by the tutee. Trainees should take turns filling these roles.

    5. Summarize.

Homework

Try to be more aware of all of the channels of communication.

Session 3 — Using Verbal Skills to Get and Relay Information
Objectives

- Develop skills in using open-ended and closed leads to collect information.
- Teach the skills needed to gain specific information from students.
- Teach the skills needed to impart information to students.

Activities

1. Get reports regarding the homework assignments. Were you a better listener? Were you able to use the skills you learned last week to respond to the people with whom you interacted? Did it seem odd or strange when you tried to respond in this way?

2. Give a minilecture regarding gathering information. Explain that there are two types of leads: open-ended leads cannot be answered with one word and closed questions or prompts that can be responded to with one word. Closed questions require one-word or simple answers. Examples follow:

   a. Open-ended: Tell me about the problem you are having with history?

   b. Closed: What did you get on your last history test?

   c. Open ended: Which areas of algebra give you the greatest problem?

   d. Closed: Are you having problems solving word problems?

   In the tutoring process you will need to use both open-ended and closed leads. However, it may be best to open the tutoring conversation by using open-ended leads and then ask closed questions to zero in on the problem the tutee is having.

3. Give a minilecture on increasing specificity in communication. You will be unable to help a student with a problem unless you fully understand the nature of the problem he or she is experiencing. It is not enough to know that a student is having trouble with chemistry or technical math. In order to get at the specifics of the problem you need to ask a series of who, what, when, and how questions such as the following:

   - Who made the assignment?
   - When is it due?
   - What difficulties are you experiencing with the assignment or subject matter?
   - How have you tried to learn the material?
   - At what point in the process of doing the work do you begin to have problems?
   - What is the best way I can help you with your work?

4. Give a minilecture on providing information. Effective techniques for imparting information include

   - being patient;

- being specific;
- using step-by-step approaches;
- using multiple examples checking for understanding (having tutee repeat verbalizations of tutor);
- asking for a skill demonstration to check for learning (tutee works problems, punctuates sentences, conjugates verbs, etc. to demonstrate learning has occurred; and
- making notes regarding students' problems for consultation with teachers.

5. Introduce students with real academic concerns. Break the group into dyads (tutors and tutess) and have them conduct a tutoring session.

6. Process what occurred in the sessions by asking

    a. tutors: What types of problems did you experience in the tutoring process?

    b. tutees: Did our tutor identify the problem you are having? If yes, were they helpful?

    c. tutees: Was your tutor a good listener?

6. Summarize.

Homework

Practice tutoring if the opportunity presents itself. Continue to work on communication skills.

Session 4 — Study Skills (I)

Objectives
- Teach study tips that can be passed on to students who are tutored.
- Teach two study habits: getting organized and getting motivated.

Activities

1. Emphasize that one of the major concerns of the tutoring process is to make students capable of functioning independently of tutors. In order to accomplish this, students who come for tutoring need to learn good study habits. Therefore, along with helping students solve their immediate problems, tutors need to help tutees learn to study.

2. If this is a peer-tutoring course, ask the students in the course to make a list of their Best Study Practices. Develop this list into a handout labeled "Study Habits of Successful Students at XYZ School." Make copies and give to tutors so they can use it as a handout to students. Encourage students and adults to draw upon their own habits when they work with students. However, tutors should remember that what works for them may not work for their tutees.

3. Introduce the study habit, Getting Organized. Begin by having

trainees discuss their own organizational skills strategies. How do they keep track of their assignments? How do they make sure that they take all needed material and books to each class? Give them Handout 10-2, Preparation and Organization of Material for Study, and discuss it. Encourage them to give copies of the handout to students who seem disorganized and to spend time with them to improve their organizational skills.

4. Give students copies of Handout 10-3, Step Approach to Major Homework Assignment Completion. This handout should also be available to tutors passed on to tutees who are disorganized and/or overwhelmed by their homework assignments. Encourage trainees to engage tutees in discussions about completing homework. The step approach to homework emphasizes

- completing homework on time - first priority is to complete homework due next day.
- looking ahead - look at the course outline and beginning to plan for the completion of homework.
- studying for mastery - this requires spaced learning sessions instead of "cram" sessions.
- Using memory aids such as flash cards, saying things to be learned out loud, and anagrams (words constructed out of the first letters of things that are be learned in sequence or lists of things to be learned).

5. Introduce study habit two, getting motivated. Discuss the importance of goals in the motivational process. Goals improve focus, give students something to shoot for, and help them understand that there is something to be gained by doing schoolwork.

Examples of goals that students set for themselves and the reasons for the goals include the following:

- I want to use my study time more effectively by becoming better organized.
- I want to learn more during the time that I study by using better study strategies.
- I want to make better grades so I can graduate from high school.
- I want to make better grades so I can go to college.
- I want to make better grades so I will feel better about myself.
- I want to make better grades to gain respect from others.
- I want to make better grades so I can get a good job after high school.

6. Encourage trainees to ask students about their goals for school and afterwards. Encourage them to help students set educational goals.

7. Motivation is also negatively influenced by the frustration that grows out of not being able to do the work. Suggest to trainees that they will play a major role in helping students overcome this particular problem.

8. Summarize the two study skills covered in this lesson

Homework

For peers: Try out the two study skills covered in this session in your own work.

For adults: If there is a school age child in your neighborhood, arrange a meeting to discuss his or her study habits. Try to determine if she or he has study and personal goals and the strategies that he or she uses when studying.

Session 5 — Study Skills (II)

Objectives

- Teach two additional study habits: note taking and test taking.
- Assess trainees readiness for assignments as tutors.
- Discuss confidentiality and have trainees sign confidentiality pledge.

Activities

1. Review success with homework assignment.

2. Provide an overview of session. The purposes of this session are to teach trainess two additional study skills and to assess your readiness to take on the tutoring role.

3. Begin with note-taking. Give trainees Handout 10-4, Note Taking. If trainees are students, have them talk about their own note-taking strategies. If the trainees are adults, go through the two handouts. Tell them that verbalizations such as the following may be cues that the tutee is not a good note taker:

    a. The teacher said that everything on the test was in the notes, but it wasn't in my notes.

    b. I can never make sense of my notes 2 days after class.

    c. I get so far behind when I am taking notes that I get frustrated.

4. Encourage trainees to inquire about the note-taking habits of the people who tutor. Ask them to give Handout 10-4, Note Taking, to students who are having trouble. Ask them to refer students who seem to be having a great deal of difficulty mastering note taking to the school counselors.

5. Discuss preparing for and taking tests. Review Handout 10-5, Test-Taking Strategies. If the trainees are students, have them talk about their own approaches to preparing for and taking tests. For example, how do they study for mastery? Do they use spaced or intensive study sessions. Encourage tutors to go over handout with students that they tutor.

6. Teach trainees to make a preliminary diagnosis of test anxiety and to make referrals when they think a student is test anxious. They can ask:

- Do you get anxious before a test?
- On a 1 to 10 scale how anxious do you get? High rankings (9 or 10) should raise concerns.
- Do you ever blank in a test, that is, forget material you have learned?

If students have high anxiety or draw a blank on tests, they should be referred.

7. Summarize note taking and test-taking strategies.

8. Ask, "On a 1 to 10 scale, with 1 being no confidence and 10 being complete confidence, how would you rate your self-confidence that you can be a successful tutor?" For those trainees who have low numbers (self-confidence), determine the reason for their lack of confidence and reteach as necessary. Some of this may have to be done outside the group session.

9. Discuss the importance of confidentiality. The confidentiality rule in tutoring is that you do not discuss the problems of the students you tutor with others. Have trainees sign Handout 10- 6, Confidentiality Pledge.

10. Discuss the next phase of the training process: observation of the tutoring process. Give trainees Handout 10-7, Tutorial Observation Rating Form, and review the form with them.

Homework

Schedule initial tutoring sessions

Note: If trainees are to tutor physically and mentally challenged students they should receive additional training (Sessions 6 and 7). If they are not expected to work with these groups, they should be scheduled for tutoring sessions where they can be observed.

Sessions 6 — Tutoring Students Who Are Mentally and Physically Challenged (I)

Objectives
- Provide background of special education movement such as PL 94-142, IDEA, and ADA.
- Introduce special education vocabulary such as IEP and resource teacher.
- Apprise students of the process by which students in special education are identified and screened.
- Provide information about special tutoring issues with mentally retarded, visually impaired and students with learning disabilities.

1. Give a minilecture with background information about special students. In 1975 Congress recognized that special students needed unusual services if they were to succeed in the classroom. At that time they passed passed a law (PL 94-142 The Education of All Handicapped Children Act) that guaranteed students who are physically and mentally challenged a right to the best education possible. This Act was amended in 1990 with a law (PL 101-476) titled Individuals with Disabilities Education Act (IDEA)

which strengthened PL 94-142. Also in 1990, Congress passed the American with Disabilities Act (ADA) which guarantees that people who are mentally and physically challenged will not be discriminated against by employers and in other places such as transportation and hotels. Our main concern here is IDEA. It guarantees a specially designed educational services, including teaching methods and a curriculum that is

- tailored to the abilities and limitations of the student.
- that all of the services needed by students to do their best in school will be provided. These include transportation, hearing services, vision services, counseling services, physical and occupational therapy, and speech and language therapy.
- all special education students must have an IEP (Individualized Educational Program) that sets forth both short- and long-term educational goals for the students, as well as strategies for achieving those goals.

Educational services must be provided in the least restrictive environment. This means that, so far as possible, educational services should be provided in a manner that does not separate the physically and mentally challenged student from other students.

2. Define and describe students who have the following problems: (1) Mental Retardation; (2) Learning Disabilities, and (3) Visual Impairments (Distribute Handout 10-7, Fact Sheet I: Defining Mental Retardation, Learning Disabilities, and Visual Impairments).

3. Identify tutorial strategies that may be helpful when tutoring students who have these problems. Refer to educational implications of Handout 10-8, Defining Mental Retardation, Learning Disabilities, and Visual Impairments.

Homework

If possible, spend time in a resource room where students in each group discussed in this session are being taught. Discuss what you observe with the teacher.

Session 7 — Tutoring Students Who Are Physically and Mentally and Challenged (II)

Objectives

- Familiarize students with the unique problems experienced by students who have hearing impairments, speech and language problems, and autism.
- Teach tutoring strategies that will be effective with each of these groups.

Activities

1. Define and describe students who have each of the following problems: (1) hearing impairments, (2) speech and language disorders, and

(3) autism (Distribute Handout 10-9, Fact Sheet II: Defining Hearing Impairments, Speech and Language Disorders, and Autism.

2. Identify and teach tutorial strategies that may be helpful when tutoring students who have these problems. Refer to the Educational Implications section of Handout 10-9.

Homework

If possible, spend time in a resource room where students in each group discussed in this session are being taught. Discuss what you observe with the teacher.

Additional Resources

Individuals who are designing peer tutoring training programs may wish to consult the following publications:

Foster, E. S. (1992) *Tutoring: Learning by helping.* Minneapolis, MN: Education Media.

Myrick, R., & Erney, T. (1992). *Caring and sharing: Becoming a peer facilitator.* Minneapolis, MN: Education Media Corp.

Supervision of Tutors

The supervisory phase of the tutoring program is an extension of the training phase. Tutors should be observed during an actual tutoring session as quickly as is practical after they begin to function as tutors. Handout 10-7, Tutor Observation Rating Form, can be used as a guide for these observation sessions. Subsequent observation sessions should be scheduled (1) if a tutor is obviously deficient in one or more of the basic tutorial skills or (2) when students request observations. Students should be encouraged to request observations if they are having difficulty with a tutee or if they believe one or more of their tutorial skills needs improvement.

One or more supervisors should be available at all times to consult with tutors. Also, if possible, group supervisory sessions should be held to allow tutors to ask questions about the unique problem that the tutors are experiencing with their tutees, their tutorial strategies, or other areas of concern. If the tutors are working with physically and mentally challenged students, a special education resources teacher should be available for both individual consultation and group supervision.

Evaluation of Tutors

Periodic notes such as the one shown in Handout 10-10, Request For Feedback On Students Receiving Tutoring, should be sent to teachers. The results of teachers' feedback should be compiled and shared with tutors, teachers, and administrators. Additionally, tutors should use Handout 10-

11, Tutor's Log, to record the names of the students they see, the dates of their appointments with the students, the length of those appointments, and a brief note about the nature of each tutorial session.

Summary

One of the major problems confronting educators is how to provide more individual attention to students, particularly those students who are falling behind their peers. A tutoring program that enlists peers, adult volunteers, or both can be used to provide this attention. From an administrative point of view, it is easier to establish a peer tutoring program because peers are easier to recruit, schedule, and supervise. Regardless of who is involved, tutors must be trained, assigned to tutees, supervised, and evaluated if the program is to be successful. Moreover, establishing a tutoring program is not without costs. One or more professional staff members must be assigned to head up the program to insure its success.

References

Anderson, R. (1976). Peer facilitation: History and issues. *Elementary School Guidance and Counseling*, 11, 16-32.

Azcoitia, C. (1988). *Structuring peer tutoring in Chicago's vocational education program.* Unpublished doctoral dissertation, University of Northern Illinois, DeKalb.

Corn, K. L., & Moore, D. D. (1992). Reach for the S.T.A.R.S.—students teaching and reaching students: A two-faceted peer facilitating program at Greenfield-Central high school. *The School Counselor, 40,* 68-72.

Dineen, J. P., Clark, H. B., & Risley, T. R. (1977). Peer tutoring among elementary school students: Educational benefits to the tutor. *Journal of Applied Behavior Analysis, 10,* 231-238.

Downe, A. G., Altmann, H. A., & Nysetvold, I. (1986). Peer counseling: More on an emerging strategy. *The School Counselor, 34,* 354-364.

Gartner, A., & Riessman, F. (1995). Peer tutoring: Toward a new model. *The Peer Facilitator Quarterly, 12,* 43-45.

Greenwood, C. R., Terry, B., Utley, C.A., Montagna, D, & Walker, D. (1993). Achievement, placement, and services: Middle school benefits of peer tutoring used at the elementary school. *School Psychology Review, 22,* 497-516.

Lazerson, D. B., Foster, H. L., Brown, S. I., & Hummel, J. W. (1988). The effectiveness of cross-age tutoring with truant junior high students with learning disabilities. *Journal of Learning Disabilities, 21*, 253-255.

Lynn, D. R. (1986). Peer helpers: Increasing positive student involvement in school. *The School Counselor, 34*, 62-66.

Morgan, R. R. (1990). *Tutoring: A description of ongoing research.* ERIC Document ED314458.

Tyndall, J. A. & Foster, E. S. (n.d.). *Peer helping research.* Huntsville, AL: Huntsville City Schools.

Vacc, N. N., & Cannon, S. J. (1991). Cross-age tutoring in mathematics: Sixth graders helping students who are moderately handicapped. *Education and Training in Mental Retardation, 26*, 89-97.

Responding to Verbal Content and Feelings of Tutees

Please write your responses to the following tutees' statements. In your responses make sure that you mirror both the verbal content and the emotion of what the tutee said (Response 1). Then respond to the statements as though the tutee is an American Indian or Asian American (Response 2).

a. Leaning back with a smile : "That was easier than I thought it would be."
   Response 1

   _____

   Response 2

   _____

b. "Geometry is so stupid. I'll never use it in real life." Drops head
      to break off eye contact.
   Response 1

   _____

   Response 2

   _____

c. Fist clenched: "If I had my way Ms. Smith would be fired. She is a
      terrible teacher."
   Response 1

   _____

   Response 2

   _____

d. Speaking slowly and softly, head down: "I really thought I would pass
      that test. I was so confident."
   Response 1

   _____

   Response 2

   _____

e. Speaking rapidly and louder than usual: "I just gotta get this stuff. If I
      don't pass I can't accept an athletic scholarship.
   Response 1

   _____

   Response 2

   _____

f. Slumped in chair: "I don't know why I keep coming to you. I'm still
      failing."
   Response 1

   _____

   Response 2

   _____

g. Head up, speaking rapidly: "I'm actually learning this stuff. It's great!"
Response 1

Response 2

Handout 10-1B

Answers to Handout 10-1A

Note: There are many correct ways to respond to the tutees in the exercise in 10-1A. What follow are some examples.

a. Leaning back with a smile: "That was easier than I thought it would be."
Response 1: You're very pleased with how easily you learned this material.
Response 2 : The material was easier than you expected.

b. "Geometry is so stupid. I'll never use it in real life." Drops head to break off eye contact.
Response 1: You're frustrated by the fact that geometry doesn't seem to have any real life applications.
Response 2: Geometry doesn't seem to have any use in real life.

c. Fist clenched: "If I had my way, Ms. Smith would be fired. She is a terrible teacher."
Response 1: Ms. Smith's teaching style really makes you angry.
Response 2: You would prefer it if Ms. Smith taught her class in a different way.

d. Speaking slowly and softly, head down: "I really thought I would pass that test. I was so confident."
Response 1: It's pretty depressing to fail something you thought you would pass.
Response 2: You failed the test when you thought you would pass.

e. Speaking rapidly and louder than usual: "I just gotta get this stuff. If I don't pass I can't accept an athletic scholarship.
Response 1: It makes you anxious just thinking about what youwill lose if you do not learn this material.
Response 2: It is very important that you learn this material.

f. Slumped in chair: "I don't know why I keep coming to you. I'm still failing."

Response 1: It is so frustrating that you are not doing better that you are thinking of giving up.

Response 2: This class is very hard for you.

g. Head up, speaking rapidly: "I'm actually learning this stuff. It's great!"

Response 1: It is really exciting to be learning the material.

Response 2. You are learning the material and that is important to you.

Handout 10-2

Preparation and Organization of Material for Study

Complete the following checklist in order to get a quick fix on your organizational skills. Successful students are ready to participate when they go to class because they have prepared by completing the assignment for the day and have the books and supplies they will need for the class. Just as importantly, they are prepared when it is time to do homework. They know the homework assignment because they have it written down.

Place an X under *Agree* if the statement describes you. Place an X under *Disagree* if the statement does not describe you. Then go back and look at the Xs placed under Disagree. These are areas that need work.

Agree   Disagree

_____   _____   1. The notes I take in class are easily understood.

_____   _____   2. The notes I take in class are thorough.

_____   _____   3. I highlight the most important points teachers make in my notes.

_____   _____   4. I review my notes before class.

_____   _____   4. The material I need to study is easy to locate.

_____   _____   5. The material I need to study is well organized and ready to be learned.

_____   _____   6. I almost always write down class assignments.

_____   _____   7. I keep a calendar that includes important dates such as dates when tests will be given

Step Approach to Major Homework Assignments Completion

The step approach to homework completion requires that you do first things first while considering the future. It requires that you schedule your study time so that you will master material to the best of your ability. This requires spaced study as opposed to cramming. Because you learn better when you are fresh, the step approach to studying also requires that you do the things that are more difficult for you first. Here is one student's plan for completing her or his homework for one evening. Initially it is a good idea to write out your homework plan as you begin using the step approach.

1. Complete the 25 math problems assigned and check answers (assignment completion - due tomorrow).
2. Identify and memorize main concepts in social studies lesson(mastery - may be quiz in class).
3. Read material and place main points on flash cards (preview - getting ready for test in 1 week)
4. Pick a topic for the term paper assigned in English or language arts (looking ahead - paper due in two weeks) .
5. If time permits, draft outline for paper assigned in English or language arts. Consider what resources or references I will need to complete this paper. (If this is not done, put on to-do list for tomorrow).

Note Taking

Rules for taking notes. Take notes when
- the teacher writes something on the board;
- the teacher gives you a definition or a date;
- the teacher uses her or his hands to make a point;
- the teacher gives you a list to remember;
- the teacher repeats a point; and
- the teacher raises her or his voice.

A Shorthand System for Taking Notes

Common Words	*Dimensions*	*Measurements*
@ = at	wd = width	" = inches
2 = to	ht = height	' = feet
2gthr = together	< = less than	yds = yards
4 = for	< = greater than	mi = miles
bef = before	blw = below	k = kilometer
ex = example	abv = above	m = meters
info = information	mny = many	c = centimeters
p = page		l = liters
v = very		ml = milliliters
w/ = with		= = equal
u = you		
thru = through		
thru/o = throughout		
——> = conclusion		
sum = in summary		

Write in some of your own shorthand:

Test-Taking Strategies

Multiple Choice Questions
- Cover answers as you read and try to answer the question without them.
- In many instances, your first impulse is correct. Put a mark by the answer that you first believe to be correct, but read all of the answers.
- Read all answers before deciding.
- Beware of answers that contain words such as *always, never, totally,* and *completely.* Try to remember if there are exceptions.
- Look for answers that contain the words *usually, sometimes,* and *frequently.*
- If two answers seem the same, one is probably correct. Study these carefully.
- Make calculated guesses after you have eliminated as many responses as possible.
- Make a mark by the answers that you are unsure of so you can check them later.
- You may get some clues from other test questions.

True/False Questions
- Look for words such as *always, never,* and *all.* These questions are often false. Questions with *frequently* and *usually* are more likely to be true.
- If the question contains two parts read them as though they were one statement and remember if any part of a question is false, the entire question is false.
- Remember, double negatives in a sentence equal a positive. The statement, "George Washington was *not unconcerned* about the battle in Boston." means that he was concerned.
- Guess after you have done your best to recall the answer.
- Mark those answers that you are unsure of so you can come back to them later
- Don't forget to check answers carefully after you have completed the entire test.

Matching Questions
- Read the directions very carefully to determine if items in the answer list can be used more than once.
- Read all questions and answers before you start.

- Look for words and phrases that provide clues to the answer.
- Answer the questions you are certain of first and as quickly as possible. If answers are to be used only once, cross them out as you use them. Then, answer the questions that you think you know.
- Guess wisely. After you have answered all the questions you know the answers to, then guess.

Essay Questions
- Read the question and ask yourself, "What is the test maker looking for?"
- Always write out a brief outline before you write the answers to either short or long essay questions. This saves time and keeps you from forgetting information as you write.
- If there are several parts to the question, make sure you answer all parts.
- Write legibly and make your points easy to find (e.g., number them).
- Read your answer to make sure you have included everything you know.
- Do not include unneeded information. Individuals scoring the test are not impressed with information that is not related to the question, and they may actually deduct points from your answer. for providing unnecessary information.

Handout 10-6

Confidentiality Pledge

My role as a tutor is to assist students improve their academic performance. I understand that disclosing information that I learn about the students I tutor to other students and adults other than teachers, administrators and counselors who need information to help students may embarrass them. Therefore, I pledge to keep the information I learn in the tutoring process confidential, with the following exceptions:

a. If a student makes a statement about harming himself or herself or others, I will report it immediately.

b. If a student discloses that he or she being abused physically or emotionally I will report it immediately.

_____   _____
            Tutor's Signature   Date

_____   _____
Witnessed by (Course Instructor's Signature)   Date

Tutor Observation Rating Form

This sheet is to be completed during an actual tutoring session. Rate the tutor's behavior as satisfactory or needs improvement by placing a check in the appropriate space. If the tutor needs improvement, write down specific suggestions for improvement. Statements such as "Should do better" are not helpful. At the end of the session, the rater's observations are to be shared with the tutor.

Initial Phase

Satisfactory	Needs Improvement		Suggestions
_____	_____	1. Is ready for student _____	
_____	_____	2. Greets the student warmly_____	

Tutoring

_____	_____	3. Asks open-ended questions_____	
_____	_____	4. Gives specifics of problem_____	
_____	_____	5. Uses interchangeable responses_____	
_____	_____	6. Gives specific suggestions _____	
_____	_____	7. Checks for understanding _____	
_____	_____	8. Encourages/reinforces student_____	

Diagnostics: When one of the following appears to be a problem:

_____	_____	9. Asks about study habits._____	
_____	_____	10. Asks about motivation/ goals. _____	
_____	_____	11. Asks about study habits._____	
_____	_____	12. Asks about test anxiety. _____	
_____	_____	13. Checks on use of step approaches to studying._____	
_____	_____	14. Shares best study practices. _____	
_____	_____	15. Provides handout. _____	

If Physically or Mentally Challenged Student is Tutee

_____	_____	16. Uses tutoring strategies that are appropriate for student given nature of handicap.	

_____

_____ _____ _____

Observer   Tutor   Date

Defining Mental Retardation, Learning Disabilities, and Visual Impairments

Definition	*Incidence*	*Educational Implications*
Mentally retarded students learn more slowly than other students and may experience social adjustment problems. In some instances their physical development may be impaired as well.	1% of general population 1.7% of school population	1. Use concrete materials 2. Present in small steps 3. Review frequently 4. Provide feedback 5. Be positive/supportive
Students with learning disabilities have difficulties understanding or using spoken language- (delays/disorders/ discrepancies in listening), written language (difficulties reading, writing, or spelling), arithmetic (difficulties understanding basic concepts), and reasoning (problems organizing thought or integrating new ideas)	5-10% of general population 4-5 % of school population	1. Give step by step instructions. 2. Use short sentences. 3. Use a simple vocabulary. 4. Be positive/patient. 5. Use multi-sensory methods. 6. Use computers for drill. 7. Teach word processing. 8. Give feedback, not criticism.
Students with visual impairments vary from partially sighted (student needs special education, often has trouble seeing at a distance), low vision (student has severe problem and may not be able to read normally close up or at a distance even with normal aids such as glasses or contacts) to legally blind (student has vision of less than 20/200 in best eye; very limited field of vision) to total blindness (student has no vision).	1.2 % of school population	For partially sighted or low vision: 1. Use large print. 2. Books on tape 3. Use "readers" that enlarge words up to 40 times or more. 4. Teach listening skills. For totally blind: 1. Use Braille. 2. Use books on tape. 3. Provide oral tutoring.

Source: Abstracted from materials published by the National Information Center for Children and Youth with Disabilities.

Defining Hearing Impairments, Speech and Language Disorders, and Autism

Definition	Incidence	Educational Implications
Hearing Impairment - a degree of hearing loss ranging from mild to severe	21 million in the general population	1. Start early (1 to 3 years) 2. Use hearing aids 3. Teach speech reading if loss is total. 4. Use sign language if loss is total. 5. Use captioned films. 6. Give computer tutorials.
Student with speech and language disorders may substitute some sounds for others, make inappropriate sounds, have restricted vocabularies, be unable to express themselves, have problems forming some sounds.	10% of the general population. Over 1 million school-age students have speech and language problems.	1. Identify specific speech and language problem. 2. Tailor speech. 3. Learn common signs. 4. Listen crefully.
Students with autism have a brain disorder that influences behavior, social interactions, and communication. They may exhibit difficulty in relating to people, make repetitive movements such as rocking, be averse to change, avoid eye contact, have limited intellectual ability, have high intellectual functioning, be averse to social interaction, be averse to touch, and have no interest in their families	.05 to .15% in the general population	1. Establish clear expectations. 2. Use positive reinforcement. 3. Teach communication. 4. Set clear rules. 5. Use step-by-step communication 6. Be consistent in tutorial style.

Sources: Abstracted from materials published by the National Information Center for Children and Youth With Disabilities and the National Information Center on Deafness.

Request for Feedback on Students Receiving Tutoring

Please help us evaluate the effectiveness of the tutoring program by providing feedback about the academic progress of the following students. Place a check in the column that best describes each student's academic progress.

	Date Tutoring	**Academic Progress**		
Student's Names	Began	Grades - Up	Grades - Same	Grades - Down
_____	____	_____	_____	_____
_____	____	_____	_____	_____
_____	____	_____	_____	_____
_____	____	_____	_____	_____
_____	____	_____	_____	_____
_____	____	_____	_____	_____
_____	____	_____	_____	_____

_____   _____

Teacher's Signature   Date

Handout 10-11

Tutor's Log

Tutor's Name _____

Log for the Week of _____

    Please record the date of each appointment, the name of the student, the length of each appointment, and a brief statement regarding what was covered in each session. This log should be handed to the program supervisor at the end of each week.

Date	Student's Name	Duration of Session	Content Covered
4/10	Robin Smith	15 min.	English I Homework

_____
_____
_____
_____
_____
_____
_____

Chapter Eleven

Achievement Motivation Groups

In every classroom there are students who are not working up to their potential. In some instances these students befuddle and frustrate even the most dedicated teachers. In other cases, teachers simply stop caring because these are students that they see as lazy, insubordinate, and disrespectful. Interestingly enough, efforts to improve the overall academic performance of our schools rests heavily on the ability of educators to motivate underachieving students.

When trying to motivate students, teachers and student support personnel have several options. One frequently used motivational strategy employed by teachers is to threaten students by telling them of the dire consequences that befall low achievers, early school "leavers," and others who do not develop good work habits and high levels of academic skills. Unfortunately, students rarely feel concerned about these threats, partially because they know they are not totally based in fact, and partly because some students erroneously believe that they have a built in immunity to the consequences associated with low academic achievement.

Achievement Motivation Groups do not rely upon threat. Instead, Achievement Motivation Groups rely upon three proven strategies to motivate achievement: goal setting, social support, and extrinsic rewards. These strategies are not fool proof because they are not replacements for intrinsic motivation, but, when employed together in an Achievement Motivation Group, they have been shown to be an effective means of increasing the academic achievement. A hoped-for outcome of Achievement Motivation Groups is that the students will become intrinsically motivated, but there are no assurances that this will occur.

The approach to developing and leading Achievement Motivation Groups presented here is a modification of the pioneering work of Silverman (1976). The modifications include placing greater emphasis on the goal-setting process and on students' evaluation of their own goals and progress toward their goals. Another modification involves the structure of the group. Silverman advocated the use of a closed-ended group, and although that is legitimate, the format outlined here is for an open-ended group. The difference between these two types of groups is discussed later.

Getting Started

As just noted above, Achievement Motivation Groups rely upon three basic strategies: extrinsic rewards, goal setting, and the establishment of a social support network. Establishing a supportive social milieu requires the involvement of significant caregivers, namely teachers and parents, as well as other students.

Support from students occurs primarily in the context of the Achievement Motivation Group, although social support will undoubtedly occur outside the group. The process of involving teachers begins when teachers are contacted to ask them to refer students whom they believe might wish to improve their academic performance if provided the right atmosphere. Notes to teacher should make it clear that the purpose of the Achievement Motivation Group is to assist students who are functioning below their academic potential. Students who are achieving at their potential and still not doing well should not be referred for inclusion in these groups. Notes to teachers should also stipulate that teachers play an integral role in the success of the group, and that they will be asked to complete brief daily progress reports. A copy of the forms for the report that teachers need to complete (see Figures 11-3 and 11-4) should be appended to the letter. Figure 11-1 is an example of a note that can be used to solicit teacher referrals.

Figure 11-1

Sample Note to Teachers

I am hoping to initiate at least one Achievement Motivation Group in the near future, and I am seeking your help. Achievement Motivation Groups are designed to help students who are achieving below their academic potential raise their grades and improve their classroom behavior. Students who are at or above normal in scholastic aptitude, but seem to lack motivation, are the best candidates for these groups.

The Achievement Motivation Group will meet for 30 minutes once or twice per week and will be led by a counselor. However, motivating underachieving students requires more than participating in a small group. The active participation of teachers in evaluating student progress and providing feedback to students is a prerequisite to success. Teachers will asked to complete brief daily reports regarding the academic and general classroom behavior of the students in the Achievement Motivation Group (see attached Achievement Motivation Weekly Progress Report form). Normally this record keeping will take less than 5 minutes per day and will often require only a minute or so per day.

The parents of the students included in the Achievement Motivation Group will be contacted and asked to help with one aspect of the motivational process, providing extrinsic rewards when students improve their academic performance. These contacts and subsequent contacts will not involve teachers unless they need be involved in meetings with parents. However, teachers will be asked to send periodic reports to parents (see attachment, Achievement Motivation Weekly Progress Report to Parents).

Finally, if you have students who might benefit from participation in an Achievement Motivation Group, please write their names on the bottom of this piece of paper and place it in the Counseling Program's mailbox. If you want more information about Achievement Motivation Groups before making referrals, call the Counseling Program Office and a counselor will set up an appointment to meet with you to answer your questions.

Names of Students Being Referred   Best Time To Contact Student

_____   _____
_____   _____
_____   _____
_____   _____

Screening Members

Once a list of referrals is received from teachers, prospective participants should be screened to determine their suitability for the group. To accomplish screening, students should be scheduled for a 15-minute screening session to determine their level of motivation, whether they fit into the group that is being formed, and whether their schedule will permit them to participate in the group. Ascertaining whether a student's schedule will permit her or him to participate in the Achievement Motivation Groups is an easy chore. Determining a student's motivational level and his or her ability to function as an effective group member is more difficult.

Motivation: Motivation can be assessed using one or more of the following questions:

1. On a 1-to-10 scale, with 1 being a very low motivation and 10 being extremely high, how would you rate your motivation to improve your school performance at this time? (Students who rate their motivation at less than a 5 should probably be rejected, particularly if the group can be filled with more highly motivated students.)

2. We have not established a meeting time yet, but would you be willing to meet during your lunch hour at least part of the time? (Students who answer No to this question may not be included, particularly if there are

other indictors that their motivational level is low).

3. Will you be willing to help other people in the group? (A *No* answer should probably result in disqualification from participation in the group because students will need to function as buddies at some points in the group).

4. If you are included in the group, what academic goal or goals would you like to accomplish? Although the answers to this questions will often be vague (e.g., to improve my grades or pass all my subjects, graduate from high school) this is to be expected. Students who cannot articulate at least some type of goal may be poor risks for the group.

Suitability: Determining a student's ability to participate in a meaningful way in the group may not be discernible from a screening interview, but some estimates about student "fit" can be made by posing the following questions:

1. If the group is to be successful, it is essential that students show respect by listening carefully to each other. Are you a good listener? Do you interrupt others? Do you sometimes make fun of others? Because I will have to remove any student who does not listen to others or makes fun of them from the group, it is probably better if you do not start the group if you have problems in this area. What do you think? Are you still interested?

2. The purpose of the group is to help you improve your grades. However, for this to happen you must agree to complete your homework and other assignments. Can you make this commitment at this time?

If a student cannot commit to being a good citizen and working to improve her or his grades, he or she probably should not be included in the group. However, the final decision regarding the inclusion or exclusion of a student in the group can often be facilitated by discussing a student's behavior with his or her teacher(s). The group of students that is selected should not be smaller than 6 or larger than 10 members.

Signing a Contract: Students who are selected should be asked to sign the Becoming a Better Student Group Contract, which is shown in Figure 11-2.

Figure 11-2

Becoming a Better Student Group Contract

While I am a member of this group I agree to
• be on time to each meeting;
• bring the Weekly Report Form and homework assignment to each group meeting;
• respect others in the group by listening when they talk;
• help others in the group; and
• do the work the teacher assigns while I am in the group.
My goal for the group is

_____

_____

Student_____
Counselor_____
Date_____

Orienting Teachers

After students are selected, the counselor should meet with their teachers to review their role and the Achievement Motivation Group Weekly Progress (Figure 11-3). This orientation should include the following information:

1. After the first group meeting and as long as a student is in the Achievement Motivation Group, the teacher should complete the Weekly Progress Form at the end of each day and send it with the student when he or she attends group meetings. The completion of the form should be done with the student present and all U's (unsatisfactory) should be explained.

2. Teachers should also inform other teachers who may have the student in class that she or he is participating in an Achievement Motivation Group, and encourage them to provide feedback to the student on an informal basis. Group leaders should also inform other teachers about the student's participation in the group.

3. All teachers (the reporting teacher and others) should provide verbal praise and encouragement to students who are involved in the Achievement Motivation Group. When possible, teachers should ignore minor problems that occur in the classroom. New, desirable behaviors should be praised verbally.

4. Teachers should keep the leader of the group informed about abrupt or dramatic changes in the student's academic progress.

5. If the student's parents are involved, teachers should send a progress

report home each week and ask that it be signed by one or both parents (see Figure 11-4) (Silverman, 1976).

6. After the first meeting, teachers should give short academic assignments that can be worked on during the Achievement Motivation Group each time the student comes to group.

Figure 11-3

Achievement Motivation Group Weekly Progress Report

Date of report _____
Student_____

Use the following symbols to indicate student's performance:
  S = Satisfactory performance
  U = Unsatisfactory performance
  NA = Not applicable

	M	T	W	Th	F
AcademicWork (General)					
1. Follows directions	—	—	—	—	—
2. Completes homework	—	—	—	—	—
3. Participates in class discussion	—	—	—	—	—
4. Test performance is acceptable	—	—	—	—	—

This student should be commended for: _____

Make one or two specific recommendations regarding areas that need improvement (e.g., solving word problems in math; punctuation of sentences and paragraphs; writing topic sentences:

_____

_____

Classroom Behavior	M	T	W	Th	F
1. Follows Classroom Rules	—	—	—	—	—

If applicable, list one or two classroom behaviors that student needs to improve:_____

_____

Teacher's Signature _____

Involving Parents

If the results of the Achievement Motivation Group are to be maximized, it is highly desirable that parents be involved in the process. As mentioned earlier, teachers may send parents notes that provide details about their student's progress as one means of keeping them informed on a weekly basis. However, parents should be more than passively involved. At a minimum they should provide positive verbal feedback and encouragement to their students. If possible, tangible rewards should be provided when students make progress toward their goals.

After students have been selected for inclusion in the Achievement Motivation Group, parents should be contacted, preferably by telephone or personal contact, and told about the functioning of the group. They should be asked to provide verbal feedback when appropriate, refrain from negative feedback when reports from teachers do not meet their expectation, and to provide tangible reinforcers for progress and goal attainment. Although providing verbal and tangible reinforcers are important roles for parents to play in the motivational process, it is extremely important that, when the teacher's report is given to them, they not allow poor performance to escalate into verbal warfare. Rather, parents should be urged to provide feedback such as, "I'm sorry that your performance wasn't somewhat better, but I have great confidence in your ability to do better in school." Parents should also be encouraged to sign the report and return it to school on a timely basis. If parents cannot agree to provide encouragement and verbal reinforcers and refrain from criticizing their students when they receive an unsatisfactory report, they should not be included in the achievement motivation process.

Parents should also be informed that, even though their student is in an Achievement Motivation Group, their interaction with their student is not discussed in the group. Explain that the purposes of the group are to help students realize academic goals, to provide feedback about their performance more frequently, and to provide a supportive environment for students who wish to do better in school. Some middle and high school students may prefer that their parents not be involved. Always check with students before involving parents.

Figure 11-4

Achievement Motivation Weekly Progress Report to Parents

Date _____
Parent's Name (s) _____
Student's Name _____
This week your student (check = Yes) (NA = Not applicable this week)

	M	T	W	Th	F
1. Handed in completed homework	___	___	___	___	___
2. Was on time to class	___	___	___	___	___
3. Participated in class	___	___	___	___	___
4. Was attentive in class	___	___	___	___	___
5. Followed directions	___	___	___	___	___
6. Worked well with others	___	___	___	___	___
7. Improved test performance	___	___	___	___	___
8. Improved performance on classwork	___	___	___	___	___

For this week, your students should be commended for his or her work in:_____
For next week, the areas of academic functioning that need the greatest improvement are:

_____

Signed

_____

Facilitating the Group: Some General Considerations

It is a general rule of thumb that small groups have from 6 to 10 members, as has already been noted, but the size of the Achievement Motivation Group should be dependent upon the amount of time available and the age of the group members. Silverman (1976) suggested that groups be restricted to eight members if at all possible and that the group should meet for about 30 minutes at the end of each day so students can get into the habit of doing homework, having it checked by the group leader, and getting feedback about their work. Although it may be possible to follow the schedule outlined by Silverman in some middle and elementary schools, it is unlikely that this schedule can be adhered to in a high school setting. Moreover, few student support personnel can spend 2.5 hours per week with 6 to 10 students, given their schedules.

It is not necessary for Achievement Motivation groups to meet every day to be successful, although it would be desirable. If students can meet daily and the group leader does not have the time to commit to the group it is suggested that either a volunteer or peer leader be recruited to act as a coleader who can be trained to facilitate the group during some of the meetings. This frees the group leader to work with other students and allows the group to meet oftener.

Another rule of thumb regarding small groups is that they are typically closed-ended, which means that the group meets for a specified period of time, and that group members who begin the group stay in the group until it is terminated. Achievement Motivation Groups can be operated as closed-ended groups, but the suggestion here is to run them as open-ended groups. Open-ended groups may meet from one to five times per week throughout the school year, but group members may choose to terminate their membership in the group once they have reached their goals. At the point of termination of a group member, another member can be incorporated into the group as a replacement. If Achievement Motivation Groups are operated on an ongoing basis, it establishes that student support personnel are committed to working with underachievers, and that teachers should routinely refer students who are not achieving up to their potential. Further, open-ended groups have no formal termination date. Achievement Motivation Groups are typically terminated at the end of the fall semester, school year, or when all interested students have achieved their goals.

Session 1 — Getting Started

Objectives
- Establish rules that govern the group's functioning.
- Review the purpose of teachers' Achievement Motivation Weekly Progress Report form (see Figure 11-3).
- Review the purpose of the Weekly Progress Report to Parents (see Figure 11-4).
- Initiate the goal-setting process.

NOTE: Group leader will need a file folder for each student in the group. These will be used as Achievement Motivation Group portfolios. Contracts, goal statements, and Weekly Progress Report forms will be kept in these portfolios.

Activities

1. Conduct a warm-up exercise called My Fantasy Future. Encourage students to let their imaginations "go wild" and forget about barriers, real or imagined.

2. Review the rules:
- Be on time.
- Bring homework assignment with you, along with your Weekly Progress Report Form from your teachers.
- Respect others by listening.
- Be willing to help others who are having problems with homework.
- Use no put-downs. This is hurtful and the opposite of respect.

• Leave the group at any time, particularly when you have attained your goals.

3. Give students copies of the teachers' Weekly Progress Report form as well as Weekly Progress Report to Parents form. Explain that these are (1) a way for them to monitor their progress and (2) a device to keep their parents informed of their progress.

4. Engage students in initial goal setting. Provide the following guidelines for writing their goals:

• A goal is measurable. You will be able to tell when you attain it.
• A goal has a timeline attached. I want to accomplish this by X date.
• A goal is realistic. When goals are set too high, they become sources of frustration when they are not achieved. Give students Handout 11-1, Academic Achievement Goal Setting. After reviewing it, have participants write a long-term and short-term goal and give them feedback about their goals using the three criteria listed above.

5. Give students Handout 11-2, My Academic Achievement Goals.

6. Have students transfer their 1-week goal to Handout 11-2, Achievement Goals.

Example: I will hand in all of my homework for the next week.

7. Collect Handout 11-1, My Achievement Goals and Handout 11-2, Academic Goal Setting sheets place them in each student's portfolio. This portfolio will contain all Weekly Progress Report forms and their goal setting sheets. Tell students that progress toward their long-term and short-term goals will be reviewed during the next meeting and each subsequent session.

Homework

Remind students to bring Achievement Motivation Weekly Progress Reports from their teachers and a homework assignment to the next meeting.

Session 2 (and most subsequent group sessions)

Progress Review/Goal Setting/Homework

Objectives

• Review students' academic progress since last group session.
• Evaluate achievement goals and reset as necessary.
• Work on homework assignment with other students.

Activities

1. Have students share their Achievement Motivation Weekly Progress Reports with other students and get reactions. This should consist of verbal reinforcement if it is good and encouragement (I have confidence in your ability to achieve your goal) if it is not particularly good. Place these reports in the students' portfolios. Other reinforces may be provided if they are

available. Elementary school children may be given stickers, free time, a supervised play period, and time to play computer games if they achieve standards set by the group. Older children like free time, supervised games, watching television programs at school, and other similar rewards. A comprehensive list of reinforcers is provided at the end of Chapter Eight (Figure 8-4).

2. Give students an opportunity to reset their goals to a higher level. Then collect their My Academic Achievement Goals sheets (Figure 11-2) and place them in the students' portfolios.

4. Have students work on their homework assignments.

Homework

Terminate the session by reminding the students to bring Weekly Progress Report forms and a homework assignment to the next session.

Sessions When Students Leave or New Students Enter the Group

Objectives
- Say good-bye to "old" students or hello to new students.
- Have students review progress toward their goals since the last session.
- Evaluate goal and reset as necessary.
- Work on homework assignment with other students.

Activities

1. If a student is leaving the group, ask him or her to share reasons for leaving. If the student has attained his or her goal, ask members of the group to give him or her a sustained round of applause. If not ask group members to commit to continued assistance outside of the group if the student wants continuing help.

2. If a new student is entering the group, have the continuing students provide the orientation to the group by going over what the student needs to return to bring to the group, the goal-setting exercise (Handout 11-2) and the criteria for evaluating goals, what happens in the periodic review sessions, and the rules.

3. Have students share their Weekly Progress Report Forms

4. Have students review the goal that they are currently working on and reset as necessary. Have the new student write his or her first goal during this time.

5. Have students work on homework together. The new student can assist one of the students with his or her homework or observe one of the students do homework.

6. Remind students to bring their Weekly Progress report forms and brief homework assignments to next session.

Summary

Achievement Motivation Groups assist students to set realistic educational goals and provide the support necessary to achieve those goals. The first step in getting these groups started is to identify underachieving students. The next step is to screen the students to determine whether they are suitable candidates for Achievement Motivation Groups. During the first group session students should begin the goal-setting process and learn how feedback is to be given. Subsequent sessions focus on goal attainment, providing support, and the completion of homework.

References

Silverman, M. (1976). The achievement motivation approach: A counselor-directed approach. *Elementary Guidance and Counseling, 2,*100-106.

Academic Achievement Goal Setting

1. Student who is failing every class: By the end of this grading period, I will be passing in two classes.
2. Student who hasn't turned in any homework: I will turn in 75% of my homework this month.
3. Student who gets all C's: I will raise my grades in science and English to B's this grading period.
4. Student who is always in trouble: I will stay out of trouble this week.
5. Student who failed math: I will pass math this semester.
6. Student who is late handing in assignments: I will hand in 85% of my homework assignments on time for the next month.

Think for a moment about what you would like to accomplish by the end of this semester. Do you want to pass every subject? Improve all of your grades by one letter? Develop better work habits such as handing in work on time? Get along better with the teachers? Write down that goal in the space below:

_____

_____

Now think about what you would like to accomplish in the next week that will start you on the road to accomplishing your goal. Write a goal that is measurable and achievable in the space below. The time line for achievement of this goal is 1 week from today.

_____

_____

My Academic Achievement Goals

Today's Date   Goal   Target Date

_____

_____

_____

_____

_____

_____

_____

_____

_____

_____

_____

_____

_____

_____

_____

_____

_____

_____

Chapter Twelve

Establishing Homework Support Programs

It is a well-documented fact that students in other countries spend more time in school than do students in the United States (Daggett, 1997). However, it is often not possible for students in this country to spend additional time in school because of the amount of time it takes them to get to school and to return home after school. Riding a bus for extended periods of time has always been a problem in rural America, a problem that has been exacerbated by the consolidation of small schools in the move to develop larger, more comprehensive schools. Since the advent of the civil rights movement and legal mandates to achieve racial balance in schools, urban students have joined their rural counterparts in spending extended periods of time on buses as they travel to and from school. The overall result of spending more time commuting not only takes away time that could be spent in the learning process but also takes students away from neighborhood schools that can be easily accessed by students and parents.

If students in this country are to achieve at the level of students from other developed nations they must spend more time on task. This can be accomplished by extending the school year and by adding homework. Unfortunately, requiring students to spend more time doing homework magnifies the academic problems experienced by poor students who have few resources at home such as books and computers. It also places students whose parents are not highly educated at a disadvantage because they cannot get the support they need as they struggle with the extra work. Providing a variety of out-of-school homework support programs such as peer and volunteer tutoring programs and achievement motivation groups can to some degree offset this problem. It can also provide students with the type of help they need with increasingly technical material. In this chapter several alternatives for establishing external homework support programs are discussed.

Designing A Homework Support Program

The goals of a homework support program are to facilitate the completion of assigned homework and to enhance the learning process. In short, like all other strategies discussed in this book, the purpose of homework support programs is to improve achievement. More specifically, homework support programs are aimed at leveling the educational playing field so that all students have access to the support they need to learn the material that has been assigned. Therefore, the position here is that homework support programs should target less-advantaged students.

If homework support programs are to be beneficial, they must be designed so that students have multiple ways to access them. For example, programs should be offered in schools and in the students' neighborhoods. Programs should also be offered at different times of the day because of the variability in students' schedules. Homework support programs, like any instructional method, should be designed to meet the special needs of the students. Students who access homework support programs come from many different achievement levels, have various types of learning deficiencies including learning disabilities, and have varying degrees of proficiency in English. Unless programs are tailored to meet these specific needs some students will be unable to take advantage of them. Homework support programs, like all educational programs, cost money. Many of the strategies discussed in this chapter utilize volunteers, but this does not mean they are free. Someone must recruit, train and coordinate the efforts of volunteers. To this end, some school districts have appointed volunteer coordinators. The appointment of a homework support program coordinator will be necessary in many instances if viable programs are to be developed. If this is not done at the individual school or district level, one or two student support professionals should probably assume this role as a part of their duties.

Homework support programs should take advantage of emerging technology when possible. For example, local cable systems are required by law to provide some free public access. Some of that access could be used by schools with uniform curricula to reteach aspects of subjects such as mathematics, foreign language, and science in after-school and before-school sessions. This would require that all schools stay on the "same page" in the delivery of lessons, which is an obvious limitation of this approach. It would also be possible to hire technicians to videotape the lessons included in an entire course. These could be duplicated, cataloged by content, and placed in the library for students to check out and review at home. Although such strategies are technically not part of homework support programs, they would facilitate the completion of homework assignments.

The homework support program must be carefully designed and staffed. As has already been noted, in order to maximize the likelihood that homework support programs will be successful, a professional building-level coordinator should be appointed. It may also be useful to have a district-level coordinator who can recruit and train volunteer tutors from the community (Corn & Moore, 1992; Rosenroll & Dey, 1990). However, the building-level coordinator will ultimately have to come to grips with staffing issues such as when will homework support be available, what types of help will be needed by students, and where will services be offered. For example, Corn and Moore (1992) reported on an in-school homework support program that was staffed by peers and offered during the school day. They found that 85% of the requests for support had to do with homework in mathematics. The remaining requests for assistance with homework had to do with English, chemistry, and history.

Questions of what expertise needs to be available, who should provide the services, when the program should be available to students, and where services should be offered can be based partly on a survey of potential users. A model survey is presented in Figure 12-1.

Figure 12-1

Sample Survey to Determine the Need for a Homework Support Program

Directions: The faculty and administration of Grady Smith High School are planning a homework support program and we need your assistance. Please answer the following questions regarding your need for help with your homework.

1. Would you consult a homework support program to gain assistance with your homework if the staff is available at a time and a place convenient to you? (Check One) Yes _____ No _____

If your answer to question 1 is No, stop and return your questionnaire. If you answered Yes to question number 1, please answer the remaining questions.

2. Think about the types of people that you would like to have available to help you with your homework problems. Then rank order the following types of people who might be used to staff a program by placing a 1 by the type of person you would most prefer, a 2 by the type of person that would be your second choice.

_____ Knowledgeable student (peer)
_____ Knowledgeable adult volunteer
_____ Teacher

3. We are interested in knowing when homework support should be made available to students. Please indicate which of the following times you could access a homework support program (Check all that apply).

_____ During school hours

	Immediately after school
	Weekday evenings (7:00 to 9:00)
	Weekends (specify best time _____)
	Other (specify best time _____)

4. Think about the type of homework support you need. Place a check by all subjects with which you feel you need assistance.

Mathematics
_____ Calculus
_____ Algebra II/Trig
_____ Algebra II
_____ Algebra I
_____ Geometry
_____ Pre-Algebra
_____ Technical mathematics

Science
_____ AP/Honors Chemistry
_____ Chemistry
_____ AP/Honors Physics
_____ Physics
_____ AP/Honors Biology
_____ Biology
_____ Physical Science
_____ Computer science
_____ Other (please specify _____)

English and Foreign Language
_____ English IV
_____ English III
_____ English II
_____ English I
_____ Spanish (specify level _____)
_____ French (specify level _____)
_____ German (specify level _____)
_____ Latin (specify level _____)
_____ Other foreign language (specify language and level
      _____)

Other subjects
_____ U.S. History
_____ World History
_____ Economics and Government
_____ Psychology
_____ Sociology
_____ Other subject (please specify _____)

5. From the above list of courses, write in the course or courses with which you most frequently need homework assistance_____

Types of Programs

Peer Homework Support Programs: In some schools, clubs such as the National Honor Society have set up homework support programs on an after-school basis (Corn & Douglas, 1992). The concern when staffing these programs, as it is with all homework support programs, is to provide an array of students who possess the expertise required to provide the diverse assistance needed. For example, it is not difficult to imagine students coming to homework support programs with questions about three or four foreign languages, several math and science courses, and an array of English literature and composition courses. If students are to get the help they need, the peers staffing the center must be familiar with their subjects.

Afterschool Programs: Many school districts have established afterschool homework support programs by either paying their teachers to stay an extra hour or two or through using volunteers. Although these programs make a great deal of sense, they are often inaccessible because of transportation issues and work best in situations involving neighborhood schools.

Parent and Community Volunteers: Many school districts use parents and volunteers from the community to staff their homework support programs. These volunteers must be recruited, trained, scheduled, and supervised if the programs are to be effective. These processes parallel those described in establishing tutorial programs (Chapter 10).

Telephone Centers: Some school districts have established telephone hotlines staffed by professionals and volunteers so that students can call during the evening to get assistance with their homework. With the advent of telephones equipped with television screens, these programs offer the promise of being even more effective in the future.

Online Services: Currently about 30 to 35% of the families in this country own personal computers, and not all of these computers are linked to the Internet. Fortunately, computers are becoming far more affordable and the technology is available to access the Internet via specially designed television sets. Many individual schools have home pages that are used for posting important information needed by students and parents such as testing dates. However, schools can hire webmasters who are responsible for posting homework assignments and tips for completing homework on a daily basis. More importantly, through the use of e-mail students can pose questions to volunteers or paid personnel who are housed in a central location and receive answers almost instantaneously. Finally, it is also possible for schools to provide chat rooms to provide interactive homework support programs on the Internet.

Community-Based Homework Support Programs: As has already been noted, many students live long distances from their schools. Using local libraries, churches, and other facilities, students can be offered homework support programs in their neighborhoods. Again, community centers can be staffed either by volunteers or paid personnel.

Mobile Homework Support Programs: In rural areas and large cities it is possible to provide face-to-face homework support programs using buses or other vehicles equipped with computers and other office equipment.

Utilizing Private Agencies: Some school districts have set aside money to send students to private companies such as Sylvan® for tutoring and homework support. This is obviously an expensive option, but it is potentially a highly effective alternative to some of the other programs listed here.

Summary

Homework support programs are necessary if the achievement level of students is to be improved. These programs can take many forms and may include teachers who are paid to provide extra hours of service, volunteers, peers, and private agencies. Just as the programs can be staffed in many ways, delivery mechanisms may vary. Face-to-face sessions, telephones, chat rooms, and e-mail are among the ways that homework support programs can be delivered. Finally, homework support programs can also be delivered at school, in community facilities such as churches or libraries, or via technology in students' homes.

References

Corn, K. L., & Moore, D. D. (1992). Reach for the S.T.A.R.S.—students teaching and reaching students: A two-faceted peer facilitation program at Greenfield-Central High School. *The School Counselor, 40,* 68-72.

Daggett, W. R. (1997). Getting schools ready for the technology of the future. *Model Schools News, 1,* 1-2.

Rosenroll, D. A., & Dey, C. (1990). A centralized approach to training peer tutors: three years of progress. *The School Counselor, 37,* 304-312.

Chapter Thirteen

Parenting for Academic Achievement: Promoting Resiliency and Academic Skills

An impressive number of authoritative observations and empirical investigations support the idea that increased parental involvement in the educational process results in higher academic achievement (e.g., Campbell & Mandel, 1990; Floyd, 1996; Keith & Lichtmen, 1994; Rak & Patterson, 1996). Parents who set educational expectations, enforce standards, offer direct assistance, and provide psychological support to students produce students who achieve at higher levels.

Many programs are available to student support personnel that focus on discipline in the parenting process. However, there is no single program designed to prepare parents to facilitate the educational growth of their children. Moreover, it seems likely that different types of programs are needed depending upon the cultural background of the parents. For example, Hispanic American parents may need to understand more fully their rights as parents, often need the skills to deal with the educational bureaucracy, and may need to provide more independence training for their children if they are to help them succeed in the typical classroom (Okagaki, Frensch, & Gordan, 1995). Tentative lists of family variables that may positively and negatively influence achievement of children from Hispanic American families (Figure 13-1), Chinese American and other Asian American families (Figure 13-2), and African American families (Figure 13-3) are presented. Unfortunately, there is very little literature dealing with the factors that influence the achievement of American Indian children. However, as noted at the outset, when Figures 13-1 through 13-3 are examined, it becomes clear that when parents value education, set expectations for achievement, and establish a family structure that supports academic achievement school performance is likely to increase.

Figure 13-1

**Family Factors Affecting the Academic Achievement
of Hispanic American Students**

Factors That Facilitate Achievement
- Parents of high achievers are upset with low grades;
- parents read to their children;
- parental involvement in the educational process;
- commitment to children;
- belief that a well-educated child is one who has learned ethical and moral behavior;
- belief that child's behavior reflects on honor of family; and
- Belief that there is a duty to care for family members.

Factors That May Lower Achievement
- Language barriers; lower proficiency in English influences participation in school;
- low SES;
- recent immigration status;
- belief in absolute authority of teachers;
- poor Hispanic Americans do not believe they have the right to question school's bureaucracy;
- parents consider it rude to intrude into the school;
- students who have a collective orientation (in traditional classroom); and
- parents fail to provide independence training for children.

Source: Okagaki, Frensch, & Gordan, 1995.

Figure 13-2

**Family Factors Affecting the Academic Achievement of Chinese
American and Other Asian American Students**

Factors That Facilitate Educational Achievement
- Parents set high standards of behavior for their children;
- more pressure and monitoring (Asian American);
- work with children to ensure diligence;
- value self-improvement;

- value education and achievement more than many European Americans; and
- greater stability in family than all others (Asian American).

Factors That May Lower Achievement
- Parents less concerned about independence; and
- acculturation of children

Sources: Campbell & Mandel, 1990; Chen, & Uttal, 1988; Chia, 1989; Ji, Jiao, & Jing, 1993; Peng & Wright, 1994.

Figure 13-3

Family Factors Affecting the Academic Achievement of African American Students

Factors That Facilitate Educational Achievement
- Parents have strong educational values;
- involvement of children in academic activities;
- optimism;
- sense of control;
- supportive and nurturing environment; and
- maternal support.

Factors That May Lower Achievement
- Parents and families live in a dangerous neighborhood; and
- students have a low SES.

Sources: Floyd, 1996; Gonzales, Cauce, Friedman & Mason, 1996; Halle, Kurtz-Costes & Mahoney, 1997; Johnson, 1992.

Parenting Education and the Resilient Child

What is not addressed in Figures 13-1 through 13-3, at least directly, is the importance of parenting to increase the resiliency of children. The issue of resiliency came to the fore when educators and others began to wonder why children coming from what appeared to be identical backgrounds, coped differently when faced with hardships such as poverty. "Resiliency in children is the capacity of those who are exposed to identifiable risk factors to overcome those risks and avoid negative outcomes such as delinquency and behavioral problems, psychological maladjustment, academic difficulties, and physical complications" (Rak & Patterson, 1996. p. 368). Research has identified a variety of family factors that are related to producing a resilient student (Adler, n.d: Rak & Patterson, 1996; Werner & Smith, 1982) including the following:

1. The family establishes clear expectations for behavior and enforces those expectations.
2. Children are monitored on an ongoing basis.
3. Parents openly demonstrate that they care about the children on an ongoing basis.
4. Discipline is evenhanded and fair, not harsh and sporadic. Love is not withdrawn as a means of punishment.
5. Parents do not abuse alcohol or drugs and do not condone their use in students.
6. The family is stable and marital conflict is minimal.
7. There are 4 or fewer children spaced at least 4 years apart.
8. There is focused nurturing during the first year of life and little separation from the caregiver.
9. A social support network including relatives and others who share similar values is available.
10. A nurturing sibling or other confidant is available to the child.

Although these general factors are undoubtedly important in producing resilient students, parents need to know the traits of resilient students and be given specific assistance in how to develop these characteristics (Rak & Patterson, 1996). The traits of resilient children are social competence, problem solving skills, autonomy, and a sense of purpose (Cowen & Work, 1988). Adler (n.d.) defined social competence as having good communication skills, concern for others, having a sense of humor, and flexibility. Problem-solving ability requires the ability to think reflexively (as opposed to impulsively), to consider options, and to try alternate solutions in social and educational situations. Autonomous children have a strong sense of their ability to "do things," can exert self-control, have high self-esteem, and can generally "operate on their environments", as opposed to responding passively to the things that occur. Further, Adler suggested that students with a sense of purpose are motivated to move forward, to achieve. These students are optimistic about the future and have realistic but healthy expectancies about the future. Unquestionably, parenting strategies can influence all of these competencies.

Each school district should offer ongoing parenting training to the parents of preschoolers as well as to parents of enrolled students. Additionally, student support personnel should be advocates of parenting training with the courts, probation and parole officers, and the department of social services. For example, some judges are asking for an evaluation of the parenting skills of the parties involved before awarding custody of the children to either parent. In addition, pregnant teens should be provided with the opportunity to participate in a parenting class prior to giving birth to their children.

A Parenting Course

A parenting course focused on developing parenting skills that will facilitate the development of resiliency as well as educational skills is presented in this section. Each session of the course should be spaced one week a apart and last for 60 to 90 minutes.

Who Should Be Involved?

Poverty and family disorganization seem to be the major factors that place children at risk. Although all parents may benefit from training aimed at helping students develop resiliency, poor parents, single parents, and families in crisis (such as those in which drug or alcohol abuse is a problem) should be targeted.

How Should Parents Be Recruited?

At the outset it is necessary to define the word *family*. The stereotypical definition of family is a mother, father, and children who are biologically related. However, in a society in which as many as half of the students live in single-parent homes, the first aspect of our stereotypical definition that must be surrendered is that there are two parents present in the home. In addition, many students live with surrogate parents. In some instances these are grandparents, aunts, and uncles. In other instances children live in foster homes. Therefore, the second aspect of our definition of family that must be given up is that a biological link exists between the caregiver and the child. Additionally, in many cultures the definition of family includes the extended family which may very well include godparents and/or members of the child's tribe (Brown, 1997). The point is simple: efforts to recruit parents must focus on the caregivers who influence the child's development, not solely on biological parents.

Some of the traditional methods of communication with parents, such as notes carried home by students or letters sent directly to parents, are unlikely to be effective means of recruiting participants. Direct contacts via the telephone are more likely to be effective than traditional approaches, but in rural areas direct contacts with parents may have to be made. During contacts, parents should be told that the purposes of the parent education class are to help parents: (1) facilitate their children's education and (2) raise students who can deal with adversity and thrive.

Recruitment efforts should also include contacts with organizations such as Parents without Partners, churches, departments of social services, and other similar organizations. Once the program has begun, contacts with past participants may also be useful in identifying parents who should be invited to attend the classes.

Scheduling a Time and Place and Dealing with Transportation

The schedule for the parenting courses must coincide with the availability of the parents. Although sessions will often be held in the evening, the best time for the courses may be during the school day. Transportation is likely to be a problem for many of the parents who wish to participate. Therefore, the schedule for the course may be linked to bus or other mass transportation schedules. It may also be necessary to organize volunteers to help with various aspects of the courses, including providing transportation for parents. Further, course sessions should be scheduled in a place that is most convenient for the parents. This may be in a church, library, or other facility in the community.

Who Should Lead the Course?

Parenting courses that involve parents from minority groups subscribing to traditional cultural values should be led or co-led by a person who is sensitive to their values system, traditions, and family expectations. Parenting courses should also have leaders or translators who speak the language of the participants. In some instances this may be a parent who has gone through the course at an earlier time. Moreover, "graduates" of parenting courses may be used as co-facilitators.

Session 1 — Raising a Resilient Student

Objectives

- Allow parents to become acquainted.
- Present a working definition of resiliency.
- Give parents a means of assessing the risk factors in their own children.

Activities

1. Have parents introduce themselves and tell about their families (e.g., how many children in the family, their ages, and some of the fun things the family does together).

2. Have parents tell what they hope to learn during parent education. If Asian American or American Indian families are involved, either skip this step or make sure that they understand that they do not have to talk about their families.

3. Explain the purpose of the group — helping parents raise resilient students— and define resiliency (Use Overhead 13-1, The Characteristics of Resilient Students). In defining resiliency, use the metaphor of inoculation against disease. Students who are resilient have been vaccinated against certain types of problems as a result of good parenting. This does not mean that every child who develops a problem has been parented poorly. However, by parenting to promote resiliency, the probability of psychological and educational problems developing is reduced.

4. Provide information on positive family factors. (Use Overhead 13-2, Family Factors That Produce Resilient Kids).

5. Provide information on family factors that put students at risk. These are to some degree the opposites of the factors that produce resilient students. Use Overhead 13-3, Family Factors That Put Students at Risk.

6. If Asian American, Hispanic American, or American Indian parents are involved, spend time discussing the differences in points of view about autonomy between these groups and European Americans. However, if students are to do well in the typical classroom, they must receive independence training. Independence does not mean that children should be oriented to being totally independent from the family. It does mean that children need to be oriented to functioning independently in the school setting. For example, in the typical classroom, students are expected to listen to an assignment and work with a minimum of supervision while the teacher works with small groups of students. Also, much of the work is done in centers. Students are expected to follow oral or written directions and work without a great deal of supervision.

7. Have parents discuss what they have learned.

8. Indicate that the best way to prepare a child to work independently at school is to allow the child to work independently at home. Parents should expect that children will do some things on their own, such as chores, picking out his or her own clothes, dressing themselves as soon as possible, deciding

how to spend their allowance if they have one, and resolving their problems with their siblings.

8. Summarize

Homework

- Think about your children. Do they have the characteristics of resilient kids?
- On the basis of what you have learned, are there things that you would like to change? Stress that parents will not be asked to disclose information about their families.

Session 2 — Raising Resilient Children
The Importance of Routines

Objective

- Develop an understanding that structure in the family is important.

Activities

1. Give a minilecture concerning Why children need order. Stress the following:

- A family schedule is important. When does the family get out of bed? Eat meals? Go shopping? Do homework? Watch television? Go to bed?
- The structure imposed by a schedule provides the child with a sense of security that grows out of feeling that the world is predictable.
- Structure is not just about schedules, however. Structure includes the people in a child's life.
- Children need to feel secure about the people in their lives. When will parents be in the home?
- Do parents who live in the home as well as outside the home keep their word? Do parents who live out of the home as a result of divorce or separation keep their word? Is the home frequented by strangers (e.g., mother's or father's boyfriends or girlfriends?) Do the children know who will be in the home when they wake up?
- Structure is about schedules and people. It is also about the roles that people play in the family. Children need know who is in charge. Boyfriends and girlfriends should be precluded from being in charge unless they are in the home on a full time basis. If possible, siblings should not be put in charge of siblings. However, if the parents are out of the house and no baby sitter is present, it may important to place one sibling in charge.
- Structure is also about safety. Children need to feel secure in their own home. They need to know what to do in threatening situations out of the home. They should know how to dial 911. They should

246

know how to answer the telephone when a stranger calls. They should know what to do when they are approached on the street to keep themselves safe. They should know what to do when they hear a gunshot and when there is a fight. Children need to be able to cope with their home and neighborhood. Use Overhead 13-4, Helping Children Feel Secure.

3. Indicate that feeling secure also means that children must believe that they are not going to be abused in their own home. Tell participants that discipline will be discussed next week but that harsh punishment takes away from the child's feeling of security. Define *harsh discipline* as ridicule, physical, and emotional abuse.

4. Stress that in training children to be safe, it is not enough to describe situations. Children need to practice if they are to act appropriately in dangerous situations. Demonstrate role-playing strategy as a tool in teaching children new habits:

- Assign one of the parents to take the role of a child walking down the street. The leader assumes the role of a would be molester in a car. The car stops by the child who is walking along the street and asks child for directions. The child gives the directions, but stranger pretends not to hear and asks child to come closer. When child gets closer the stranger grabs the child (this takes a millisecond).
- After the role-play discuss why practice is necessary to avoid the situation they just observed. Children are too trusting and too naïve. They must be taught that not everyone can be trusted and that certain situations should be avoided or handled carefully.

5. Have parents share what they do to cope with establishing schedules, defining roles, and ensuring security. Ask for examples regarding ways parents use to prepare their children to cope with strangers. Be alert for inadequate strategies. Most parents do not do a good job in this area. They provide simple warnings, and children need to be prepared with specific strategies.

6. Summarize.

Homework

Think about the nature of your interactions with your children. What percentage of them are positive, encouraging, or reinforcing, and what percent are negative? Are any of them harsh?

Session 3 - Disciplining for Resiliency (I)
Objective
- Introduce alternatives to harsh punishment.

Activities

1. Give a minilecture regarding the impact of harsh punishment which is defined as verbal abuse (you're a fat cow), emotional abuse (I don't love you because you are so stupid), and physical punishment that leaves marks

or is excessive in any way (better not to use at all). These approaches

- teach the child that they are powerless and lower self-esteem;
- legitimize aggression by teaching children it is okay to verbally or physically abuse others;
- result in displaced aggression, that is the children may verbally or physically abuse others;
- alienate children from their parents - we avoid abusive people; and
- Strengthens the peer group (as parents' influence wanes and that of peers grows).

2. Explain that sometimes the home environment is punitive, even when there is no verbal or physical abuse. Children need positive interactions with the adults in their lives for their emotional development.

3. Explain that children may conclude that no one cares because there is no expression of love and may seek it elsewhere.

4. Discuss what to do if a child misbehaves. Distribute Handout 13-2 Disciplining without Violence and use Overhead 13-6, Positive Approaches to Discipline. Positive approaches to discipline include

- positive reinforcement (rewards for appropriate behavior);
- encouragement (focus on the efforts and the overall worth of the child); and
- non-contingent rewards (positive expressions of love not related to behavior).

4. Discuss what if the child misbehaves (Handout 13-2, Disciplining without Violence). Review the five approaches on this handout. Ask parents to tell when they have used each of them.

5. Summarize.

Homework

Consider ways that you might use some of the approaches discussed in this session.

Session 4 — Disciplining for Resiliency (II)

Objective

- Continue to teach parents how to replace harsh methods of punishment with positive approaches.

Activities

1. Discuss the importance of setting expectations for how children are to behave at home and in school. For example, children should be told how they are expected to treat their siblings, other children, and adults. This behavior should be taught through modeling. Children should also be told how they are expected to behave in school. Behavior such as punctuality, thoroughness, accuracy, and demonstrating respect for others should be reinforced. When these behaviors are not practiced, the children should be

punished using logical consequences or restitution.

    2. Discuss the importance of consistency. Use the following techniques:

- Tell parents to set expectations and enforce them every time the child does not meet them.
- Catch your children being good. Reinforce them when they do not expect it.
- Use at least one encouraging statement each day.
- Negotiate consequences.
- Tell your children that you love them and that you are glad they are yours.

    3. Emphasize that it is not necessary to use all of the techniques. Note: Be sensitive to cultural differences in beliefs about the roles of children. For example, some Asian American parents may like the idea of negotiating logical consequences. Stress that they can still use this approach, but without the negotiation, by setting logical consequences in advance.

    4. Summarize.

Homework

Try one of the approaches that has been discussed.

Session 5 — Helping Your Child Be A Better Student

Objective

- Provide parents with specific strategies for improving their children's academic performance.

Activities

    1. Emphasize to parents that children draw conclusions about the importance of school from their family and peers. Ask, have you ever

- talked about how little your education meant?
- talked about how you misbehaved in school?
- attributed your success to luck instead of school?
- diminished the importance of schooling in getting a job?
- told how you just got by in school or didn't take school seriously?

    2. If the answers to these questions are Yes, you are teaching your child that school is not important with your verbal behavior. Then ask participants if they

- read to their children?
- take them to museums, zoos, or other places where they will learn new things?
- buy educational toys or games for them?
- talk to children about current events?
- encourage them to watch educational television, or better yet, watch it with them?
- talk to them about the role education played in the lives of famous people?

If the answers to these questions are yes, tell parents they are teaching their children that education is important through your behavior.

3. Pass out Handout 13-3, Helping Your Student at Home. Have parents share successful strategies that they have used on their children.

4. Summarize this session as well as others.

Homework

Try some the new strategies introduced in this session to promote children's achievement.

Summary

Involving parents in the educational process can lead to positive results in the classroom. Parents who have the most chaotic home situations should be targeted because their children are risk both educationally and psychologically.

References

Adler, A. (n.d.). *Building resiliency.* Palm Beach, FL: Palm Beach County School District.

Brown, D. (1997). The implications of cultural values for cross-cultural consultation with families. *Journal of Counseling and Development, 76,* 29-35.

Campbell, J. R., & Mandel, F. (1990). Connecting math achievement to parental achievement. *Contemporary Educational Psychology, 15,* 64-74.

Chen, C., & Uttal, D. H. (1988). Cultural values, parents' beliefs, and children's achievement in the United States and China. *Human Development, 31,* 351-358.

Chia, R. C. (1989). Pilot study: Family values of American versus Chinese American parents. *Aapa Journal, 13,* 8-11.

Cowen, E. L., & Work, W. C. (1988). Resilient children, psychological wellness, and primary prevention. *American Journal of Community Psychology, 16,* 591-607.

Floyd, C. (1996). Achieving despite the odds. A study of resilience among a group of African American high school seniors. *Journal of Negro Education, 65,* 181-189.

Gonzales, N. A., Cauce, A. M., Friedman, R. J., & Mason, C. A. (1996). Family, peer, and neighborhood influences on academic achievement among African American adolescents: One-year prospective effects. *Journal of Community Psychology, 24,* 365-387.

Halle, T. G., Kurtz-Costes, B., & Mahoney, J. L. (1997). Family influences on school achievement in low-income African American children, *Journal of Educational Psychology, 89,* and 527-537.

Keith, P. B., & Lichtman, M. V. (1994). Does parental involvement influence academic achievement of eighth graders? Results from the National Education Longitudinal Study. *School Psychology Quarterly, 9,* 256-273.

Ji, G., Jiao, S, & Jing, Q. (1993). Expectancy of Chinese parents and children's cognitive abilities. *International Journal of Psychology, 28,* 821-830.

Johnson, S. T. (1992). Extra-school factors in achievement, attainment, and aspirations among junior and senior high-school-age African American youths. *Journal of Negro Education, 61,* 99-119.

Okagaki, L., Frensch, P. A., & Gordan, E. W. (1995). Encouraging school achievement in Mexican-American children. *Hispanic Journal of Behavioral Science, 17,* 160-179.

Peng, S. S., & Wright, D. (1994). Explanation of academic achievement of Asian American students. *Journal of educational Research, 87,* 346-352.

Rak, C. F., & Patterson, L. E. (1996) Promoting resiliency in at-risk children. *Journal of Counseling and Development, 74,* 368-373.

Werner, E. E., & Smith, R. S. (1982). *Vulnerable but invincible.* New York: McGraw-Hill.

Positive Approaches to Discipline

1. Positive reinforcement includes nonverbal verbal praise, monetary rewards, food, or the offer of a fun activity for doing a job well. Examples are:

    a. You did a great job when you cleaned up your room. (verbal praise)

    b. Because I got a nice note from your teacher, I'm taking you to MacDonald's for lunch. (food)

    c. I'm adding a dollar to your allowance because you did so well this grading period. (money)

    d. You did such a great job on the test I've arranged for you to go to the park to play with your friends. (fun activity)

    e. A smile when the child has done well or a pat on the back. Hugs, kisses, and winks can also be used.

2. Noncontingent positive reinforcement is positive verbal and nonverbal interactions that are not related to behavior. Examples are:

    a. I love you.

    b. I'm proud that you are my child.

    c. We have problems, but I still think you are great.

    d. A touch of any kind.

3. Encouragement involves expressing faith in the child's ability to do school work or deal with a difficult situation. Examples are:

    a. I know the test will be hard, but I'm sure you do well if you do your best.

    b. I know you have trouble getting along with Mykala, but I have confidence in your ability to deal with your problems.

    c. No matter what others say, I have faith in you.

Disciplining Without Violence

1. Time out: Children are removed from situations in which they are causing problems (e.g., fighting with a brother or sister) and placed in a quiet place (with no radio, TV, computer games for a specified period of time). For example, "Both of you go to your quiet places for 15 minutes. I'll tell you when time is up." This should be done firmly, but without physical or verbal abuse.

2. Ignoring: Minor misbehavior (slamming a door) should be ignored. Later, show the child how to close the door properly.

3. Natural consequences: This is when parents allow the social or physical environment to punish the child. For example, the child does not put on warm coat on cold day. The result is the child gets cold and learns that it is wise to dress warmly. Do not use natural consequences with schoolwork or when the child's health or well-being is in danger.
4. Logical consequences: Punishment for misbehavior is logically linked to the misbehavior. This works best when the punishment is negotiated in advance with the child. For example, a child might be asked:
    a. What should I do if you fail to do your schoolwork? (logical consequence = more time on school work.)
    b. What should happen if you are late to dinner? (logical consequence = no dinner or cold dinner.)
    c. What should happen if I have to do some of your work? (logical consequence = you do something for me.)
5. Restitution - This is a special case of logical consequences (see 4-c above). It involves making up in some way the results of misbehavior. Examples:
    a. A child breaks a another child's toy. (restitution = replace the toy out of allowance)
    b. School property is damaged. (restitution = repair or replace the damaged property)
    c. A student leaves the kitchen in a mess and mom cleans. (restitution = help mom prepare dinner)

Handout 13-3

Helping Your Student At Home

1. When your child goes to preschool or kindergarten tell and teach him or her to:
   • Follow the rules
         • Listen to the teacher
         • Do all of the assigned work
         • Do his or her best
         • Treat everyone with respect
         • Ask questions
2. Restate all of these expectations regularly until they are learned.
3. Make statement to show you value education on a regular basis.
4. Do things that show you value education such as
         • Read instead of watching TV and you read to the child.
         • Watch educational TV
         • Buy educational toys
         • Take your child to plays and museums.

- Share your own educational experiences with the child in a positive way

5. Monitor your child's education by:
- Meeting with teachers and others to check on the progress of your child (It is your right.).
- Making sure that your child is being taught in his or her first language.
- Ask that your child be evaluated if you believe he or she has a learning problem.
- If your child is on an Individual Educational Plan check to make sure it is implemented.
- Asking for biweekly progress reports if your child is having problems.

6. Collaborate with the teacher if the child is performing poorly academically.

7. Teach preschoolers to:
- Count to 10 and higher as the child gets older.
- Recognize the letters in the alphabet and the sounds associated with them.
- Pick out simple words (e.g., boy, girl, dog, cat, cow, sheep, etc.).
- Identify colors.
- Recognize different types of animals.
- Put puzzles together.
- Recognize shapes such as circles and triangles and to match these shapes to similar shapes.
- Cut and paste.
- Draw simple figures such as animals, people, houses, etc.
- Sit quietly and work alone for up to 15 minutes.
- Listen to what is said and repeat it (e.g., question child about the content and meaning of fun and interesting television programs.)
- Anticipate what will happen next in a story (e.g., read a part of a story and then ask the child, "What will happen next?")
- Match the words in stories with the pictures in the book (e.g., where is the cow?)
- Identify the feelings the characters in a story have? (e.g., how was the boy feeling when his friends left him?)
- What is good and bad in stories? (e. g., should the girl in the story have taken the toy?)

8. Children in kindergarten and first grade should be asked about school each day. If they seem to be having trouble, teachers should be contacted and suggestions obtained for improving learning at home. For example, if a

child is having trouble with alphabet, have the child circle all the As in a newspaper or magazine article. Then all the Bs and so forth. If the money is available, purchase toys that teach the letters of the alphabet and play games with the child. These toys are often available used at garage sales.

9. Have children read to you on a regular basis. Check for comprehension by asking questions about what was read.

10. When a child is assigned homework, ask the child to establish a time to do the homework. Check the homework for completion and accuracy. Tutor the child if necessary. Never do the homework for your child.

Overhead 13-1

Characteristics of Resilient Students

- Has good interpersonal skills and can deal with social problems.
    - Is alert and can function independently. *
    - Can gain attention in positive ways. **
    - Is an active problem solver.
    - Is optimistic.
    - Enjoys new experiences.
    - Is cheerful.
    - Is self-confident.
    - Understands the feelings of others. ***
    - Has a sense of humor. ****
    - Cares about other people.
    - Is responsible.
    - Is self-disciplined.
     * In cultures with a collateral value the resilient student functions within the family structure at home, but can function independently at school.
    ** In families that value humility, resilient children will not call attention to themselves.
   *** In cultures that value self-control, children may not acknowledge that they understand the feelings of others because they do not wish to embarrass them.
  **** A sense of humor is culturally appropriate.

Family Factors That Produce Resilient Students

1. The family establishes clear expectations for behavior and enforces those expectations.
2. Children are monitored on an ongoing basis.
3. Parents openly demonstrate that they care about the children on an ongoing basis.
4. Discipline is evenhanded and fair, and not harsh and sporadic. Love is not withdrawn as a means of punishment.
5. The family does not abuse alcohol, use drugs, and does not condone their use by their students.
6. The family is stable and marital conflict is minimal.
7. There are four or fewer children spaced at least four years apart.
8. There is focused nurturing during the first year of life and little separation from the caregiver.
9. A social support network including relatives and others who have similar values is available.
10. A nurturing sibling or other confidant is available to the child.

Family Factors That Put Students at Risk

- Drug and alcohol abuse
- Witnessing physical and verbal violence at home
- Physical or emotional abuse or neglect
- Sexual molestation
- Negative and conflicted relationships with parents
- Frequent moves
- Poverty
- Child feels unloved
- Child has no role in home (e.g., chores)
- Child has no space of his or her own
- Family membership unstable
- No clear roles for parents and children
- Erratic, inconsistent discipline
- Interactions with parents mostly negative
- Not enough social support from relatives and others

Overhead 13-4

Helping Children Feel Secure

SITUATION	WHAT CHILD SHOULD DO
1. Home alone	Lock all doors and windows
2. Fire, attempted break in	Dial 911
3. Sibling becomes very ill	Dial 911
3. Stranger calls	Tell them an adult is in but unavailable
4. Stranger knocks	Do not answer the door
5. Approached by stranger	Maintain distance; run and yell; dial 911
	Go to safe house (community watch signs)
6. Gunshot	Run away from the shot
7. Fight	Stay away from the fights
8. To be picked up at school	Only ride with approved people
9. In the neighborhood	Walk in groups, not alone

Overhead 13-5

Positive Interactions with Children

Positive reinforcement: Saying positive things to children when they have done things well. Also involves giving children money, food, or arranging for fun events when they do something well. It is also called contingentreinforcement.

Noncontingent positive reinforcement: Saying positive things or doing positive things to children that are not relate to their performance such as telling a child, "I love you."

Encouragement: Verbally focusing on the worth or potential of the child. Examples of encouragement are: "I have faith in your ability to work out your problems with your sister" or "I am confident that you can do well in first grade if you work hard."

Chapter Fourteen

Resisting Peer Pressure to Underachieve: A Refusal Skills Group

Peer pressure results from the subtle and overt attempts by students within the same general age range to influence the attitudes and behaviors of other students. Peer group pressure occurs when students in cliques, clubs, teams, or other associations engage in efforts to influence the functioning of specific group members. Although the concept of peer pressure is often thought of in negative terms, peer group pressure on students can also be positive (i.e., you should refrain from cheating). Helping students cope with peer pressure is often associated with the prevention of substance abuse (e.g., Jensen, 1992; Sabatini, 1989), sexually transmitted diseases such as AIDS (e.g., Votey, 1989), or smoking (Herrmann & McWhirter, 1997). However, anecdotal reports from school counselors suggest that peer pressure plays a major role in underachievement for many students.

Susceptibility to peer pressure seems to go up as self-esteem, assertiveness, parental support, and the availability of positive role models go down (Isaacs & Duffus, 1995). Moreover, many students have neither thought about the need to resist peer pressure nor developed the skills to do so (Herrmann & McWhirter, 1997). Fortunately, as the literature review by Herrmann and McWhirter (1997) suggested, as early as third grade students can be taught refusal skills that will enable them to resist pressure to engage in self-destructive behaviors. Their review also suggested that programs of this type work best when they are supported by the participants' peer group(s), and when they are a part of a comprehensive effort to deal with a specific concern.

Core Refusal Skills

Goldstein, Reagles, and Amann (1990) identified 20 core refusal skills. These core skills were selected from among a broader set of social skills because they seemed to be most pertinent to the refusal skills of students. The skills they identified are:

1. Asking for help	11. Responding to teasing
2. Giving directions	12. Avoiding trouble with others

3. Persuading others	13. Staying out of fights
4. Understanding your feelings*	14. Dealing with embarrassing situations*
5. Communication your feelings	15. Dealing with rejection*
6. Coping with the anger of others	16. Responding to persuasion
7. Coping with your own fear*	17. Responding to failure*
8. Exerting self-control*	18. Dealing with accusations
9. Standing up for your rights	19. Preparing for a confrontation
10. Responding to peer pressure	20. Making a decision

The core skills marked with an asterisk (*) involve teaching students to deal with their own thoughts and emotions. These skills must be used in emotionally charged, dynamic situations involving other students or adults. In order to learn the 20 skills listed students must learn to STOP their thoughts and behaviors and gain control of their emotions, LISTEN to others to determine what is being asked of them, DECIDE what they wish to do about the request that is being made, and ACT, either by refusing to comply or responding positively to the request or pressure. Many of the skills just identified will be addressed in the following section.

Selecting a Leader

Professionally-led groups can produce some excellent results, but there is some evidence that peer leaders get better results than professional leaders (Herrmann & McWhirter, 1997). Peer leaders did as well or better than groups led by professionals across cultural contexts and age-groups according to these authors. Although Herrmann and McWhirter did not mention refusal skills groups co-led by professionals and peer leaders, this is an option. Co-leading should be considered as a leadership strategy that may make refusal skills groups more effective.

Establishing a Refusal Skills Group

The typical approach to forming groups is recruiting group members from throughout the school, placing them in closed-ended groups, and terminating the group after a specific number of sessions. The recommendation regarding underachievers is somewhat at variance with this procedures. Begin by identifying cliques of underachievers and place them in a group together. Cliques are informal groups of 2 or more friends that influence each other's behavior. If possible, groups should be composed of a single clique, but more than one clique can be placed in a group. There are some dangers associated with this approach, the main one being that a clique may decide to resist efforts to redirect their achievement behavior, but proper screening can reduce this problem.

Teachers should be surveyed and asked to identify groups of underachievers who seem to be friends or associates. Once groups are identified, all members of the groups should be invited to a screening interview that involves the following steps:

1. Discuss confidentiality: No confidentiality can be guaranteed in this group.
2. Explain the purposes of the group. These are to help students improve their academic achievement and to develop refusal skills that can be used to resist peer pressure.
3. Identify the refusal skills to be taught. These include
   - out right refusal,
   - out right refusal with a rationale,
   - refusal with an excuse (preferred by many adolescents),
   - leaving the situation,
   - negotiation (increasingly used as students get older), and
   - avoidance (although not assertive preferred by many adolescents).

Another objective is for the group to develop "peer pressure" for higher levels of achievement.

This will be done by encouraging cooperation in the academic achievement area.

4. Get commitment to participate in the group by all members of the clique. However, if most students agree to participate, the clique can be included although those that do not agree should be excluded from the groups
5. If other cliques are to be included in the refusal skills group, determine if there are groups of students in the school that should not be placed in the same group.
6. Determine the tentative meeting time and the length of the meetings. (30 minutes for elementary school students and 30 to 45 minutes for older students).
7. Discuss the rules and sign contracts.

Figure 14-1

Sample Group Contract

1. We agree to participate in the group.
2. We agree to abide by the following rules:
    a. Be on time.
    b. Respect others by listening.
    c. No put-downs such as laughing at someone or making fun of others.
3. We agree to provide support for others, particularly our friends, who are trying to improve their grades.

Signed
Student 1 _____
Student 2 _____
Student 3 _____
Student 4 _____
Student 5 _____
Student 6 _____
Leader _____
Date _____

Group 1 — Getting Started

Objectives
- Introduce students to each other (if more than one clique is involved in the group).
- Review group objectives.
- Review the rules.
- Define peer pressure and discuss how other students apply it.
- Define refusal skills

Activities

1. Conduct an introductory exercise that requires each student to tell the group members one thing about himself or herself that they may not know.

2. Give a minilecture outlining the objectives of the group and why they are important. The objectives of the group are to
- teach about peer pressure;
- teach strategies for resisting peer pressure to do things that will lower your grades; and
- help all students set higher achievement goals and attain those goals.

3. Brainstorm a definition of peer pressure and have students give examples of when they have been pressured by other students. Then ask

them to tell what they did in response to the pressure. Ask students if they have ever done anything that they really didn't want to do as a result of peer pressur. Ask if peer pressure is always bad. Have them give examples of times when peer pressure has helped them.

4. Distribute Handout 14-1, Six Ways to Say No When You Do Not want to Do Something! Ask if students have ever used any of the techniques identified in the handout in their efforts to resist pressure.

5. Why does peer pressure work? Why would people do things that they really don't want to do?

- Students want to "fit in."
- Students want to be included.
- Students do not want to feel odd or different.
- Students do not want to be lonely.
- Students do not want to be bored.
- Students want friends, sometimes boyfriends or girlfriends.

Homework

Observe peer pressure at work this week. Bring in examples of peer pressure to discuss next week.

Session 2 — Understanding Peer Pressure

Objectives

- Increase students' understanding of how peer pressure is applied.
- Raise students' awareness that they are involved in applying peer pressure.
- Begin the process of developing the skills needed to resist peer pressure.

Activities

1. Discuss what students observed as a result of the homework assignment.

2. Ask, "When and where did you observe students trying to pressure others and how were they doing it?"

3. Brainstorm a list of methods that people use to pressure others..

4. Ask if girls apply peer pressure differently than boys? Now give students Handout 14-2, How Peer Pressure Is Applied. Ask if any of the students engage in any of the behaviors that are listed on Handout 14-2.

Homework

Observe yourself this week. When friends ask you to do things you do not wish to do,what do you do?

Session 3 — Reasons to Resist Peer Pressure to Underachieve
Objectives
- Have students identify the reasons why people apply pressure to others.
- Have students identify the reasons why they may wish to
  resist peer pressure and the skills they will need to resist pressure.

Activities

1. Discuss why some students try to pressure others to do as they wish. Why would a friend want you to do poorly in school? Possible answers include

- power trip: Some people like to manipulate others.
- misery loves company: If they have low grades they may not want to see others succeed.
- phony friends: They do not respect you as a person.
- may want to get you into trouble: Some people are mean to others.

2. Follow up on the homework assignment. What are the reasons why you may want to resist peer pressure that will lead to lower academic performance?

- you may be embarrassed by what you do (e.g., cut class) or by a low or failing grade.
- you may make teachers/parents angry and lose their support.
- you may bring shame to your family, group, or tribe.
- you may not be allowed to participate in school activities if GPA is too low.
- you may not be promoted or graduate from grade level.
- you may have to go to summer school to make up failing grades or low test scores.
- you may be suspended from school for some things.
- you will feel better about yourself if you do what you think is right because you are in charge.
- you will gain respect for being strong.

3. Discuss the skills students will need to develop to resist pressures that will lower your academic achievement.

You need to know your rights. You have a right to
- (a) say no to any request without giving the reasons (although you may wish to explain);
- (b) to do as well in school as your ability allows;
- (c) to go to school in a hassle free environment;
- (d) to leave any situation in which a person is asking you to do something you do not wish to do; and
- (e) to have friends that do not pressure to do poorly in school.

- You need the skills to communicate that you do not want to do what is asked.
- You need the skill to walk away, even when being verbally attacked

by one or more students.
- You need the skill to seek help if you are being threatened.
- You need the skills to make friends and to end relationships with friends that are not helpful.

Homework

For next week, think about your ability to refuse requests aimed at getting you to do something you do not wish to do..

Session 4 — Assessing the Skill to Resist Peer Pressure

Assess students' refusal skills using paper and pencil and role-playing. Introduce the STOP-LISTEN-DECIDE-ACT model.

Activities

1. Explain that people who have good refusal skills STOP when they feel that others are trying to persuade them to do something they do not wish to do (peers applying pressure), LISTEN to make sure what is being suggested, DECIDE if they wish to do it, and ACT by either refusing to do or doing what is asked. Today you will be asked to use these steps in the group.

2. Ask, "What did you decide about your ability to refuse suggestions or requests to do things that you do not wish to do?" Go around the circle and ask students to rate their ability to refuse requests using a 1 to10 scale, with 1 meaning almost no ability and 10 meaning a very high ability to refuse requests

3. Ask students to complete Handout 14-3, Do I Give Into Peer Pressure? Have group members provide feedback. Are they good answers? Would they work? What would work?

4. Select one student at a time to role-play his or her refusal skills. Select the individual who is to demonstrate his or her skills first and ask him or her to leave the room. Tell two of the students that they are going to try to apply pressure on the student to skip school tomorrow. The other students in the group are asked to observe the student who is demonstrating his or her skills and give feedback about whether they do a good job and to make suggestions for improvement. Tell the students to ask themselves did the student who is demonstrating refusal skills STOP, LISTEN to get the facts, DECIDE, and ACT. Bring student back into room and tell him or her that two friends have a request.

During role-playing, the leader should serve as a director. For example, if the students who are applying the pressure are not being persuasive enough, ask them to turn up the heat and be more demanding and persuasive.

5. Repeat the role playing with each student using the following situations:
- Ask a student to allow another student to copy during an examination.

- Ask a student to cut a class and smoke (select students who smoke for this role-play).
- Have students make fun of student who has just gotten a good grade.
- There is an important test the next day. A student is asked to go to a party that will last past midnight.
- Take homework from a student and step on it.
- Call a student on the telephone and ask him or her to come over during studytime.
- A student has asked teacher for help. Other students make fun of him for trying to "get over" (get on the teacher's good side) with the teacher by asking for help.
- A student answers a very difficult question. Other students snicker and whisper "nerd."

Homework

Practice responding to students who put you down when you do something well in the classroom.

Session 5 — Learning Refusal Skills

Objective

Students will learn refusal skills through role-playing.

Activities

1. Reintroduce Handout 14 -1, Six Ways to Say No When You Do Not Want to Do Something! and tell students they need to master all of the strategies on the handout and apply them in the STOP, LISTEN, DECIDE, and ACT approach.

2. Reintroduce the role-plays from last week. Role-play each of the situations again several times with students responding with each of the strategies listed on the sheet. Have the students who are applying peer pressure be very insistent that the student who is the target of the role-play do as they wish. Ask students who are observing determine if the role player has used one of the strategies suggested in Handout 14-1 and the STOP, LISTEN, DECIDE, ACT. In all of the role-playing situations listed below, the student should decide to refuse the request. Show Overhead14-1, Stop, Listen, Decide, Act to illustrate how they are to respond.

a. Outright refusal.	No thank you. I don't want to do that.
b. Refusal with a rationale.	I don't want to do that. I have other things to do.
c. Refusal with an excuse.	I don't want to do that. My parents would be angry.
d. Leaving the situation.	I'm leaving now.

| e. Negotiation | I'll go over to your house, but I don't want to drink. |
| f. Avoidance | (You stay away from people who ask you to do things you do not wish to do.) |

3. Have students generate situations that they encounter and role-play methods of responding.

Homework

Ask students to commit to monitor each other's refusal skills. This means that all they do is observe, not intervene by commenting and giving advice.

Group 6 — Doing Better in School Through Cooperation and Support

Objectives

- Increase the academic goals of the participants.
- Gain peer support for attaining these goals.

Activities

1. Review the results of the homework assignment. What did the students observe?

2. Bring in reports from teachers, end of grade tests, and report cards and other data that will allow you and the students to determine their current achievement level.

3. Discuss the implications of students' current achievement patterns, but do not dwell on them if they are poor.

4. Ask students to think about what they are capable of doing and have them reset their academic goals.

5. Ask students to brainstorm how they can assist each other to achieve their goals. Make a list of strategies that they might use to help others.

6. Ask students to set one or more goals to improve their behavior and write these on Handout 14-4, Setting Goals for Increased Achievement. Make sure that their goals meet the following criteria:

    a. Goal is measurable: You will be able to tell when you attain it.

    b. Goal has a timeline attached: I want to accomplish this by X date.

    c. Goal is realistic: When goals are set too high, they become sources of frustration when they are not achieved.

7. Have students who agree to help students with their goals sign Handout 14-4 and collect these.

Homework

Cooperate with each other to improve your achievement. This means not applying pressure to do things that will interfere with do better in school

267

and helping others with schoolwork whenever possible.

Sessions 7 to 10 — Follow Up (these sessions can be shorter that previous sessions)

Objectives
- Monitor progress toward academic goals.
- Determine if refusal skills are being utilized.

Activities

1. Review progress toward goals using student self-reports and reports from teachers.

2. Ask if students are using their refusal skills.

3. Ask students if there are other areas of peer pressure they would like to work on. Stress that habits such as drinking and use of other illegal substances (alcohol usage is illegal for individuals under 21 years old) keep people from doing their best in school.

4. Practice refusal skills in role-playing as needed.

5. Congratulate those students who are making progress and encourage those who are not.

Homework

Continue to work toward academic goals and be supportive of each other. Use refusal skills. "Use them or lose them" applies here.

Summary

In this chapter, one of the problems that causes some able students to underachieve–peer pressure–was addressed. Refusal skills groups made up of cliques of underachievers can be used to build positive pressure for increased achievement.

References

Bleuer, J.C. (1987). *Counseling underachievers.* Greensboro, NC: University of North Carolina at Greensboro, ERIC Clearinghouse on Counseling and Student Services.

Bleuer, J.C., Palomares, S., & Walz, G.R. (1993). *Activities for counseling underachievers.* Greensboro, NC: University of North Carolina at Greensboro, ERIC Clearinghouse on Counseling and Student Services.

Goldstein, A. P., Reagles, K. W., & Amann, L. L. (1990). *Refusal skills: Preventing drug use in adolescents.* Champaign, IL: Research Press.

Herrmann, D. S., & McWhirter, J. J. (1997). Refusal and resistance skills for children and adolescents: A selected review. *Journal of Counseling and Development, 75,* 177-187.

Isaacs, M. D., & Duffus, L. R. (1995). Scholars' club: A culture of achievement among minority students. *The School Counselor, 42,* 204-210.

Jensen, M. A. (1992). School programming for the prevention of addictions. *The School Counselor, 39,* 202-210.

Lavin, P. (1997). A daily classroom checklist for communication with parents of children with attention deficit hyperactivity disorder. *The School Counselor, 44,* 315-318.

Sabatini. L. (1989). Preparing eighth graders for the social pressures of high school. *The School Counselor, 36,* 203-207.

Votey, S. (1989). Helping sophomores to say "no": An assertiveness training program for sophomores. *The School Counselor, 36,* 198-202.

Six Ways to Say No When You Don't Want to Do Something!

Method	*How It Sounds*
• Outright refusal.	No thank you. I don't want to do that.
• Refusal with a rationale.	I don't want to do that. I have other things to do.
• Refusal with an excuse.	I don't want to do that. My parents would be angry.
• Leaving the situation.	I'm leaving now.
• Negotiation	I'll go over to your house, but I don't want to drink
• Avoidance	(Avoid people who ask you to do things you do not wish to do.)

How Peer Pressure is Applied

a. Modeling the behavior they want you to imitate by "showing off" and calling attention to it: Look at this great shirt (these shoes, this car, or this tattoo). I'm cool (bad or some other complement to themselves).

b. Threat: If you don't do as I tell you I will hurt you.

c. Subtle pressure: If you don't do as I suggest "we" won't let you come to "our" party. (I won't like you anymore or you won't be my best friend).

d. Verbal abuse: You're a nerd (chicken, momma's boy or much worse) if you don't do as I suggest.

e. Avoidance: When you do (not do) as they wish, they avoid you.

g. Phony praise: You find yourself the object of their attention and they say nice things. Then they make requests directly or subtly.

Do I Give Into Peer Pressure?

Several situations that you may face are listed below. In the lefthand side is a request from a friend. You are to assume that you do not wish to do what the friend asks. What would you say? Write what you would say in the space provided after your "friend's" request.

You know you have homework to do, and your friend makes one of the following requests:

Simple Request: *Your answer:*
Let's go over to my house and   _____
play with our new computer.   _____

Let's cut class. It's boring anyway._____

Let me copy your homework?
I forgot to do mine.   _____

Incentive Request
If we go over to my house and
play with our new computer,
I'll let you use it first.   _____

Let's cut class. I'll let you drive
my car.   _____

If you let me copy your homework,
I'll do it next time and you
can copy it.   _____

Altruistic Request to Do Good
You'll learn a bunch of good stuff
if we go over to my house and play
with our new computer.   _____

Let's cut class and go visit Jamal.
He's at home sick and could use
the company.   _____

Let me copy your homework. You'll be saving my
life if you do because my parents are going to be real
angry if they find out I didn't do it. _____

Coercive Request
I'm not going to be your friend
if you don't go with me to play
with our new computer.   _____

Let's cut class. I'll tell our friend
what a momma's boy or girl you are
if you don't go with me.   _____

Let's cut class. I'm going to tell
your mom what you did last Saturday
if you don't.   _____

Handout 14-4

Setting Goals for Increased Achievement

Name _____   Date _____

My goal for improving my academic achievement is as follows:

_____

_____

I want to achieve this goal by (date): _____
We agree to help
(student's name)_____
   achieve his goal being helpful, supportive, and not pressuring him
or her to do things that will interfere with her or his schoolwork:
   Student 1_____
   Student 2 _____
   Student 3 _____
   Student 4 _____
   Student 5 _____
   Student 6 _____

Chapter Fifteen

Helping High-Potential Underachieving Students Set Career and Educational Goals Using the Internet

The Internet is an exciting technological development that allows student support personnel and teachers to provide relatively inexpensive learning experiences for students. Sampson (1997) identified four specific uses of the Internet when providing career development services: (1) surfing the Internet to determine the range of information that is available, (2) using Internet addresses to obtain specific information, (3) searching using search engines, and (4) communicating via e-mail, chat rooms, and teleconferencing to gain information. For the most part, this discussion will focus on conducting searches on the Internet with addresses and search engines.

Advantages of using the Internet to facilitate the learning process include the immediacy of the response to queries, the interactive nature of the Internet, and, in some instances, the use of graphics to make the learning experience more interesting. Many students will have surfed the net for a variety of purposes, some of which may have related to schoolwork (e.g., conducting research for a term paper). However, it is unlikely that most students, particularly bright underachievers, have used the Internet as a personal planning tool.

The use of the Internet to facilitate career and educational choices is largely unexplored. However, because of the nature of online resources, students can take inventories such as Career Key (http://www.ncsu.edu/careerkey) (Jones, 1997), gain access to resources such as the Occupational Outlook Handbook (http://stats.bls.gov.ocohome.htm) (BLS, 1998-1999), and get valuable information about scholarships and loans (e.g., http://www.studentservices.com.fastweb). Students can also explore college majors by visiting the home page of institutions that are of interest to them. This can be done by going to the home page of American Universities (http://www.clas.ufl.edu/CLAS/american-universities.html) and clicking on the first letter of the name of the college that the student wishes to explore. This will take the student to the home page of the college. After the home page of the college is reached, a student can point to appropriate topics and click with the mouse until the desired information is found. The American

Universities home page also provides "hot links" to the home pages of community colleges and international universities. This chapter addresses the use of Internet resources to help students set career and educational goals.

Why the focus on life goals? One reason is that underachievers often fail to set meaningful educational and career goals (Rathvon, 1996). Another reason that has already been noted in several places in this book, is that goals are an important source of motivation for students (Brown, 1998; Locke & Latham, 1990). This is particularly true of career goals. However, career goals must be established in tandem with educational goals if they are to be achieved because many of today's careers require education beyond high school. Students can use the Internet to measure their interests, find occupational information, get estimates of job trends, explore college majors, apply to colleges, find out about and apply for financial aid, and explore specific careers.

Establishing the High-Potential Underachiever/Internet Group

This small group activity is aimed at high potential, underachieving students in grades 7 through 12. Teachers should be asked to identify students who have the potential to go on to post-secondary education, but are achieving at one or two grades below their potential. This includes students who are getting Cs, but have the potential to get As, students who are getting Ds but have the potential to do Bs and students who are failing, but have the potential to get Cs.

Screening

After the names of high-potential underachieving students have been received they should be screened individually in 15-minute sessions. During the screening interview the students should be told that their teachers believe they have the potential to go on to postsecondary education, but that their current achievement levels may not be sufficient to pursue their goals. Then explain that the purpose of the group is to help students set goals to pursue careers that require attendance at community or 4-year colleges. Also tell students that much of the work of the group will take place on the Internet, but they are not required to have a computer at home to participate. However, include as many people in the group as possible that have a home computer connected to the Internet. If at least 50% of the students in the group have a computer, the group can form buddy teams and work on homework assignments together.

Signing a Contract

Students who wish to join the group should be asked to sign the contract shown in Figure 15-1.

Figure 15-1

Sample Contract for High-Potential Underachieving Students

I _____ agree to attend the group regularly and abide by the rules as established by the group and the leader. My goal for the group is to choose an occupation that requires some postsecondary education and draft a preliminary plan for attending a community or 4-year college to prepare for that occupation.

Signature	Date

Session 1 — Introduction to Educational and Career Planning

Objectives
- Provide an overview of the purposes of the group.
- Provide an opportunity for students to get acquainted.
- Introduce the Internet as a career and educational exploration tool.

Activities

1. Introduce the group session by highlighting the importance of goals. Ask students to share goals that they have set and pursued. Then ask them to share their educational and career goals at this time. Many will be unable to share these goals because they have not taken time to consider their options. If this is a classroom group, ask students to indicate if they plan to pursue some form of postsecondary education by raising their hands. Ask those students who have a definite career in mind to raise their hands. Ask students who are unsure about their plans for the future to raise their hands.

2. Indicate that an expected outcome of the group is that some students who have career and educational goals will change their minds and others will become more certain of their goals. Also, many of the students who are now unsure of their future will develop tentative plans.

3. Ask students to adopt as their goal for the group to identify possible educational and career goals and strategies for reaching their goals. If the students are juniors and seniors in high school, they should be asked to develop specific goals for their educational and career futures including the choice of a specific career and educational plan for entering that career.

4. Ask students how instrumental their parents will be in their educational and vocational choices. For some minorities, particularly Asian Americans, it is likely that parents will be heavily involved in the choice-making process. Encourage all students to discuss the options they are considering with their parents.

5. Identify the common mistakes of educational and career planning. These are:

- Students do not plan at all. Only one-third of today's workers planned to be in their current jobs. Not surprisingly, most of these people would plan if they had another opportunity.
- Students defer planning until later and miss opportunities. Some students believe that some life event will arouse their interests and tell them what to do. It doesn't happen that way.
- Students do what their friends do. Unless you are identical to your friend this is a big mistake.
- Students plan for their education but not their careers. Many students erroneously believe that their community college or 4-year college experience will automatically allow them to identify the career they should enter. Often this doesn't happen, particularly in liberal arts colleges.

6. Introduce the Internet as a source of information that can help students in their career and educational planning. Review Handout 15-1, Internet Terms Defined. If possible, provide a computer that is connected to the Internet for each student. If this is not possible, have the student who is most adept with computers show other students how to get online and use keyword searches and addresses to get information about careers using the following steps:

- Get online.
- Connect to the World Wide Web (www) using either NetScape Navigator, Microsoft Internet Explorer, or the software that your school is using to connect to the web.
- Show students how to enter a website address such as http://stats.bls.gov/ocohome.htm to find occupational information. This address is for the Occupational Outlook Handbook. For example, to enter a website address using Microsoft Internet Explorer, students would connect to the Internet and then click on an icon of the world under a magnifying glass. This brings up a screen with the word *Address* near the top of the screen. Click on the address it will turn blue. Then hit *delete* or *backspace* and the word *Address* will disappear. Then type in the address of the website the student wishes to visit and hit *enter* on the keyboard. The website will appear.
- Define *hot links* and show students how to surf the net using these links.

- Show students how to use keyword search strategies to find information when they do not have an address.

7. Summarize and give students Handout 15-2, Using the Internet in Educational and Career Planning.

Homework

Pair students who have computer skills and those who do not. Ask them to practice getting online and using addresses and keyword search strategies to find information on the web.

Session 2 — Exploring Interests Using the Career Key

Objectives

- Have students identify their interests using the Career Key.
- Teach students to go from the Career Key web site to the Occupational Outlook Handbook website to get occupational information.

Activities

1. Ask students to report their experiences on the Internet. If they have problems, reteach the skills they need to get on the Internet and use it as a source of information.

2. Introduce the idea of taking the Career Key on the Internet. (This exercise requires that every student have a computer that is linked to the Internet.) If not enough computers are available for all students, have some people take the online version of Career Key and others take a paper-and-pencil version of it. In order to give students a pencil-and-paper version of career key you must either download it from the Internet on to your computer or get a hard copy from the NC State Occupational Information Coordinating Committee) can be reached 919-733-6700 in Raleigh, NC). Adobe Acrobat Reader software must be downloaded from the website (http:www.adobe.com/prodindex/acrobat/readstep.html) before a usable hard copy can be printed. This software is available free of charge at the website.

Note: The Career Key was developed by Lawrence Jones of North Carolina State University to measure the dimensions of John Holland's typology. It yields scores on each of Holland's types: realistic, investigative, artistic, social, enterprising, and social types. If you are not familiar with Holland's ideas, you may explore them by reading his book *Making Vocational Choices* (3rd Ed.) (1997). Psychological Assessment Resources, Odessa, FL publishes this book.

3. The website address for Career Key (Jones, 1997) is http://www.ncsu.edu/careerkey (do not enter a period at the end of the address). Have students enter this address and follow the directions as they take the Career Key.

4. Once students have identified several occupational choices, have

them click on one of the hot links that takes them to that occupation in the Occupational Outlook Handbook. This process should be repeated until they have identified two or three occupations that they would like to explore further. Have them complete Handout 15-3, Occupational Summary Sheet, as they explore occupations.

5. Summarize.

Homework

Have students continue to explore the occupations that that they have identified. This can be done on the Internet or by talking to people in the occupation. They should complete Handout 15-4, About Your Career. It may also be possible for students to go into one of the chat rooms and ask if anyone in the room is in the occupation they are interested in pursuing. However, if at all possible, students should be asked to identify people in the occupation that they have chosen who can be interviewed face to face.

Session 3 — Choosing A Career

Objectives

- Have students make tentative career choices.
- Compare the women's choices to the men's choices.
- Provide information about the impact of sex-role stereotyping on women's career choices.

Activities

1. Ask students to report the results of the homework assignment.

2. Ask students to write down their top three occupational choices based on their Career Key results. Also ask them to place their gender (M=male; F=female) on the sheet, but not their names.

3. Record the choices, by gender, on the board. If you are working in a computer lab have students go to the Occupational Outlook Handbook (OOH) (http://stats.bls.go.ocohome.htm) and look up the average salary of each of the occupations listed. If not, bring in as many copies of the Occupational Outlook Handbook as possible and look up the average salaries of the occupations listed. Compute the average salaries for the boys and girls in the group. The typical result will be that the average salaries of the occupations selected by the males will be higher than the average salary of the occupations selected by females.

4. Introduce the fact that women make about 70% as much as men. The reasons for this are:

- An initial job choice with less earnings potential;
- less participation in the workplace because of childbearing and child rearing responsibilities; and
- discrimination in the workplace (e.g., accounting and law firms; management positions in business and industry (the glass ceiling).

5. Ask both boys and girls if they were considering the role that they

may play in family life when they made their choices.

6. Suggest to girls in group that they will spend as much time in the labor force as the boys and that they may wish to reconsider some of their choices to take potential earnings into account.

7. Summarize.

Homework

Women in the group should look at their Career Key results and try to select occupations that will pay more and still be commensurate with their interests. Men should consider the roles they might play in families that will allow spouses to pursue nontraditional careers.

Session 4 — The Education I Need

Objectives

• Show the linkage between educational and career goals.

• Initiate the process of developing a long-term educational goal.

Activities

1. Have students share progress on the homework assignment. Ask if there have been any changes in occupational choices as a result of the assignment. Their top two choices should be used in the exercise in this meeting.

2. Go to Handout 15-3, Occupational Summary Sheet. If they are to pursue any of the occupations they identified on that sheet, what level of education must they complete?

3. Where must you go to get that education? Does your favorite school have the major or training program that you need to enter the occupations you have identified?

4. For information about 4-year colleges have students go to the website <http://www.clas.ufl.edu/CLAS/american-universities.html>. At this website they can identify a college or university of interest and link to that school's website by clicking on the name. Once students have linked to the websites of their favorite schools, they should determine the majors available.

5. For information on community colleges, go to <http://www.mcli/ dist.maricopa.edu/cc/>. Once the students have located the websites of their favorite schools, they should determine the majors offered. If the school does not offer the major they are interested in, they should check other schools by returning to the original website. This can be done by clicking *Back* at the top of the page.

6. Students should complete the bottom section of Handout 15-3, Occupational Summary Sheet, during this exercise.

7. Students should visit the page(s) of the college's website that includes information about the majors offered. In some instances, career planning and placement services and/or university counseling centers have posted information about the careers that students graduating from the institution

enter with some frequency. This information can be particularly helpful for students who major in liberal arts, because it allows high school students to choose majors that do not have obvious links to occupations such as engineering and education. To find these postings, students may have to visit the page of the college's website that concerns career planning or placement or the information may be listed under *career* on the home page. The *home page* is the page that comes up first in the search and typically has extensive listings that are linked to other pages in the website. To get to these pages, have students click on the titles that wish to visit (e.g., careers).

8. Summarize.

Homework

Continue to work on locating information about institutions that offer training for the careers of interest to you.

Session 5 — Financial Aid I: Scholarships

Objective

Teach students how to use the Internet as a tool for finding financial aid.

Activities

1. Ask students to report on their homework assignment. Ascertain whether they have identified a postsecondary educational institution that provides the training they need to enter the career of greatest interest to them. If not, spend some time helping them identify at least one institution that offers the training they need.

2. Have students return to the websites they visited last week by repeating steps three and four from Session 2. Once they get to the website of the institution they wish to explore, have them click on *financial aid* and/ or *scholarships* and explore the sources of aid at the institution of interest to them, particularly how to apply for aid. Information gained at the institution's Website should be recorded on Handout 15-1 Occupational Summary Sheet.

3.Students should also access:

<http://www.studentservices.com.fastweb>if they wish to do a more comprehensive search for financial aid. Because this search requires approximately 30 minutes, students may wish to pursue it on their own.

4. Students interested in mathematics, science, and/or engineering should visit <http://www.cs.cmu.edu/afs/.cmu.edu/user/mkant/Pub/Fin/Aid/finaid.html>

Another site that offers a comprehensive listing of financial aid complete with links to other sites is <http://www.cs.cmu.edu/afs/.cmu.edu/user/mkant/Pub/Fin/Aid/search/search>

6. All students should have completed Handout 15-3, Occupational Summary Sheet, by the end of this session.

7. Summarize.

Homework

Have students discuss what they learned about scholarships with their parents and continue to work on sources of finical aid.

Session 6 — Financial Aid II: Loans

Objective

Have students learn about loans as a means of financing education.

Activities

1. Ask students to report their progress on identifying sources of aid that can be used to finance a college education.

2. Identify loans as a sources of finance. Identify the types of loans available through the Federal Student Aid Program. These are:
   • Pell Grants;
   • supplemental Educational Opportunity Grants;
   • subsidized and unsubsidized Stafford Loans;
   • Perkins Loans;
   • work study; and
   • Title VII and Public Health Act Programs.

3. Have students sign on to <http://www.cs.cmu.edu/afs/.cmu.edu/user/mkant/Pub/Fin/Aid/search/search> and click on the *hot link* to federal financial aid. This will take them to the federal financial aid website where they can use the directory to explore each of these programs.

4. Students should record the names of the loans that would help them finance their education on the Occupational Summary Sheet. They can also call 1-800-4-FED-AID and receive a student guide to these programs.

5. Students should look at the online application for federal loans and be allowed to ask questions.

6. Summarize.

Homework

Have students talk to parents about what they learned about student loans on the Internet.

Have students think about their educational and career goals. Come to group next week prepared to set some tentative goals.

Session 7 — Setting Goals for the Future.

Objective

Have students set post-secondary educational and career goals

Activities

1 Give students Handout 15-5, My Goals for the Future.

2. Assist them to fill out this sheet. When questions such as the number of Advanced Placement and honors courses needed for admission to certain

colleges arises, encourage students to consult the website of the college they are considering to gain information about admission requirements. Also encourage students to write directly to the colleges to get this information.

3. If students need financial aid, encourage them to think in terms of packages. Financial aid packages include parent support scholarships, loans, their own savings, and earnings from part time jobs while they are in school.

4. Information about the class rank and GPA needed to get into a particular school will need to be gotten from an admissions counselor at the institution or a knowledgeable school counselor.

5. Summarize.

Homework

Complete Handout 15-5, My Goals for the Future.

Session 8 — Wrapping Up

Objectives

- Insure that students have completed Handout 15-5, My Goals for the Future.
- Encourage additional planning.

Activities

1. Have students share the information they have entered on Handout 15-5, My Goals for the Future.

2. Identify the reasons for incomplete information and have students assist others to develop a plan to complete Handout 15-5.

3. Review factors such as the need to graduate from high school and the need to achieve certain GPAs and class ranks in order to achieve goals. Ask students if it is realistic for them to achieve these and have them set goals to do so if they are realistic

4. Identify barriers to achieving their academic goals and strategies for overcoming these barriers.

5. Summarize all sessions.

Homework

Continue to think about their career and educational goals and how they can work to achieve them.

Summary

The Internet is an exciting new tool that can be used to facilitate the planning of students. The advantage of using the Internet is the speed with which students can get information, the interactive nature of the Internet, and the types of information available that are more diverse than provided by any other source of educational and occupational information. This chapter has addressed the use of the Internet to help underachieving, high-potential students engage in meaningful career and educational goal setting by using the Career Key (Jones, 1997), the *Occupational Outlook Handbook*, and the home pages of colleges and universities, the federal loan programs, and two scholarship databases

References

Brown, D. (1998). *Hanging in or dropping out* (2nd Ed.). Lincolnwood, IL: VGM Books.

Brown, D. (1996). Brown's values-based, holistic model of career and life-role choices and satisfaction. In D. Brown, L. Brooks, and Associates. *Career choice and development* (3rd Ed., pp. 337-372). San Francisco: Jossey-Bass.

Bureau of Labor Statistics (1998-99). *Occupational outlook handbook.* Washington, DC: Author.

Holland, J. L. (1997). *Making vocational choices: A theory of vocational personalities and work environments* (3rd Ed.) Odessa, FL: Psychological Assessment Resources.

Jones, L. (1997). *Career key.* Raleigh, NC: North Carolina State University.

Locke, E. A., & Latham, G. P. (1990). *A theory of goal setting and task performance.* Englewood Cliffs, NJ: Prentice Hall.

Rathvon, N. (1996). *The unmotivated child.* New York: Fireside Books.

Sampson, Jr., J. P. (1997). Effective Internet use in career services. Unpublished manuscript. Center for the Study of Technology in Counseling and Career Development, Florida State University, Talahassee, FL.

Internet Terms Defined

• Internet: A global network of computers that are capable of sharing data with other computers. This network is comprised of specially designed hardware that connects these computers and allows them to communicate. The World Wide Web (www) is one component of the Internet.

• World Wide Web (www): A network of computers on the Internet that support specially formatted documents. These documents are in a format called hypermedia which is a combination of clickable text and pictures that provide links or "jumps" from one document to another. An application called a web browser is needed to view these documents.

• Home page: The main page of a website. It usually serves as an index or table of contents for the other pages contained at the website.

• Hyperlinks: A part of an electronic document that links to another place in the same document or to an entire new document. These are usually represented by text or graphics and are "clickable."

• Icons: Pictures or graphics that are used as symbols in a document. They can sometimes be hyperlinks.

• Web Address or Uniform Resource Locator (URL): The address of a website, page, or other electronic element accessible through the www It is analogous to the street address for a person. Most web addresses (or URLs) are case sensitive which means that upper and lower case letters can make a difference. Most of the addresses use hypertext transfer protocol (http). This is why you might see <http://> prior to the web address. This is required for the browser to understand how to handle and/or display the document. Many of the newer browsers will automatically add the <http:/ /> for you if you leave it out. It may be better to include it when typing the web address in to make sure you get to the website you want.

• Search Engines: A program or a system of programs that searches documents on the www and returns a list of documents that contain the specified keywords. Many search engines have a rating system and will order them from the most relevant to the least relevant. Each search engine has a different rating system.

• Web Browser: A software application used to locate and display web pages. Most modern browsers have the ability to display graphics while all browsers are capable of displaying text. Web browser's specifically are able to read hypertext and hypermedia documents found on the web. Examples of web browsers are Netscape Navigator and Microsoft Internet Explorer.

Using the Internet in Educational and Career Planning

In order to use the various resources on the Internet, you must be connected via an Internet service provider (ISP). ISPs provide a connection from the Internet to the local computer through the combination of hardware such as modems, and special software. Two popular ISPs are America Online (AOL) and Mindspring. There are many available and your school may use a different one.

One component on the Internet is the World Wide Web (www). To view objects on the web, you need to use a special application called a browser. The two most popular browsers are Netscape Navigator and Microsoft Internet Explorer. Your ISP should provide this application and documentation on using it. If you need further assistance, the browsers have help menus to answer common questions.

When you are online, there are several ways that you can search for information on the www. If you already know the *uniform resource locator* (URL) or address of the www page that you wish to visit, you can type the address in the *address bar* and press *enter*. This will take you directly to the website or page for the address you specified. If you do not know the address of a web page, you can use search engines to help you find the information you seek. With a search engine, you enter keywords for a particular subject and it will return a list of web pages that correspond to those words. In order to perform a keyword search, you need to enter your keywords in the box provided on the search engines web page and then click on the button *Search* or *Find*. Your search engine will yield better results most of the time if you provide more keywords or you are more specific. For example, searching using the keywords *career development* can provide a list of web pages numbering more than 5 million documents.

1. There are many different search engines available, and they all search for documents in different fashions. For more information on the different syntax used by search engines find the *Help* link on the page. As stated, there are many different search engines available. Here are some of the commonly used search engines and their web addresses:
- AltaVista (http://www.altavista.digital.com)
- Excite (http://www.excite.com)
- HotBot (http://www.hotbot.com)
- Yahoo (http://www.yahoo.com)
- Lycos (http://www.lycos.com)
- Metacrawler (http://www.metacrawler.com)
- Internet Sleuth (http://www.isleuth.com)

The two web browsers mentioned above, Netscape Navigator and Microsoft Internet Explorer, have *hot buttons* that, when clicked, link you to a page that lists several of the popular search engines. If you are using ISPs like Mindspring or AOL, you will find similar hot buttons, such as *Search* or *NetFind* which will also link you to a list of search engines.

One final piece on search engines. If you are having difficulty finding information specific to your topic, first consult the *Help* that the search engines provide (mentioned before). You may also want to look on the search engines web page for options to do advanced searches. These provide additional search boxes that help you narrow your topic search by either including or excluding specific words or phrases.

Occupational Summary Sheet

Title of Occupation 1 from Career Key _____
Education Required _____
Working Conditions _____
Average Salary _____
Employment Outlook _____
Other Information of Interest _____
_____
Institutions That Offer Training _____
_____
Costs _____
Sources of Financial Aid _____
_____

Title of Occupation 2 from Career Key _____
Education Required _____
Working Conditions _____
Average Salary _____
Employment Outlook_____
Other Information of Interest _____
_____
Institutions That Offer Training _____
_____
Costs _____
Sources of Financial Aid _____
_____

Title of Occupation 3 from Career Key _____
Education Required _____
Working Conditions _____
Average Salary _____
Employment Outlook _____
Other Information of Interest _____
Institutions That Offer Training _____
_____
Costs _____
Sources of Financial Aid _____
_____

Title of Occupation 4 from Career Key _____
Education Required _____

Working Conditions _____

Average Salary _____

Employment Outlook _____

Other Information of Interest _____

_____

Institutions That Offer Training _____

_____

Costs _____

Sources of Financial Aid _____

_____

Handout 15-4

About Your Career

This sheet should serve as your guide when you talk to people about their career. The first step in this process is to make an appointment to discuss the person's career either by telephone or in person. If possible, arrange to interview the person in their work setting so you can get a firsthand view of the workplace. Always ask the worker for the interview.

Interview Questions:

1. What is your job title?
2. Specifically, what type of work do you do?
3. How many hours do you work each day? When does your work day begin? End?
4. How did you prepare for this job? What preparation is needed today to get this type of job?
5. If you know it, how much money does a beginning worker make in your job? An experienced worker? (If the information is not volunteered, do do not ask the worker her or his salary)
6. How would you describe the working conditions for your job?
7. Does this job ever interfere with your family or leisure roles?
8. What are the best things about your job?
9. What are the worst things about your job?
10. If you had it to do over, would you enter this job?
11. Are job opportunities in your field growing?
12. Would you recommend that one of your children enter your job? Why or why not?

My Goals for the Future

1. At this time the occupation that I plan on entering is _____
2. The education required to enter this occupation is _____
3. In order to get the education I need, I plan to enroll in

   _____
4. At this time the estimated cost of my education will be _____
5. The following scholarships may be available to me:

   _____
6. I may qualify for the following loans:

   _____
7. My parents or relatives will contribute _____ dollars
   toward the cost of my education.
8. I will need to save or earn the following amount of money in order
   to complete my education:
9. In order to reach both my educational and occupational goals I will
   have to
   • graduate from high school. Yes _____ No _____
   • graduate with a GPA of at least _____
   • graduate with a class rank of at least _____
   • have the following score on the SAT/ACT _____
   • complete the following AP and Honors courses_____

   _____
   • Participate in the following extracurricular activities _____

   _____
   Other _____

Note: If it will be more than 1 year before you plan to pursue
your post-secondary education, add 5% to the present cost for
each year that will elapse before you go to school. For example,
if it will be 5 years before you enroll in school, the cost of a
$5,000 education may have risen by 25% to $6,125.

Chapter Sixteen

Summing Up:
Principles and Practices

The educational reform movement has placed pressure on student support personnel to demonstrate that they can contribute directly to the academic achievement of students. Fortunately, there are many strategies that can be employed by school counselors, school psychologists, and school social workers to facilitate and improve student achievement. In some regards, the principles that have guided the discussions in Chapters 1 through 15 are more important than the techniques that have been outlined. To summarize, the principles that should underpin efforts to improve academic achievement and the strategies or practices that are associated with them are as follows;

1. *The family has a major role to play in facilitating the achievements of students.* Although parents are seen as adversaries by some educators, without their assistance and support it is unlikely that the efforts expended by school personnel to improve academic performance will be successful. Schools must take the lead in teaching parents basic parenting skills and in teaching parents how to facilitate the learning process of their children. In order to involve parents, student support personnel can

(a) sponsor or deliver parenting classes designed to improve basic parenting skills and to improve their skills in facilitating their children's academic performance;

(b) involve parents as tutors in homework support programs;

(c) provide feedback to parents regarding their students' academic performance as a component of achievement motivation groups;

(d) become advocates for parents who are unfamiliar with the educational bureaucracy;

(e) involve parents to provide reinforcers in the contracting process;

(f) send notes home to parents as a part of the process of establishing a success environment when students improve their performance; and

(g) involve parents in the orientation process.

2. *The overall atmosphere of the school is as important as the strategies employed by student support personnel or teachers.* Students need to see

the school as user friendly. This means that they need to feel valued, the policies of the school need to be administered fairly, institutional and individual racism and sexism need to be eliminated, and the curriculum and the activities of the school need to be inclusive. In order to accomplish these ends, student support personnel may

(a) provide or arrange for in service training for teachers that will help them gain skills in communication with students, encouragement, and reinforcing effort;

(b) consult with teachers regarding the implementation of cooperative education;

(c) advocate curricula that allows students, regardless of their race and ethnicity, to "see themselves" in the curriculum by using material, texts, and teaching approaches that illustrate the roles of minorities and women in the subjects offered;

(d) advocate a zero tolerance for racism and sexism;

(e) advocate policies that facilitate development such as in-school suspension programs;

(f) advocate policies that allow bright students who are capable of doing the work in advanced placement and honors courses to enroll in those courses regardless of their past performance;

(g) advocate fairness in admission to clubs like the National Honor Society;

(h) advocate students' rights, including due process, in the disciplinary process;

(i) establish transition seminars and support groups for new students as needed;

(j) organize programs designed to recognize effort and achievement that goes beyond giving grades periodically; and

(k) Sponsor or deliver prejudice reduction workshops.

3. *Interventions, whether by teachers in the classroom or by student support personnel outside the classroom, should be strategic interventions.* A strategic intervention is one that is crafted to meet the unique characteristics of the learner. In devising interventions the cultural, psychological, and socioeconomic status of the individual need to be taken into consideration. The language proficiency and immigration status of students also need to be considered in the development of educational interventions. Student support personnel can

(a) conduct periodic needs assessments and circulate the results of these surveys to teachers, administrators, and parents making sure that English proficiency is taken into consideration as a need;

(b) establish a goal-oriented programs that utilize interventions that are based on identified needs;

(c) evaluate the outcomes of all interventions; and

(d) make certain that when ESL students are included in any

intervention that there is a translator present, if the English proficiency of the students dictates it.

4. *All students need long- and short-term goals.* Goals are powerful motivational forces (Locke & Latham, 1990), and without them many students will lose interest in school. Important short-term goals include completing schoolwork, establishing achievement level goals, and managing time more effectively. However, more important goals have to do with long-term educational and career goals. A variety of educational problems ranging from underachievement (Rathvon, 1996) to dropping out of school (Brown, 1998) have been linked to deficits in this area. Student support personnel can

    (a) help students become aware of the expectations associated with any intervention and have them set goals to meet the expectations that have been established;

    (b) incorporate goal setting exercises into every intervention with students;

    (c) emphasize educational and career goal setting should begin in the sixth grade;

    (d) focus on students' goals in all routine meeting such as course selection;

    (e) use parent education classes and other meetings with parents as a means of stressing the importance of their involvement in the goal-setting processes of their students; and

    (f) schedule goal setting groups regularly to assist students who are having trouble in this area become more goal oriented.

5. *Innovation is important.* The Internet provides school personnel with exciting opportunities to engage students in learning experiences that were heretofore unavailable. Similarly, problems such as homework support programs can be attacked using the Internet and various other resources.

    (a) Schedule in-service training regularly to help student support personnel and others keep up with innovations such as the Internet that may facilitate the educational process.

    (b) Attend professional meetings to identify educational innovations that may be useful to students.

6. *If schools are to raise the overall level of achievement, the educational playing field must be leveled.* Students who come from poor homes, who have low English proficiency, or who have cultural values that are not commensurate with those of teachers are at a decided disadvantage. Individualization is already difficult given the range of abilities and other problems present in each classroom. Fortunately many of the potential solutions to the problems associated with cultural differences, also address the problem of what to do with differences in achievement (Slavin, 1990). Unfortunately, these solutions do not address the issue of language proficiency. Student support personnel must plan for language differences

in their work and they must advocate for more native speakers to assist students who speak English-as-a-second language (ESL). Student support personnel can

(a) establish homework support programs which are essential if the educational playing field is to be leveled for poor students and these courses must be multifaceted to be successful;

(b) include speakers who speak the first language of the students in the ESL program ;

(c) establish support groups for ESL students;

(d) target ESL students when establishing a success environment. However, the delivery of reinforcers must be geared to the cultural values of the ESL students; and

(e) include the parents of ESL students in all parenting programs.

7. *Students need a wide variety of tools if they are to succeed in the educational arena.* It is often erroneously assumed that students understand the strategies needed to gain knowledge in the classroom and in their studies at home. Similarly, because students take tests all of their academic lives, it is assumed that test taking is a skill possessed by all. This is not the case. Study skills, test-taking skills, tutoring skills, and the skills needed to resist peer pressure to underachieve are not part of all students behavioral repertoire. In the development of these skills, student support personnel can

(a) schedule study skills groups on an ongoing basis;

(b) offer time management groups to all students. Time management is essential if students are to succeed in are succeed in school environments that are increasingly demanding;

(c) help students develop refusal skills so they can resist peer pressure aimed at lowering their academic achievement;

(d) teach test-taking skills. The ability to deal with tests is an essential skill in today's schools, and students need to be aware of strategies that will help them to maximize their performance when they take tests; and

(e) develop programs that will increase scores on college admissions tests. Scores on college entrance examinations such as the ACT and SAT are important to students who plan to go on to college. Unfortunately, many poor students cannot afford expensive preparation courses that will help improve scores on these tests. Schools should develop and offer these courses at affordable prices.

8. *Many students need help in mastering subject matter that goes beyond what the typical teacher can provide.* In order to supplement the instructional efforts of teachers student support personnel and others can

(a) develop peer and volunteer tutoring programs;

(b) help parents learn how to facilitate the achievement of their children;

(c) organize and deliver achievement motivation groups on an ongoing basis; and

(d) consult with teachers to insure that they are sensitive to the fact that cultural minorities may benefit from alternative instructional strategies such as cooperative learning and group contracts.

Summary

In this chapter, eight principles for increasing academic performance are outlined. Specific strategies for acting on these principles are also identified. The techniques discussed in this book are important, but it is following the principles outlined in this chapter that student support personnel will make a favorable impact on student achievement.

References

Brown, D. (1998). *Hanging in or dropping out* (2nd ed.). Lincolnwood, IL: NTC Publishing Group (VGM Books).

Locke, E. A., & Latham, G. P. (1990). *A theory of goal setting and task performance.* Englewood Cliffs, NJ: Prentice Hall.

Purkey, W.W., & Schmidt, J.J. (1996). *Invitational counseling.* Pacific Grove, CA: Brooks-Cole,

Rathvon, N. (1996). *The unmotivated child.* New York: Fireside Books.

Slavin, R. S. (1990). *Cooperative learning: Theory, research and practice.* Englewood Cliffs, NJ: Prentice Hall.

ERIC...for all your information needs!

ERIC

ERIC (Educational Resources Information Center) is a national information system that provides ready access to an extensive body of education-related literature. Through its 16 subject-specific clearinghouses and four support components, ERIC provides a variety of services and products including acquiring and indexing documents and journal articles, producing publications, responding to requests, and distributing microfilmed materials to libraries nationwide. In addition, ERIC maintains a database of over 800,000 citations to documents and journal articles.

ERIC/CASS

The ERIC Counseling and Student Services Clearinghouse (ERIC/CASS) was one of the original clearinghouses established in 1966. Its scope area includes school counseling, school social work, school psychology, mental health counseling, marriage and family counseling, career counseling, and student development.

Topics covered by ERIC/CASS include the training, supervision, and continuing professional development of counseling, college student services and development professionals, as well as adult counseling and mental health professionals. Other up-to-date and relevant topics include:

(a) counseling theories, research methods, and practices;
(b) the roles of counselors, social workers, and psychologists in all educational settings at all educational levels;
(c) career planning and development;
(d) self-esteem and self-efficacy;
(e) marriage and family counseling; and
(f) counseling services to special populations such as substance abusers, pregnant teenagers, students at risk and public offenders.

ERIC/CASS exists to serve anyone who has a need to access information related to counseling and student services with quick and friendly assistance to retrieve information related to counseling and human services.

Print indexes (RIE and CIJE), on-line searches, and ERIC on CD-ROM can be helpful in locating what is needed.

How To Access Information

The most convenient method of gaining access to the information is to contact a local public, college, or university library that provides ERIC database search services. The customer service staff at **1-800-LET-ERIC (538-3742)** can provide information about the location in your area.

Customers can also access ERIC Clearinghouses or the central ERIC facility via the Internet at **http://www.accesseric.org:81/** You may conduct your own search of the ERIC database on the Internet by visiting the ERIC Document Reproduction Service at: **http://edrs.com/**.Complete instructions and tips for targeting your search are provided.

You can send an e-mail question and receive a return e-mail usually within 48 hours. The reply will contain a mini-search of the ERIC d atabase with references to ERIC documents and journal articles as well as suggestions for other sources of information relevant to your question. Send an e-mail to: **askeric@ askeric.org** or search the website at: **http:askeric.org**.

Contact Us Directly

Should these options be unavailable to you, contact ERIC/CASS directly for your information needs. We are able to electronically search and retrieve information based upon descriptors and key words as well as bibliographic information such as author, publication date, etc. You may request a search via a letter or fax indicating subjects, topics, key words or phrases, etc., that you wish to focus upon. You may also contact us by telephone **(800/414-9769)** or e-mail **(ericcass@uncg.edu)** so that we may discuss your needs and assist you in focusing your search in order to provide results as specific as possible.

More Resources From ERIC/CASS

ERIC/CASS is an active user of electronic communication. The CASS website features an array of targeted virtual libraries that offer users access to an unparalleled abundance of resources on priority educational topics including materials from the U.S. Department of Education and the National Library of Education. These on-line functioning libraries provide a wealth of free, full-text resources which can be downloaded and instantly put to use.

Access the user-friendly ERIC/CASS virtual libraries website at: **http://www.uncg.edu/edu/ericcass/libhome.htm**

INTERNATIONAL CAREER
DEVELOPMENT LIBRARY

Where to Go When You Want to Know...developed and managed by NOICC & ERIC/CASS.

The *ICDL* is a Virtual Library available to anyone with an Internet connection. It features a wide range of books and resources covering all aspects of career development for all age levels and for practitioners, researchers and educators, as well as students and parents. With the ongoing assistance of professional organizations and Department of Education components such as NLE and ERIC, it has exceptionally comprehensive and intensive coverage. Some of its present features as well as ones which will be added in the future are listed below. Like any new major development, it has to be seen and experienced to appreciate it, so check it out now!

SPECIAL FEATURES

- Access hot links to international web sites
- Easily download full text resources
- Customize every search using the special search engine
- Participate in the discussion of compelling career issues
- Engage in interactive, multimedia learning activities
- Learn for credit & ceu's
- Acquire requisite competencies for the cyber age
- Network with like-minded colleagues around the world
- Be a knowledgeable contributor as well as a user
- Participate at any level—new or experienced
- Utilize regularly appearing special condensations of major new publications
- Dialogue with world authorities
- Visit the topical "shelves" and browse the special collections, e.g., exemplary career development practices & programs, innovations in career development, etc.

Access the International Career Development Library at:
http://icdl.uncg.edu/

ERIC Publications: In Print And On-line

ERIC/CASS publications provide resources which respond to your needs. Written by expert researchers, scholars, and practitioners, they range from two-page information digests to in-depth monographs and books. ERIC/

CASS publications are well-known for their intensive and up-to-date analyses of high priority topics. We also offer selected publications from other professional associations and commercial sources.

For information on ERIC/CASS publications, call for a catalog **(800/414-9769)** or you may order from our on-line catalog at: **http://www.uncg.edu/edu/ericcass**.

The ERIC/CASS Newsletter

ERIC/CASS regularly announces new publications and digests, important developments in OERI and the Department of Education, and the availability of specialized training through workshops, conferences, and conventions. The CASS newsletter is the usual way of updating members of the CASS network as to available resources and future developments. Call the CASS 800 number and request to join the network.

Appendix II
Handouts

1-1   Needs Assessment Questionnaire for High School Students
1-2   Assessing Academic Needs–Parent Survey
1-3   Assessing Academic Needs–Elementary School Teacher Survey

2-1   Your Cultural Values

4-1   Am I a Good Friend?
4-1   Operung Exercise for In-Service Training of Teachers
4- 3   Rate the Achievement Climate of Your School

5-1   Weekly Study Log
5-2   Study Skills Inventory–High School/Middle School
5-3   Two-Week Assignment Sheet
5-4   Study Skills Inventory--Elementary School
5-5   Work Habits Sheet
5-6   Work Habit Stars
5-7   Am I a Good Listener?
5-8   Am I a Responsible Student?
5-9   Responsible Students Nomination Form
5-10   My Study Habits
5-11   The 10 Rules for Test Taking

6-1   Test-Taking Strategies
6-2   My Symptoms
6-3   What Happens to Your Body When You Get Anxious
6-4   Measuring Your Test Anxiety
6-5   Thought Stopping
6-6   Controlling Your Breathing
6-7   Relaxing Tense Muscles
6-8   Plan for Coping With My Test Anxiety

7-1   Visions of My Future
7-2   My Time Management Style
7-3   Values Card Sort
7 4   My Important and Unimportant Activities
7-5   My Time Management Habits
7-6   Time Management Record

10-1A   Responding to Verbal Comment and Feelings of Tutees

10-1B   Sample Answers to Handout 10-1A

10-2   Preparation and Organization of Material for Study

10- 3   Step Approach to Major Homework Assignments Completion

10-4   Note Taking

10-5   Test-Taking Strategies

10-6   Confidentiality Pledge

10-7   Tutor Observation Rating Form

10-8   Fact Sheet I: Defining Mental Retardation, Learning Disabilities, and Visual Impairments

10-9   Fact Sheet II: Defining Hearing Impairments, Speech and Language Disorders, and Autism

10-10   Request for Feedback on Students Receiving Tutoring

10-11   Tutor's Log

11-1   Academic Achievement Goal Setting

11-2   My Academic Achievement Goals

13-1   Positive Approaches to Discipline

13-2   Disciplining Without Violence

13-3   Helping Your Student at Home

14-1   Six Ways to Say No When You Don't Want to Do Something!

14-2   How Peer Pressure Is Applied

14-3   Do I Give In to Peer Pressure?

14-4   Daily Classroom Checklist

14-5   Setting Goals for Increased Achievement

15-1   Internet Terms Defined

15-2   Using the Internet in Educational and Career Planning

15-3   Occupational Summary Sheet

15-4   About Your Career

15-5   My Goals for the Future

Appendix III
Overheads

5-1   Step Approach to Major Homework Assignment Completion
5-2   Rules for Note Taking
5-3   A Shorthand System for Taking Notes
5-4   SQ3RT Method of Studying

6-1   The Escalating Panic Reaction to Tests
7-1   Time Management
7-2   The Importance of Values
7-3   Steps to Taking Control of Your Time
7-4   Time Management Record

13-1   Characteristics of the Resilient Student
13-2   Family Factors That Produce Resilient Students
13-3   Family Factors That Put Students At Risk
13-4   Helping Children-Feel Secure
13-5   Positive Interactions With Children

14-1   STOP, LISTEN, ACT, DECIDE

Appendix IV
Figures

2-1   Value Orientations of Five Major U.S. Cultural Groups
2-2   Assessing Your Knowledge
2-3   Skills and Attitudes Needed to Make Interventions With Minority Students
2-4   Cultural Factors That May Influence the Achievement of Hispanic American Students (Cuban, Puerto Rican, Mexican, Central and South American)
2-5   Cultural Factors That May Influence the Achievement of African American Students
2-6   Cultural Factors That May Influence the Achievement of Asian American Students (Chinese, Japanese, Korean, Vietnamese, Cambodian, Filipino, Laotian)

2-7   Cultural Factors That May Influence the Achievement of American Indian Students (Likely Variability Across the More Than 500 Tribes)

3-1   Preliminary Team Assignments Based on Test Averages
3-2   Preliminary Tearn Assignments Based on Grades
3-3   Individual and Team Improvement Scores for the Devils
3-4   Sample Cooperative Learning Team Summary Sheet
3-5   Teams From Figure 3-1
3-6   Sample Student Tournament Scorecard
3-7   Sample Tournament Score Sheet for Each Team
3-8   Reassigning Students

6-1   Testing Guidelines for ESL Students
6-2   Outline of a SAT Preparation Course
6-3   Request for Referrals for Test Anxiety Group

8-1   Sample Behavioral Contract–Individual With Individualized Reinforcer
8-2   Sample Individual Contracts
8-3   Sample Behavioral Group Contract
8-4   Examples of Reinforcers
8-5   Sample Individual Contract With Incentive Clause
8-6   Troubleshooting Guide for Monitoring Behavioral Contracts
8-7   Sample Notes to Parents

9-1   Academic Extra Effort Award Nomination Form
9-2   Sample Letter to Parents
9-3   Sample Academic Extra Effort Award Certificate
9-4   Sample Most Improved Group Award Certificate
9-5   Sample Letter to Parents of High School Students–Near Miss
9-6   Sample Note to Parents of Elementary School Student

10-1   Determining the Need for tutorial Services
10-2   Sample Note to Teachers: Peer Tutor Recruitment
10-3   Sample Parental Permission Note for Volunteer Peer Tutors
10-4   Sample Notice of Need for Adult Tutors

11-1   Sample Note to Teachers
11-2   Becoming a Better Student Group Contract
11-3   Achievement Motivation Group Weekly Progress Report
11-4   Achievement Motivation Weekly Progress Report to Parents

12-1   Sample Survey to Determine the Need for a Homework Support Program

13-1   Factors Affecting Hispanic American Families
13-2   Factors Affecting Chinese American and Other Asian American Families
13-3   Factors Affecting African American Families

14-1   Sample Group Contract

15-1   Sample Contract for High-Potential Underachieving Students